T.L
DA

THE GOSPEL ACCORDING TO T.L. & DAISY

Classic Documentary

P.O. Box 10, Tulsa, OK 74102 USA
Tel: 918/743-6231
Fax: 918/749-0330   E-Mail: OSFO@aol.com
www.OSBORN.ORG

Canada: Box 281, Adelaide St. Post Sta., Toronto M5C 2J4
England: Box 148, Birmingham B3 2LG
(A Registered Charity)

WE DEDICATE this book to YOU, the reader, with our sincere prayer that as you hold it in your hands and read it, the power and presence of Jesus Christ will be shown to YOU in a way that you will know that **He is the same yesterday, today and forever.** He came to us. He wants to visit you too. He met our needs — miraculously. He wants to do the same for YOU.

Dr. T.L. Osborn
Dr. Daisy Osborn

Crusade photographs by
Dr. Daisy Washburn Osborn

CO-AUTHORS

BIBLE QUOTATIONS IN THIS BOOK ARE FROM THE KING JAMES AUTHORIZED VERSION (1611) UNLESS OTHERWISE NOTED. OTHER LANGUAGES AND VERSIONS HAVE BEEN CONSIDERED. SCRIPTURES MAY BE PERSONALIZED, PARAPHRASED, ABRIDGED OR CONFORMED TO THE *PERSON* AND *TENSE* OF THEIR CONTEXTUAL APPLICATION, TO FOSTER CLARITY AND INDIVIDUAL ACCEPTANCE. CHAPTER AND VERSE REFERENCES ENABLE THE READER TO VERIFY LOYALTY TO THE BIBLICAL TEXT.

THE AUTHOR

ISBN 0-87943-021-4
Copyright © 1985 by T.L. & Daisy Osborn
Printed in the United States of America
All Rights Reserved

CONTENTS

PREFACE	13
PART 1 — HE WILL COME TO YOU	19
PART 2 — THE PROOF IS IN THE MIRACLES	23
PART 3 — QUESTIONS TO FACE	25
PART 4 — FROM FAILURE TO SUCCESS	27
PART 5 — WHAT WE DISCOVERED ABOUT THE MOSLEMS	31
PART 6 — WE FACED THE SAME ISSUE THAT PRIMITIVE CHRISTIANS FACED	39
PART 7 — BACK TO AMERICA — AND WHY	43
PART 8 — WHEN JESUS VISITED OUR HOUSE	47
PART 9 — OUR TEST OF LOYALTY	51
PART 10 — DAISY LED THE WAY	57
PART 11 — THE GREATEST REVELATION	59
PART 12 — A THOUSAND VOICES	65
PART 13 — THE LORD SPOKE AGAIN	69
PART 14 — THE FIRST MIRACLE	79
PART 15 — T.L.'S SOLUTION BECAME DAISY'S PROBLEM	85
PART 16 — THIRTEEN WEEKS	91
PART 17 — MINISTRY TO AMERICA	97
PART 18 — EVERYWHERE THE RESULTS WERE THE SAME	101
PART 19 — PROOF FOR THE MOSLEMS	107
PART 20 — RETURN TO INDIA	119
PART 21 — THE HINDU WHO SAW JESUS	125
PART 22 — 100 PEOPLE SAW THE LORD	127
PART 23 — WHY NOT AT YOUR HOUSE?	131
PART 24 — PRAYER	133

PART 25 — ACCOUNTS OF JESUS — ALIVE 137
  KINGSTON, JAMAICA 140
  PONCE, PUERTO RICO 143
  CAMAGUEY, CUBA 148
  PONCE, PUERTO RICO 152
  PUNTO FIJO, VENEZUELA 158
  SAN JOSE, COSTA RICA 159
  GUATEMALA CITY, GUATEMALA 162
  SANTIAGO, CHILE 170
  DJAKARTA, JAVA, INDONESIA 172
  SURABAJA, JAVA, INDONESIA 178
  BANGKOK, THAILAND 183
  KYOTO, JAPAN 188
  ACCRA, GHANA 193
  IBADAN, NIGERIA 197
  RENNES, FRANCE 204
  THE HAGUE, HOLLAND 209
  LOME, TOGO 215
  LUCKNOW, INDIA 220
  MANILA, PHILIPPINES 227
  SAN FERNANDO, TRINIDAD 233
  KINSHASA, ZAIRE 243
  BENIN CITY, NIGERIA 248
  UYO, NIGERIA 255
  NAKURU, KENYA 270
  MONTERREY, MEXICO 286
  NJORO-MENENGAI, KENYA 303
  EMBU, KENYA 323

PART 25 — ACCOUNTS OF JESUS — ALIVE (cont'd)
    U.S.A 333
    ACCRA, GHANA 348
    KAMPALA, UGANDA 361
PART 26 — DAMIANO'S MIRACLE 433
PART 27 — THE MIRACLE OF PAPA MUSOKE 445
PART 28 — MARIA THERESA'S HEALING 459
PART 29 — BETTY ANDIRU'S MIRACLE 463
PART 30 — MIRACLE OF CHRIST'S APPEARANCE 467
PART 31 — ALIVE IN THIS CENTURY 472
PART 32 — THE GOSPEL ACCORDING
           TO T.L. AND DAISY 475

THE OSBORNS, ON THE G

WITH HOPE & LIFE FOR MILLIONS

PREFACE

This book is an expression of *the Gospel according to T.L. and Daisy.* It is **our** story of how Jesus Christ came to **us.** It is a small portion of the wonders and miracles of Christ's compassion and love which **we** have witnessed among the hurting and lonely peoples of the world.

The Gospel according to Matthew is the story of Jesus, as told by a converted tax collector called Levi.

The Gospel according to Mark is the record of how **he** saw the Lord's ministry among the people of **his** day.

The Gospel according to Luke is a physician's account of the events and happenings in the life of Christ.

The Gospel according to John is **his** story of Jesus Christ, perceived as the life and love of God being incarnated in the man from Nazareth.

Each of those men recorded what **they** knew and witnessed as followers of Jesus Christ. John said it was what they had seen and heard, what they had witnessed with their eyes and handled with their hands of the Word of Life. (1 Jn. 1:13)

The Gospel according to Paul is the account of how Jesus Christ came to **him** and of **his** revelations about Christ's continued ministry through those who believed on Him.

Paul talked about **"my gospel"** in Ro. 2:16, 16:25 and 2 Ti. 2:8.

The Gospel according to T.L. and Daisy is **our** story of how Jesus Christ came to **us,** showed Himself alive to **us,** called **us** to follow Him, and how He has worked with **us,** confirming His word with signs following. (Mk 16:20)

The photographs we have included are part of **our** story.

We are convinced that if photographic technology had existed in Jesus' day, it would have been utilized to record the wonders of His ministry. Alas, it did not! So to record the facts, the Holy Spirit used the available technology of that day — the ability to write. In graphic word-pictures, Christ inspired His followers to record, for all time, the message and ministry of the Son of God among people.

In *The Gospel According to T.L. and Daisy,* we have utilized the technology of **photography** together with the Holy Spirit's anointing upon our **words,** to give **our** generation a living record of the life and ministry of Jesus Christ as WE have been privileged to witness Him at work, during nearly four decades of evangelism in over 70 nations of the world.

PART 1

HE WILL COME TO YOU

T.L.: We are publishing details of some remarkable experiences we have had, because of a question which Daisy posed to me.

DAISY: It was the year that we were in the midst of **the greatest crisis of our lives** — and it was climaxed by the **Lord's visit to our home** when T.L. saw Jesus alive and real.

T.L.: I remember it as though it was yesterday. The power of Christ's presence — looking right at me — was so great that **I lay at His feet like I was**

dead. There is no way to explain what His presence is like.

DAISY: I had been thinking about that experience and I asked T.L. if we had ever recorded or published the details of what happened to us through that supernatural visitation, so that other people could be helped.

T.L.: As soon as Daisy asked me that, I realized that we had never done it. We have told it in crusades around the world.

DAISY: And what is amazing is that **every time we have shared that experience, some of the greatest miracles we have ever witnessed have taken place.**

T.L.: That is true, and I believe that the reason God impressed us to publish the details is because He wants that visitation to be known, and **He is going to confirm it by doing miracles wherever anyone listens to it or reads about it.**

DAISY: Jesus has appeared at least once, and often many times, in practically every crusade we have conducted.

T.L.: I believe He has done it to confirm that He is as alive and real today as He ever was. I expect Him to make **you,** the reader, aware of His presence right where you are, as you read this.

Scenes like those (next page), captured during an Osborn crusade, are reminiscent of Bible days when *they brought to him many that were possessed with devils: and he cast out the spirits with his word, and healed all that were sick.* (Mt.8:16)

Great multitudes came together to hear, and to be healed by him of their infirmities. And it came to pass as he was teaching, the power of the Lord was present to heal. (Lu.5:15-17)

Dr. T. L. and Dr. Daisy Osborn believe that God's power is in His word. Most of the great miracles they have witnessed worldwide have taken place as the people heard them teach, and as they received faith to be healed out in the multitude — like those shown on the next page. *He sent his word, and healed them.* (Ps.107:20)

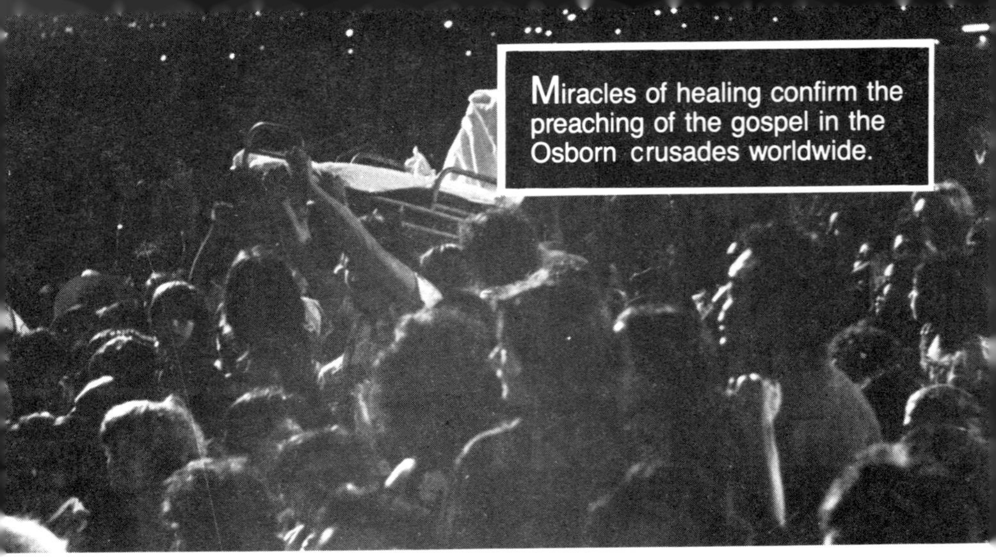

Miracles of healing confirm the preaching of the gospel in the Osborn crusades worldwide.

PART 2

THE PROOF IS IN THE MIRACLES

DAISY: As T.L. was preaching the other day, I heard him read a scripture which I would like to read right now.

Jesus was attending a celebration at the Temple in Jerusalem and *The Living Bible* says in John 10:24, *The Jewish leaders surrounded him and asked him, "If you are the Christ, tell us plainly."*

T.L.: Then in verse 25, Jesus replied: *The proof is in the miracles I do in the name of my Father.* (v.32) *At God's direction I have done many miracles to help people.*

DAISY: In verses 30 to 38 Jesus talked to them about His relationship with God.

They were angry because He had called God His Father and, by doing so, claimed to be the Son of God. The religious leaders viewed the idea so scandalous that they tried to stone Him.

T.L.: That is when He told them that the **proof** of His being God's Son was in the **miracles.**

In verse 37, He said, *Do not believe me unless I do the miracles of God. And if I do, then believe them even if you do not believe in me.* (v.25) **The proof is in the miracles I do in my Father's name.**

Is there any need for miracles today?

Is Christianity provable?

DAISY: What was the need for miracles when Jesus was here? Even people of other religions agree that He did do miracles. Is it any different now?

PART 3
QUESTIONS TO FACE

T.L.: We were very young when we accepted Christ, and right away we wanted to help others know about Him.

Should that be normal? At what age? How can one know when such questions should be faced?

DAISY: There are the great sacred books of the Orient — Confucius' writings, Buddha's sayings, Mohammed's teachings — and, of course, the Bible.

How can we know what is truth?

T.L.: How do we know that the Jesus-life is supernatural — or different, for that matter, from other religions?

Is not there a danger of being branded a fanatic — if you are different from your peers?

DAISY: How does the Lord come to us in the now and make our lives count?

How can we know that the dreams we are dreaming or the goals we are setting are right for us?

What is real success? Is success wrong?

T.L. Osborn at age 18 (one of 13 children), the 7th son of a 7th son, who was an Oklahoma farmer, married Daisy Washburn (one of 11 children), a 17-year-old farmer girl, in Los Banos, California on Easter morning, 1942, and the young couple started out together to win souls.

PART 4
FROM FAILURE TO SUCCESS

T.L.: Well — that is why we decided to tell this story.

We have found the answers to those questions, and our lives came into focus during the period between two crises — the time we faced our greatest dilemma, and the experience of discovering the answer to our life's challenge.

Since then, we have known nothing but success, happiness, peace and fulfillment. We have known beautiful love together, harmony and tranquility — and most of all, our lives have had real purpose. We have known real success!

Dr. T.L. and Dr. Daisy Osborn may have preached the gospel to more non-Christian people, and they may have witnessed more miraculous healings among the UNchurched multitudes, than any couple who has ever lived.

DAISY: It all started with what seemed to be a terrible failure. In the midst of our crisis, we picked up the pieces of our lives, we searched until we got the answer, and we turned that failure into a beautiful lifetime of success and true fulfillment.

T.L. and Daisy Osborn with Tommy Lee, Jr. and LaDonna Carol, in the early days of their ministry.

After almost four decades of world evangelism sharing Christ with millions, face to face.

PART 5

WHAT WE DISCOVERED ABOUT THE MOSLEMS

T.L.: Daisy and I were both converted when we were only 12 years old. From that time we wanted to help people find Christ.

From our early marriage, at very young ages, we set out in soulwinning ministries.

I remember the superintendent of the denomination to which we belonged. He was a man who had gone to India as a missionary. Whenever this man preached, he preached about India and about missions until he literally branded India on our spirits.

T.L. Osborn and Daisy Marie Washburn were married at ages 18 and 17, and began their life together in evangelism.

The Osborns pose for a photograph to give to churches and friends who helped sponsor them as young missionaries to India.

DAISY: We had just become pastors for the first time. Who should come as a guest to our church but a missionary from India. Clearly, we were facing the call of India's millions.

T.L.: We decided that the people of India needed Christ more than the people in our country.

If ten persons were lifting a log, nine of them on the small end and only one on the big end, and if we wanted to help lift the log, on which end should we lift?

It was logical to us that we should help where there was the greatest need and the fewest people to meet the need.

But the problem was, we were not prepared.

I remember how shocked I was when I discovered that the Moslems believed in the same God we believed in. They called Him **Allah** and we called him **God.** I thought "Allah" was a heathen god. Then I learned that it was the Arabic word for **God.**

They worshipped the God of Abraham, the same God the Jews worship — and whom we worship.

We thought they were worshippers of dead gods,

but we found that they were wonderful believers in the true and the living God.

They prayed five times a day. They loved to talk to God. We made many friends among them. Merchants with whom we dealt were Moslems.

I remember that many times they would shake my hand and say, "Good morning, **Brother** Osborn." And they might add, **"Praise God."** I was shocked.

DAISY: I remember how amazed we were when we discovered that they believed that Jesus was a good man.

T.L.: I will never forget it.

DAISY: They loved to come and study the teachings of Jesus with us because they had great admiration for Him, **as a prophet and as a teacher.** They loved His teachings and even respected Him **as a miracle worker.**

T.L.: They would stay for hours — sometimes all afternoon.

DAISY: They accepted Jesus as a prophet, as a great teacher — and as a healer.

T.L.: But they did not accept Him **as the Son**

of God, raised from the dead, or as the Savior of the world.

We knew that if they did not believe these facts about Jesus, there was no way that they could be converted, because the Bible says, *If you confess with your mouth that **Jesus is Lord,** and believe in your heart that **God has raised him from the dead, you shall be saved.*** (Ro.10:9)

These people did not believe either of these facts, so they could not be saved according to the Bible. We did not know what to do.

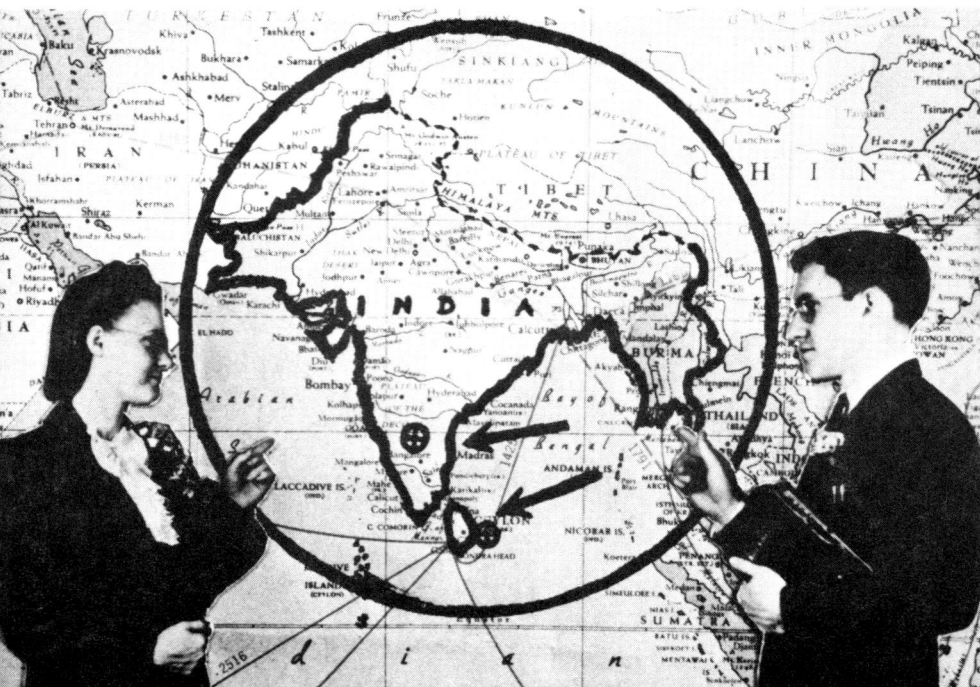

As young missionaries, T.L. and Daisy's goal was clear: To share Christ where the need was greatest and the workers were fewest.

"The Hindus had their Vedas. The Moslems had their Koran. We had our Bible. Without miracles, we could not prove that the Bible was the word of God. We were in despair."

"The Hindus were wonderful people, and were kind to us, but we could not prove to them that Jesus is alive."

PART 6

WE FACED THE SAME ISSUE THAT PRIMITIVE CHRISTIANS FACED

T.L.: We suddenly realized that **we faced the same problem**, or the same issue, that the Early Church had confronted after the resurrection of Jesus Christ. He was risen, but the people did not believe He was risen.

We were in the same situation, among the same kind of people.

DAISY: That was the real issue. We

preached. We studied the language. We entertained visitors. We spent long hours in religious discourses.

T.L.: But we could never convince them **that Jesus was the Son of God.** They were friends. They were lovely people.

I remember a group of Moslems who came one afternoon. We were having such a great visit. And they said, "All right, Mr. and Mrs. Osborn, prove to us that Jesus is the Son of God and that He is risen from the dead."

I said, "Sure, I can do that." And I reached for my Bible and I started opening the pages to locate the scriptures. But they interrupted me and said, "Wait, Mr. Osborn. We don't believe the Bible is God's word."

And they reached for their black book and started to show me what their book said.

There we were with two black books on the table. One of them was called the **Bible.** The other was called the **Koran** — according to them, the word of God that came through the prophet Mohammed.

But which was God's word? Ours said that Jesus is the Son of God, risen from the dead. Theirs denied both. We both had black books with gold print on the covers.

I will never forget that shock as long as I live. We could not prove which was God's word.

DAISY: That was our crisis. We were no good for India in that condition.

T.L.: We were in utter confusion and did not know how to minister to these wonderful people.

DAISY: Because we could not convince them of the fundamentals on which our faith is based.

T.L. and Daisy Osborn, soon after their return from India to their homeland.

PART 7

BACK TO AMERICA — AND WHY

T.L.: We decided to go home. We felt that it would be better to go back to America where most of the people already believed the Bible (or at least claimed to believe what the Bible says about Christ). So we returned home, but in unbelievable turmoil.

We had seen the masses. We had seen the need. We had seen the people who knew nothing of the gospel.

That began our search. That was the beginning of our crisis.

As we were coming home, a wonderful church elected us as their pastor, which was a great encouragement to us, because we felt terribly discouraged and ashamed to be coming home before our term had ended.

DAISY: In those days you did not go to a foreign country and preach for a few months, then come back. People just did not do that in those days. When you went, you went for five years. Some went for seven years. Some even went for ten years or more.

We had gone for five years. To come home ahead of our time really meant disgrace. But we were determined to find the solution to our dilemma.

T.L.: I always marvel at that epoch of our lives. How merciful God was to us!

Those wonderful people in that beautiful church elected us as their pastor. It was the headquarters church of a four-state district.

ABOVE: The church in Oregon where T.L. and Daisy were elected as pastors on their return to America from India.

BELOW: Comfortable in a lovely parsonage, the Osborns were discontended in their hearts as they searched for God's answer to reaching the UNreached.

The Osborn residence in Portland, Oregon.

SUPERIMPOSED PHOTOGRAPH

PART 8
WHEN JESUS VISITED OUR HOUSE

DAISY: We continued our search.

We read biographies of men and women who had been used of God. We studied our Bibles. We read sermons. We went to hear evangelists, preachers, teachers.

We were really searching. We **had** to find the answer to the dilemma we faced.

T.L.: I will never forget the convention where we began to discover the solution to our problem.

The Lord spoke to us through the convention speaker who said: **"If you ever see Jesus, you will never be the same again."**

I knew God said that. It was real.

We went home and prayed late that night and then went to bed.

The next morning at 6 o'clock sharp, **the Lord appeared in that room. I looked on Jesus just as one looks at anyone.**

He was real. He stood there. I lay at His feet as a dead man. I could not move a finger or a toe.

Water poured from my eyes, yet I was not conscious of weeping. It was an overwhelming experience. The human body cannot stand the presence of Christ.

I do not know how long it was before I was able to move my toes and my hands. I do not remember how I got on my face on the floor, and I do not know how many hours I lay there.

But I know one thing. Jesus Christ became **Lord** of my life that morning. He changed me forever. I knew He was alive, and I knew He was **Lord**. I was a totally renewed person.

DAISY: I had gotten up early that morning to feed the babies and to take care of their baths — all of the things a wife and mother must do.

I was real busy all morning. Then I was feeding

the children their lunch and getting ready to put them down for their afternoon naps.

About that time, I remember that T.L. came out of that room. **And when I looked at him, I knew I had a new husband. Something had happened. He was changed.**

T.L.: Yes, I was a new man. Jesus was **Lord** of my life.

Previously, I had become a successful denominational man. It had affected me.

Though I had seen the need of the people in India, I suppose that, having failed as a missionary — or at least it seemed to us that we had failed — I suppose that as a husband and as a leader of the home, I was grasping for success. I responded to the denominational attention that was given to me.

I became almost possessed by a drive to go to the top in that field. I wanted the favor of my superiors. My world was my organization.

I felt I had failed as a missionary, so success in my church organization helped my self-image.

I was active in official functions. I loved it. I had an almost unnatural esteem for our district and national officials. They were my leaders, my ideals, **almost my lords.**

But when I walked out of that room, I was delivered from that obsession to become something that

was not what God wanted for me.
Jesus had become Lord of my life.
From that morning, nothing else mattered.
It no longer mattered what my church officials thought about me. I do not mean that I disrespected them. I just mean that Jesus Christ had become my **Lord.**

He was real. He loved **me.** He came to **me. I** was important to Him. God had a plan for my life. God had created **me.** God believed in **me.**

I saw **myself** in a different light. Something had happened to **me.** Everything had changed. I had a new perspective on life. I knew God loved **me.** He sent Jesus to **me.** Jesus was real to **me.** He was alive and He cared about **me.** He had come to **our** home. He had appeared to **me.**

PART 9
OUR TEST OF LOYALTY

T.L.: Then the most marvelous thing happened right after that profound experience.

A very wonderful, humble man of God came to our area, whose ministry was known across the nation. He was a man who really represented Jesus in a wonderful way.

He came to our city praying for the sick. He had a wonderful gift of healing, and when he prayed for the people and touched them, marvelous miracles took place.

He came to a great auditorium in the city of Portland, Oregon, and we attended.

DAISY: That was our real test of loyalty. Up until then, T.L. was so loyal to our denomination that he never would have left the convention we were in the midst of, to go to another meeting.

T.L.: Certainly not!

DAISY: That is the real test of whether or not Jesus Christ has truly become **Lord** of one's life.

And I would like to interject here:

When that happened in T.L.'s life, he did not lose respect for our denominational officials. But **he gained a new respect** for **himself** as an individual. He could see **himself** as someone important in God's plan.

I wonder if that is not a key for Jesus to become **Lord** of one's life.

He lets you actually see that **you** have infinite value. He needs **you.** He has a plan for **you.**

T.L.: That has now become **the crusade of our lives — the passion of our lives. To help people**

The Osborns, as young pastors, in Portland, Oregon, after having returned from India in apparent defeat.

Church in Portland, Oregon, where T.L. and Daisy were pastors during the time when they had their first real experience of seeing instant miracles wrought in Jesus' name.

realize that each individual is unique and valuable to God — that each one has an important role to play in God's plan, that each person has a divine destiny to fulfill.

And as you read this, I trust that something happens today that will cause **you** to realize that Jesus loves **you** and wants to come to **you** just like He came to us — because **you have value.**

He has a plan for **you. You** are going some place. He designed **you** for a purpose. If you can catch that spark, **it will change your life like it did ours.**

What made our situation awkward was that we were pastors of the headquarters church, and we were responsible to host the people attending the convention. That was the very week during which this man of God came to our city for the great miracle meeting.

Since I was not only the official host to the convention, but was also a member of the official board — one of the presbyters and the Secretary-Treasurer of the District — I saw no way to go to that miracle meeting. It would be disloyal.

PART 10
DAISY LED THE WAY

T.L.: I had seen the Lord. Jesus had become my **Lord** and I longed to go see the miracles. But how could I just walk out of our own convention?

DAISY: But I knew that I had to go see what God was doing. I was so hungry.

T.L.: Yes, Daisy went first, then she came back and gave me a report.

DAISY: I went with my dear friend who was almost 90 years old — a great woman of God.

T.L.: Isn't that remarkable? An old woman — 90 years of age, as eager as a young person to learn new truth and to see God at work.

DAISY: She really had the spirit of a young woman. She was a real **believer.**

T.L.: That is true. And ever since we have known that woman, we have prayed that as long as we live, we will be **young enough in our faith and in our spirits** to hear God's voice and to move with Him, even if no one understands us.

Young enough **to believe.** Young enough **to take risks.** Young enough **to reach out and make decisions.** Young enough **to start again.** Young enough **to know that anything can be done if it is for God's glory and for the good of people.**

That old woman went with Daisy and they saw miracles. Then Daisy came back and told me about it.

We talked late that night and I knew I **had** to go see the wonders of God. We could have conventions anytime, but an opportunity to see miracles might not come again. I decided that, whether my organization understood or not, **I had to go.**

PART 11
THE GREATEST REVELATION

DAISY: It was the first time in my life I had ever seen miracles, even though I had accepted Jesus at the age of 12. I was a grown woman, a wife, a mother, and had been a missionary in India, yet I had never seen an instant miracle.

T.L.: We had faithfully prayed for the sick wherever we ministered. But it was almost a ritual.

DAISY: It **was** a ritual. That is right.

As a young pastor, having failed as a missionary, T.L. informs the convention which he is hosting, about his wife's report, and announces that he **must** go see the miracles for himself.

T.L.: Every Friday night in our meetings, we prayed for the sick — not Tuesday or Sunday; only Friday. We did not see much happen, but we prayed.

DAISY: I had never seen deaf ears come open, or blind people receive their sight, or cripples get up and walk.

T.L.: That is what we wanted to see. So, I made an announcement to our convention that **I had to go see the man of God and the miracles.** I told them that I did not want to be disloyal or to be misunderstood, but that in India **I had failed as a missionary because my good sermons were not enough to prove to non-Christians that the gospel is true.**
I needed miracles. I had prayed for the answer. The Lord had appeared to me and I knew that He was alive. But now I had to chance to see His miracles in action, and I must go.
So I handed over the church to the officials. I gave them the funds and the checkbook and every facility we had, but excused myself and **went to hear the man of God and to see the miracles.**

DAISY: And we saw them when we went to that meeting. That was the beginning of our answer.

T.L.: I had seen the Lord. I knew He was alive. I knew the Bible was real. **I knew that Jesus had become Lord of my life, and now we had a purpose for living. We had a destiny. We had a goal.**

I remember what impressed me: Everybody else was talking about the man's gift of healing, but what attracted me was how **he preached about Jesus.**

DAISY: God had said to T.L., **"If you ever see Jesus, you will never be the same again."** Well, he saw Him in that vision. Jesus was so merciful that He actually stood before him.

T.L.: And, what a change took place in me! Jesus became **Lord** of my life.

DAISY: Then at that meeting, we were getting a chance to see Jesus **together,** because we were seeing Him demonstrate Himself in miracles. We were seeing His power in action ...

T.L.: ... through an ordinary person.

DAISY: Yes, we were actually seeing Jesus at work through a human person.

T.L.: That is really what Christianity is. It is Jesus working through human persons.

He uses our hands, our lips, our ears, our eyes, our tongues. He speaks **through us** and loves **through us.**

DAISY: The people in Bible days saw God **through Jesus.** Today people see Jesus Christ **through us.**

T.L.: **I think that is the greatest revelation of true Christianity.** That is what we saw in that man. It was not the gift of healing that impressed us, although there was obviously a wonderful gift at work in that man, and we know that God has established those gifts in His church. But that was not what attracted us. It was that the man **exalted Jesus and demonstrated HIS love in action.**

Hundreds of people came forward and accepted Christ that night. **That** was what we had wanted so much in India. We loved those people but we could not convince them to accept and to believe on Jesus Christ.

We knew He was real ourselves, but we had to surrender our goals and return to the USA where we thought most everybody already believed in Him.

But I will never forget that yearning inside of me. It was an agony.

T.L. and Daisy had dedicated their lives, when they were married, to obey Christ and to preach His gospel.

BELOW: Now they had been to India and failed, because they did not understand faith and miracles. As pastors in Portland, now they had a chance to see miracles, and **nothing would deter them from following the Lord.**

PART 12
A THOUSAND VOICES

DAISY: Something very wonderful happened to T. L. as we sat there in that balcony beholding the wonders of God.

T.L.: Oh, what an experience! Those who were sick formed a long line and each one came before that man for prayer. Remarkable miracles took place.

People whose backs were curved, became straight in a moment — like the woman in the Bible. People with braces on their legs, took them off and walked away well.

The man stopped a little girl who was deaf and

dumb from birth.

Very kindly, that man of God said to the audience: **"Everyone, please bow your heads and close your eyes. This little girl is possessed of a deaf and dumb spirit.**

"Be very reverent because this spirit will come out of her when I speak in Jesus' name, and we do not want it to enter into someone else who is irreverent or unbelieving!"

I had never heard anyone talk like that in my life. I knew Jesus talked like that in Bible days.

But, wow, this was for real!

He prayed a very simple, quiet prayer, speaking with absolute authority.

He put his fingers in the girl's ears, and said, **"You dumb and deaf spirit, I adjure you by Jesus Christ the Son of God, that you come out of the child and enter her no more."**

And then he was quiet. That was all he said.

Then the man of God heaved a sigh of relief and said, **"The evil spirit has gone from the girl now. You can lift your heads and look. The spirit has gone out of her. She is well."**

I could not believe my ears. How did he know she was healed? He had not examined her. He had not checked her ears.

DAISY: I looked at T.L. about that time, and

his eyes were a fountain of tears.

T.L.: I will never forget it.

We have seen that happen hundreds of times since that experience, in our own meetings, **but that was the FIRST time.** I was overwhelmed.

Over my head, a thousand voices whirled and said, **"You can do that! You can do that! You do not have the gift of healing like he has, but you can do that! You have the same word of God that he has preached! That is what Jesus did! That is what Peter did! That is what Paul did! That proves that the Bible is good today! You can do that!"**

Oh, I knew Jesus was alive!

I knew I did not have that gift, but I knew that man had spoken in the name of Jesus, and that was what God's word said that **any believer** could do.

A gift is a sign from God.

A sign must point to something.

A true gift from God **always points to His word.** It points to Jesus who is the living Word.

We went home revolutionized. Oh, what a change! We sat down and talked most of that night.

"Blessed are they which do hunger and thirst after righteousness: for they shall be filled." Matthew 5:6. T.L. and Daisy Osborn were determined to find God's way to convince the NON-Christian world about Jesus Christ.

PART 13

THE LORD SPOKE AGAIN

DAISY: That was when we decided to begin reading our Bibles with a new attitude.

I said, "Honey, let's read the New Testament as though we had never read it in our lives — like it was a brand new book."

T.L.: Yes, that is what we decided to do. I shut myself in our basement to read and to pray. Daisy would have, but the children needed her care, which kept her from spending days alone in prayer as I did. It is often more difficult for a woman than for a man, but she committed herself to the same goal — between taking care of the babies and answering the phone.

DAISY: We were both experiencing a spiritual revolution.

T.L.: We had seen Christ. I had seen Him in a vision, and now we had both seen Him in a human person. What we had seen made the Bible a new book for us.

DAISY: How true that is!

T.L.: As we read the New Testament, I will never forget the shock as we discovered scripture after scripture where Jesus gave us authority over demons, over diseases, to speak in His name — **just exactly like that man of God had done in that public meeting which we attended.**

But, in spite of that, I wanted the Lord to speak to **me,** personally. So, I shut myself in a small bedroom and for three days and nights. I was there without food or a drop of water.

DAISY: That frightened me because T.L. said, "Honey, take the church, pastor it. Preach or do whatever you want. But don't look for me. I don't know how long I'm going to be in this room, but I'm not coming out until I have heard from the Lord."

I was petrified because I had never had the responsibility of the church and of doing all of the preaching myself.

T.L.: We both grew stronger those days. Something **had** to happen.

When I went into that room and dropped on my knees and opened the Bible, **in that instant** God spoke to me.

DAISY: Isn't that amazing?

T.L.: But I did not know it was God. I did not recognize His voice. I stayed in that room for three days and nights, without food or water, asking the Lord to speak to me, and every time, the same message would come to me again and again — until I finally accepted it.

This is what the Lord said.

"As I have been with others, so will I be with you. Wherever you go, I will give you the land for your possession. No demon, no disease, or no power can stand before you all the days of your life, IF you can get the people to believe my word."

And in reality, that was just a repeat of the

revelation I had received in that meeting when that man of God spoke and demonstrated that wonderful gift of healing.

Those voices over my head said, **"You can do that! That is the way Jesus did it! That is what Peter and Paul did! You can do that! That proves the Bible is for today!"**

I knew I could do that because I saw proof that what happened in the Bible was for today.

Then we discovered all of those scriptures where the Lord had given us power and authority over devils and diseases, to cast them out and to heal the sick.

Now the Lord had said to me again and again: **"As I have been with others, I will be with you. No demon or disease or power can stand before you, IF you can get the people to believe my word."**

Everything pointed to **God's word of promise,** and His word was for **everyone.**

I did not have a gift of healing, but I had the living Word of God, and the healer was living in me and in that word which I could give to people.

Others marveled at that man's **healing gift,** but his gift only pointed me to God's **healing word.**

In other words, that gift, like all of God's gifts, was a sign. A sign does not point to itself but to something else. **That healing gift pointed me to God's healing word — to His promises.** They were for us as much as for anyone else. That is why God spoke and said that **I could do that! No power could stand before me, IF I could get the people to believe His word.**

That was the secret — to get the people to believe HIS WORD!

The Holy Spirit, working in us, would help us to teach the word and would anoint us with power to show the proof of that word.

DAISY: That was when we discovered **what the Holy Spirit was for in our lives** — that it was not just to make us feel good or to speak in tongues or to be holy, but that the Holy Spirit was in us **to help us prove to the people that Jesus is the Christ, the risen Son of God.**

T.L.: Yes, and that was what caused us to write the book, *The Purpose of Pentecost.*

DAISY: Yes — our own experience.

T.L.: Christian leaders and laypersons have told me around the world that it is one of the greatest messages we have ever published. It has been a great blessing.

We saw what the Holy Spirit is for.

What a change took place in our lives!

OSBORN CRUSADE

OSBORN CRUSADE

OSBORN CRUSADE

OSBORN CRUSADE

OSBORN CRUSADE

LUBUMBASHI, ZAIRE, AFRICA

CABANATUAN, LUZON, PHILIPPINES

MADURAI, SOUTHERN INDIA

THE HAGUE, HOLLAND

BOGOTA, COLOMBIA, SOUTH AMERICA

WHAT A MIRACLE! T.L. Osborn shows the audience at Embu the crutches and braces which a cripple in the audience had discarded and sent to the platform as evidence of healing.

While everyone waited for the person who had discarded the crutches and braces to arrive at the platform, suddenly Mr. Osborn spotted another pair of crutches being held aloft, and pointed toward them to signify another miracle God had wrought among the people.

This Osborn Crusade in Nigeria is typical of the multitudes which have been drawn to hear the gospel confirmed by miracles, in over 70 nations during **almost four** decades of their miracle evangelism ministry.

At last the woman whose braces and crutches Mr. Osborn had been holding arrived to show what God had done for her. Crippled by polio when she was a child, she had been left paralyzed. Now she is healed and her legs are strong. Thousands glorified God, saying like the people at Capernaum, *We never saw it on this fashion.* (Mark 2:12)

A great multitude followed him, because they saw his miracles which he did on them that were diseased. (John 6:2)

Wheel chairs, crutches, braces, stretchers and canes are hoisted above the people's heads indicating miracles that have taken place as T.L. and Daisy share the gospel and pray for the people.

PART 14

THE FIRST MIRACLE

T.L.: When I came out of that room, I knew we had to DO something. God was with us. He would back up His word. We **had** to DO something.

So we began to make announcements on the radio and in the paper. We became bold enough to invite the people to come to our church and to bring those who were sick, assuring them that God would heal them.

That would have frightened me terribly to have made an announcement like that before. But we were revolutionized!

I knew Jesus was with us and that He would do what He had done in Bible days. The people came from everywhere. The church was packed to the door.

I preached to them, and then the sick people came

for prayer. One after another was miraculously healed as we prayed for them.

DAISY: The first person T.L. and I prayed for was a woman who had walked on crutches for 14 years.

T.L.: Yes, I shall always remember her.

DAISY: Surgically and medically she was considered an impossible case.

T.L.: But God specializes in "IMpossibilities."

DAISY: She had been injured in an accident and her hip was broken so badly that the bones could not be set. It had become rigid.

T.L.: They had operated to correct the problem but were unable, at that time, to help her. She could never walk normally again. So she used crutches to move herself about.

DAISY: While we were ministering to her, she

took her crutches and started to hand them to T.L., and I remember that I took them from her and tossed them on the floor.

T.L.: We knew God wanted her well.

DAISY: Then T.L. commanded her, **"In the name of Jesus, walk!"** She raised her hands high, and with her eyes closed, she began walking as perfect as anyone. Her face was shining like an angel! Her rigid hip became flexible and free.

She kept walking and she acted as though she was listening to something marvelous.

> Her eardrum had been removed in an operation, leaving her with no physical faculty for hearing. After T.L. and Daisy prayed, she can hear a watch tick — a creative miracle of God.

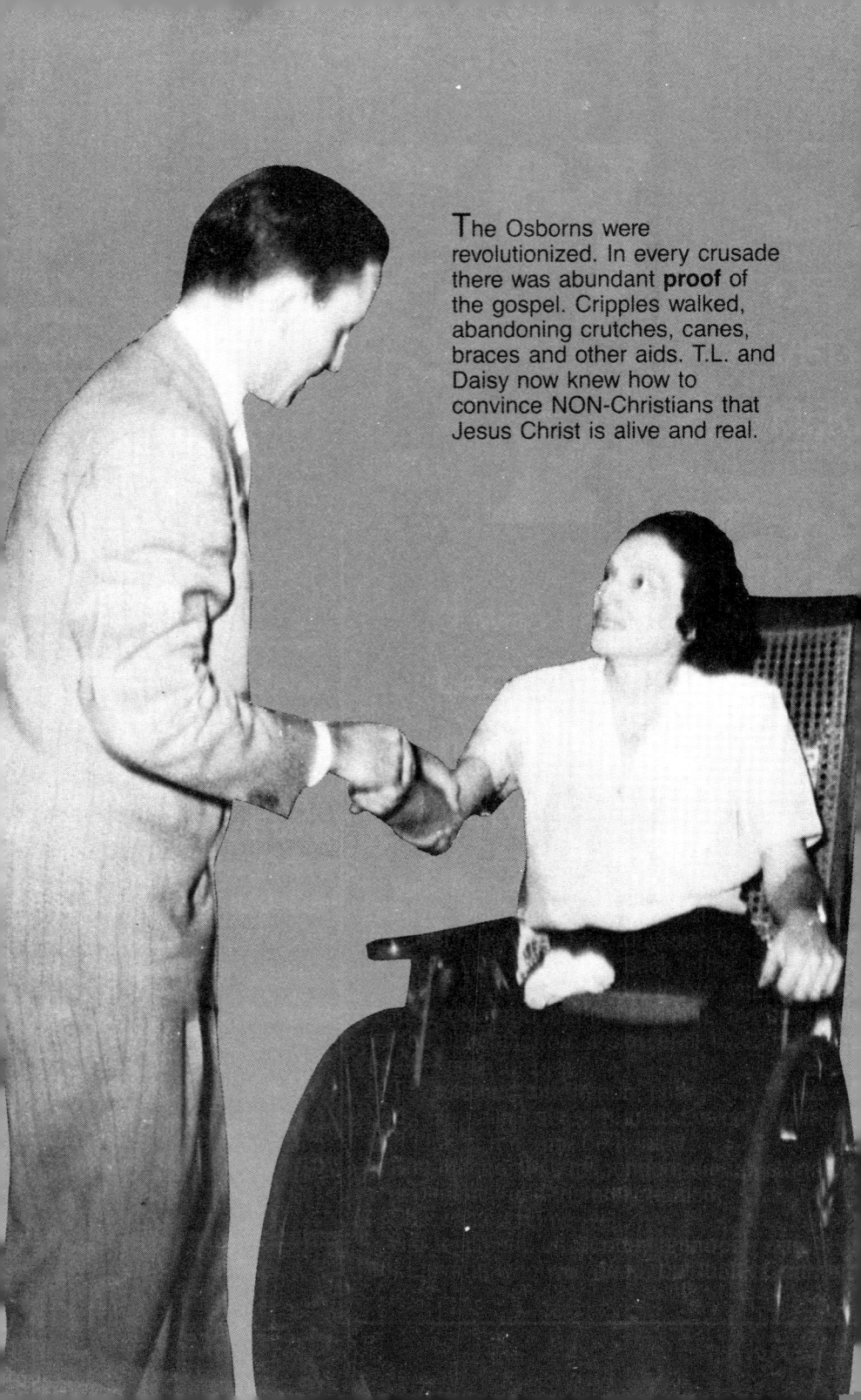

The Osborns were revolutionized. In every crusade there was abundant **proof** of the gospel. Cripples walked, abandoning crutches, canes, braces and other aids. T.L. and Daisy now knew how to convince NON-Christians that Jesus Christ is alive and real.

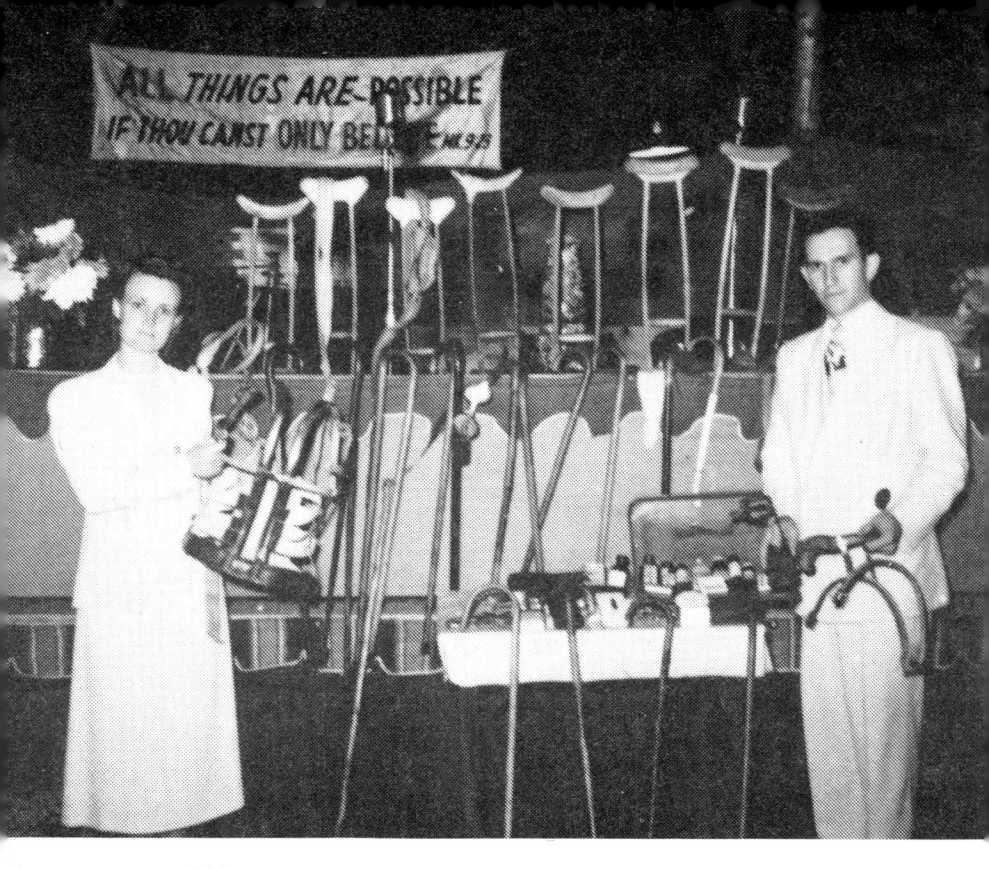

T.L. and Daisy Osborn teaching faith in one of their first tent crusades in Pennsylvania, standing amidst crutches, canes, braces, etc., discarded by those miraculously healed.

All the time that we were ministering to the others, that woman kept her hands up and kept on walking about. Then we found out that she had been hearing a choir of angels singing. She said, **"I've been listening to the heavenly hosts singing praises to our Lord."**

Well, that was the beginning of a change for our lives.

"All I could think about were those masses in India — those wonderful people who knew nothing about the living Christ. Now we had the answer. Now, we could help them." T.L. Osborn

PART 15

T.L.'S SOLUTION BECAME DAISY'S PROBLEM

T.L.: For us, that was our real discovery of Christ at work in **our** lives.

Our search had been richly rewarded. Our crisis — was over. **We had the answer.**

But what were we going to do about it?

All we could think about were those masses in India — those Moslems, those Hindus — those wonderful people who knew nothing about the living Christ.

DAISY: It was really **for them** that we started our search. Now we could help them.

T.L.: We loved them and we knew that they needed Christ, but we had not been able to prove to them that Jesus is the Son of God, risen from the dead.

Now we could prove it! As Jesus said, **"The proof is in the miracles."**

DAISY: We say, "Every problem contains the seed of its own solution." You can reverse that and say, **"Every solution brings with it the seed of a bigger problem!"**

T.L.: That is really true. That helps us grow.

DAISY: So **our** search had ended, but **my personal** problem had just begun.

T.L.: I remember that you felt that way.

DAISY: Here I was in the security of a lovely home — which every woman wants — happily married, with lovely children.

I had everything a woman could desire. And now it seemed that everything would be uprooted — **because my man had seen Jesus.**

Our lives had been changed and he had been called to go to the uttermost parts of the earth. That was my problem.

T.L.: The thing that impressed me about Daisy at that time was the fact that she wanted the Lord to appear to **her** too.

DAISY: That's what I wanted. I needed that.

T.L.: Most women would say, "Well, whatever my husband does, I'll join him." And to a certain extent we understand that.

DAISY: To a point, yes.

T.L.: But what I liked about Daisy — and I remember how it impressed me even as a young husband — **she was determined that God was going to speak to her too.**

DAISY: I really felt that Jesus was obligated to say something to me too because, though I was part of T.L., I was also an **individual** and **I** would have to stand before God some day and answer for **my own life, my own decisions, my own attitude. T.L., as my husband, certainly could not answer to God for ME.**

T.L.: But, that is another story — and I have urged Daisy to write it and to record it for the good of so many others who are searching.

DAISY: Yes, I will publish it. And Jesus **did** speak to me. I **did** have my spiritual experience.

T.L.: That is true, and how real and wonderful it was!

DAISY: So I have been a **GO-along**, not a **TAG-along**, in God's No. 1 Job.

T.L.: I wish every woman could understand how she counts with God — **as an individual** human person, accountable to Him.

If women could believe in their own value to God, He would raise up thousands of them and use them in His ministry to humanity.

Daisy Washburn Osborn, proclaimer of the good news of Christ to multitudes around the world.

Teaching

Preaching

Ministering

Witnessing

Healing

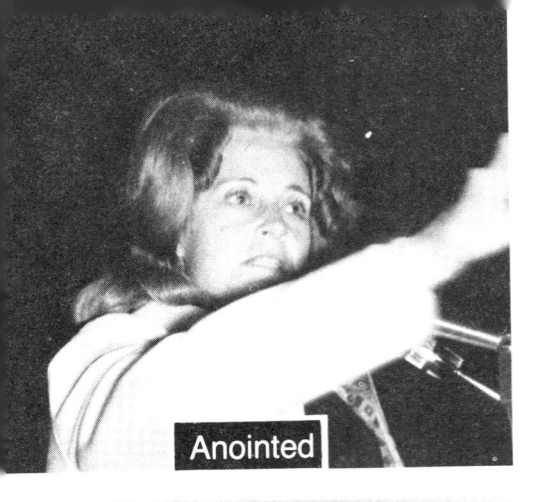

Anointed

Chosen of God

Commissioned

Preacher of the Gospel

PART 16
THIRTEEN WEEKS

T.L.: We knew we had to DO something. We had to GO to the peoples of the world.

We had no funds to go to India. It was too far and would cost too much. But we had been invited to the island-nation of Jamaica, in the Caribbean. That was near enough to the USA that we could get enough money to go there.

DAISY: So we left our house full of furniture. All we had was our **car, kids** and **cases,** and our destination was Jamaica. We were on our way.

T.L.: Yes, and how God did lead us!

We ministered in Jamaica for 13 weeks and we preached and prayed for the people, individually, night after night.

Although Daisy's story must wait for another publication, I want to explain how we worked and ministered **together**. Hundreds of people would line up, even out to the street, waiting for us to pray for them, one by one.

DAISY: We prayed for them, hour after hour.

T.L.: That was the only way we knew to do.

DAISY: Mass healing was unknown.

T.L.: It was impossible for me to pray for so many people by myself.

So we would set our two children in chairs, beside one of the pastor's wives. Daisy would stand on one side of the platform and pray for a line of people while I stood on the other side and prayed for the other line.

People with crossed eyes, blind eyes, deaf ears, cripples — **they were healed just the same in Daisy's line, as in mine. The people did not care which one of us prayed for them.**

DAISY: *One can chase a thousand; two can chase ten thousand,* the Bible says in Deuteronomy 32:30.

T.L.: It was wonderful! For 13 weeks it was like that.

DAISY: Thousands were healed.

T.L.: During that time, over 9,000 people came forward, knelt and prayed the salvation prayer and accepted Jesus Christ as Savior.

Over 90 totally blind people received their sight instantly — hundreds of others gradually.

Over 125 deaf mutes instantly talked and received their hearing. Scores of others were gradually healed.

And the Lord only knows how many thousands of other people were healed as we prayed for them.

DAISY: We saw more fruit from our labors in a single night than we had seen in the seven years of our ministry before the Lord appeared to us.

And it was **the miracles that made the difference!**

T.L.: Many times, in one night, three or four hundred people would accept Christ.

MIRACLES IN JAMAICA

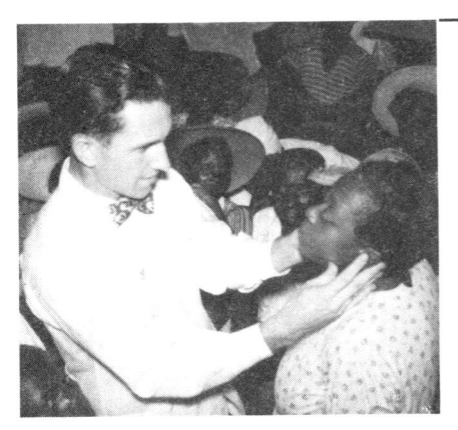

TOTALLY BLIND & DEAF INSTANTLY HEALED

Lady totally blind and totally deaf since a small girl receives her hearing first, then after T.L. rebukes the blind spirit, she receives her sight.

Being totally blind and deaf, the poor lady had no idea where she was or why she was there, but when able to hear and see, it is doubtful if there was ever a woman happier in the world.

She literally screamed, jumped, squealed and yelled for joy.

She would look at the light and scream, "Look at de lite! Look at de lite!"

Then she would jump and bow completely to the floor, clapping her hands as fast as she could, for joy.

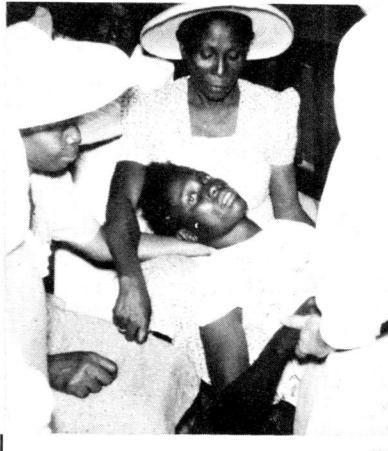

MIRACLE OF VEDA McKENZIE

"I was like Lazarus; now I am ALIVE!"

Veda McKenzie was stricken with a complete stroke on a Sunday, which rendered her totally unconscious and helpless. From Sunday until Thursday, she lay in a coma, unable to eat or drink. Her eyes rolled back in her head.

Three women loaded her into a wheelbarrow and brought her across town and into the building, laid her on the floor, and waited patiently from 4 p.m. until 10:45 that night when her turn finally came for prayer.

T.L. rebuked the demon, charging it to leave the woman's body. He called out with a loud voice, "Veda, open your eyes and look at me, and be healed."

She immediately responded, sat up, stood up, walked, and was perfectly and instantly healed.

She walked home well.

Her testimony on Sunday afternoon was: "Folks, look at me. I am Lazarus who was dead, but thank God I am alive."

DAISY: I guess that answers the questions that we posed at the beginning of this testimony. **Are miracles really important today?**

T.L.: Yes, they are important.

DAISY: Do we really need them today?

T.L.: People who are being born **today** need them. They need to see Jesus the same as people who were born in Bible days.

The church was established for the people then, but God re-establishes Himself for every new generation. He is as real today as He ever was, **and He wants to prove it.**

That is why the theme of our crusades around the world has always been, *Jesus Christ the same yesterday and today and forever.* (He. 13:8)

PART 17
MINISTRY TO AMERICA

T.L.: After the Jamaica crusades, we returned to America, and received an urgent call from Rev. F. F. Bosworth, asking us to come to Flint, Michigan to continue Rev. William Branham's crusade in the large city auditorium there, inasmuch as he had become exhausted and was physically unable to minister to the thousands attending.

DAISY: That Flint crusade marked the real beginning of our ministry across the USA.

T.L., a powerful teacher and preacher of faith, and proven in miracle evangelism overseas, influenced hundreds of preachers to turn from dull religion to dynamic redemption with faith and power.

In crusade after crusade, after T.L. and Daisy taught the word of God and prayed for the sick people, hundreds left braces, crutches and other aids behind as testimonies of the miracles they had received from God.

Wherever the Osborn tent was erected across Pennsylvania, New York state, Maryland and then westward into Tennessee and on to Texas, it was packed and surrounded by thousands eager to hear T.L. and Daisy teaching faith, and to see and to experience the miracle power of Jesus Christ through their anointed ministries.

PART 18
EVERYWHERE THE RESULTS WERE THE SAME

T.L.: After the summer in the USA, we went to Puerto Rico, to Cuba and to Central and South America. Everywhere the multitudes and the miracles were the same.

Then, we went to Japan. They told us: "Oh, it will be different here. The people here are Shintoists."

But it was exactly the same in Japan!

DAISY: Everywhere was the same.

T.L.: In our first crusade in Japan, 44 deaf mutes were healed, and the Japanese were as excited and as emotional as anyone in the Western Hemisphere.

DAISY: Maybe even more so. We found them very emotional.

OSBORN CRUSADE

BELOW: Eight of more than 44 deaf-mutes healed during the Kyoto Campaign.

Osborn crusades in Japan. The Shintoists were no different from people of other religions.

KYOTO, JAPAN

OSBORN CRUSADE MATSUYAMA, JAPAN

TOTALLY BLIND 21 YEARS

INSTANTLY HEALED, READS BIBLE BEFORE AUDIENCE IN OSBORN'S KYOTO CRUSADE.

This man had been totally blind for 21 years. He was led to the crusade at Kyoto. As the Osborns prayed for the blind, commanding the blind spirits to leave, he received his sight immediately. Several persons confirmed his testimony.

A man in the audience who doubted that such a miracle could be genuine came to the platform. He shoved a calling card before the formerly blind man and demanded: "Read that! He read the card perfectly.

He asked for a Bible, and to the amazement of the audience, read it as well as anyone could.

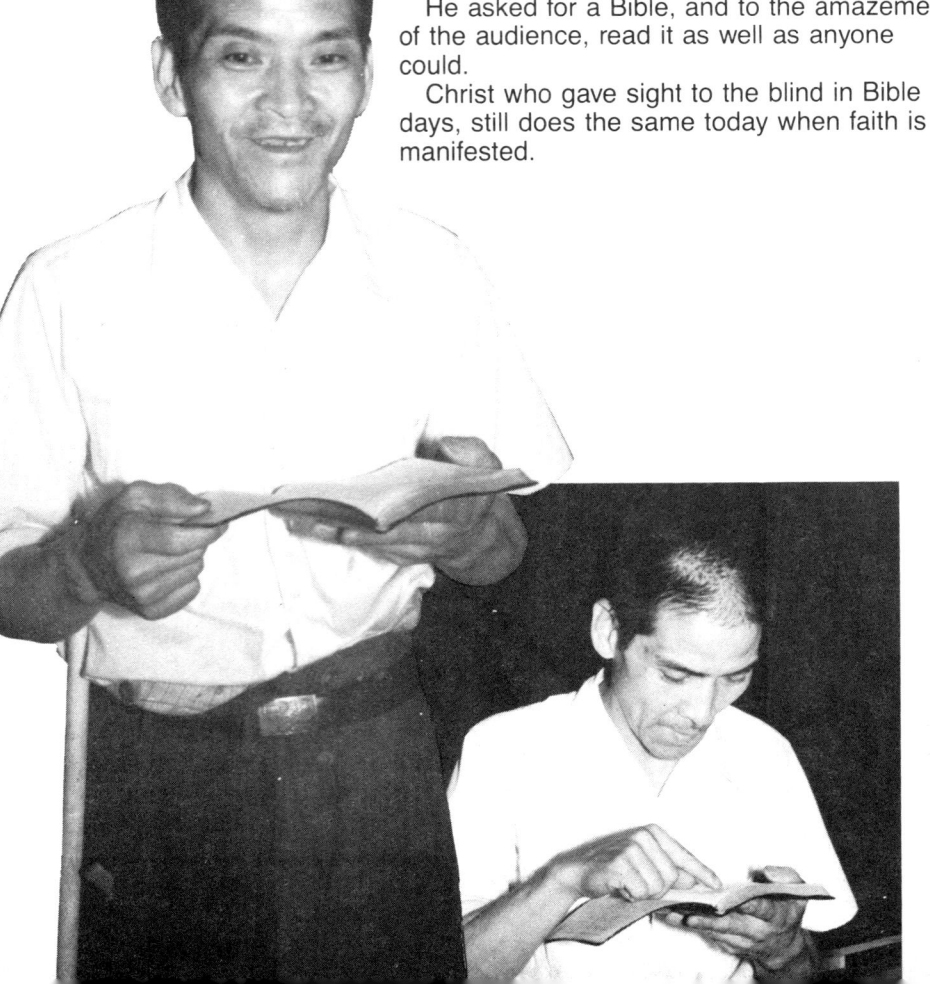

Christ who gave sight to the blind in Bible days, still does the same today when faith is manifested.

This Japanese lad fell and broke both hips when he was four years old. Since then he had only been able to walk with the aid of a brace and crutches. After the healing prayer, in the Osborn Crusade, he was completely healed and could walk normally.

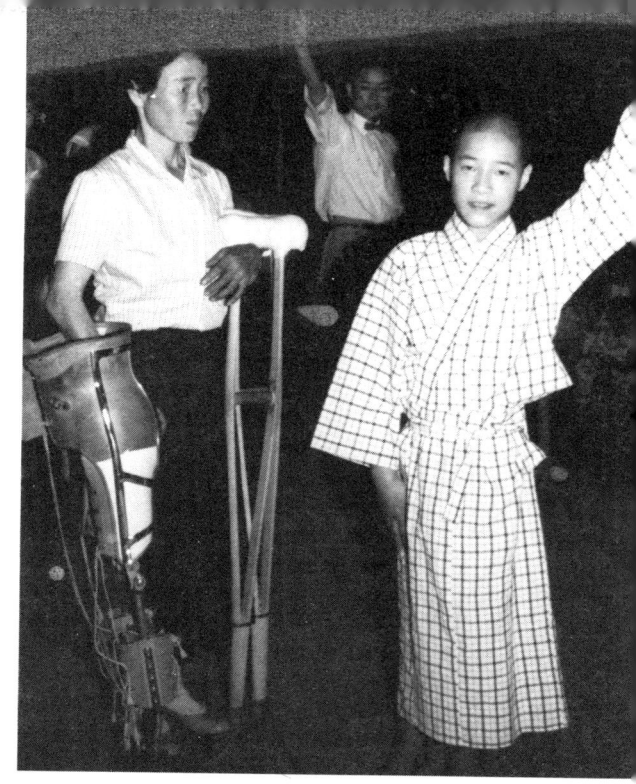

Victim of polio since childhood. Miraculously healed.

Five years paralyzed. Perfectly healed.

T.L.: Next we went to Thailand, a Buddhist monarchy.

DAISY: It was no different among the Buddhists. God is the same everywhere.

T.L. rejoices with a man in Thailand who had been a leper for four years. He was totally healed in the Osborn Crusade at Bangkok.

PART 19
PROOF FOR THE MOSLEMS

T.L.: After the nation-changing Thai crusades, we went to Java where the population was 95 percent Moslem.

Some of the Christians there were frightened. They did not know if it was wise to go out on a public field and call thousands of Moslem people together and talk to them about Jesus and pray for the sick, expecting miracles to confirm that Christ is alive.

DAISY: That was our first time to preach, with miracles, to the Moslems.

T.L.: We did not believe they were different.

The first night I preached in Java, I thought it would be good to tell them **that I did not expect them to accept Jesus unless they saw proof that He was risen from the dead.**

Actually, people are the same today as they were in Bible days. They need to see **proof** that Jesus is alive. Otherwise, all we have is a **religion** — a ritual, a tradition, a ceremony.

DAISY: That is right. They believed on Jesus in Bible days **because they heard and saw His miracles.** (Jn.2:23; 6:2)

T.L.: And it is the same today! In fact, we have proven that to be true in over 70 nations of the world. There has never been an exception.

In Java I asked for anyone who was deaf in one ear, to come to the platform.

Quite a group responded and each one was instantly healed as we prayed for them. The very first person to respond was a Moslem teacher, a man about 60 years old.

He had been born with one ear totally deaf. He had never heard out of it in his life. I will never forget that experience.

I told the people that if his ear did not come open, they would know that I was a false teacher, and that

Jesus Christ had not risen from the dead as the Bible claims.

DAISY: That shocked all who heard T.L.

T.L.: But I explained that if Jesus is alive, **He would make Himself known; He would do the same miracles that He had done before He was crucified.**

DAISY: There were over 100 pastors on the platform. They said, afterwards, that they were frightened about what the multitude might do if that Moslem teacher was not healed.

T.L.: They were petrified. They viewed it as a radical and dangerous challenge.

DAISY: Yes, rather careless and extreme. They felt it was almost irresponsible.

T.L.: Well, I started to put my hand on his ear.

DAISY: But T.L. never touched him. The man did not even stand very close to my husband. T.L. just stretched his hand toward him.

T.L.: Christ is the healer — not me.

DAISY: I remember that T.L. did not want the people to think that there was something mystical about his touch or that he had some strange power.

T.L.: I wanted them to realize that Jesus Christ was there in their presence.

DAISY: Other times we would touch the sick and lay our hands on them.

T.L.: I wanted those people to understand **that this was the power of the Living Jesus, who, though He had been crucified, was alive again, and was present in that meeting.**
Our position was simple and it seemed totally logical to me: **If Jesus is alive, He will do the same things that He did before they killed Him. But if He is dead, He can do no miracle and His name has no power.**

DAISY: Two things I remember about that case: One was that my husband did not touch him, and the other, that he did not close his eyes.

T.L.: I wanted that Moslem teacher to believe that Jesus Christ is alive.

DAISY: T.L. wanted everyone to witness that he was doing nothing mystical.

T.L.: That is why I did not ask the people to close their eyes.

DAISY: We wanted them to watch everything we did. Usually we bow our heads.

T.L.: I looked at him and said, **"In the name of Jesus Christ whom God has raised from the dead according to the scriptures — Jesus who is the Son of the Living God — I adjure the deaf spirit to leave your ear and I command your ear to hear now, so that all here may know that the Bible is true, that Jesus is the Son of God, that His blood was shed for the remission of our sins, and that He is risen from the dead to be the Savior of the world. Amen."**

I spoke with authority. The Holy Spirit was present. When I finished, you could hear a pin drop. It was an apostolic moment.

DAISY: We knew Christ was with us.

T.L.: Across that field was total silence.
Then I pulled the man to me. I stopped up his good ear and faintly whispered in his deaf ear, and

he jumped.

DAISY: It was obvious to everyone.

T.L.: He repeated every word. I told him: "Say what I say, and say it out loud." He agreed.
Then I made him confess what the Bible says about Jesus.
I said, **"Jesus is the Son of God."** He said, "Jesus is the Son of God."
I said, **"He must be risen from the dead."** He repeated, "He must be risen from the dead."

DAISY: By that time he was weeping.

T.L.: As he broke into tears, the crowd started clapping, and I think the preachers were greatly relieved.

DAISY: Then T.L. turned to the multitude to help them accept Christ.

T.L.: Immediately I turned to the audience and asked, "Now, is Jesus Christ alive, or is He dead?"
We called on them to make a decision.
Thousands raised their hands to accept Jesus Christ as their Lord and Savior.
It was marvelous — probably the greatest gospel

demonstration in all of the history of Christian evangelism in Java up to that time.

DAISY: We stayed there for several weeks, preaching, teaching and praying, day after day, conducting two and three meetings per day. We proved afresh that, **when you see Jesus, you can never be the same again.**

MIRACLES AMONG THE JAVANESE

Dumb four years. Healed instantly.

15 months unable to walk. Completely healed.

Totally deaf many years. Miraculously healed

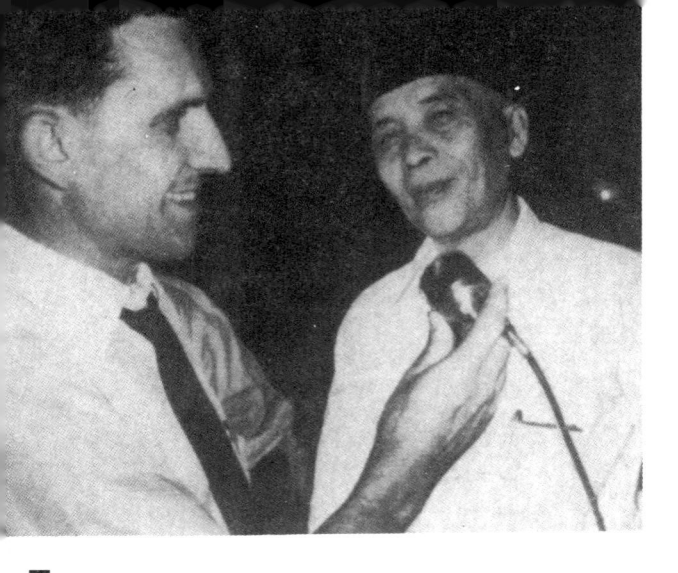

OPPOSITE: The Osborn family during the Java crusades.

The first person who came for prayer was a Moslem teacher, born with one ear totally deaf. When his ear was opened, thousands believed on Jesus Christ.

OSBORN CRUSADES

JAVA, INDONESIA

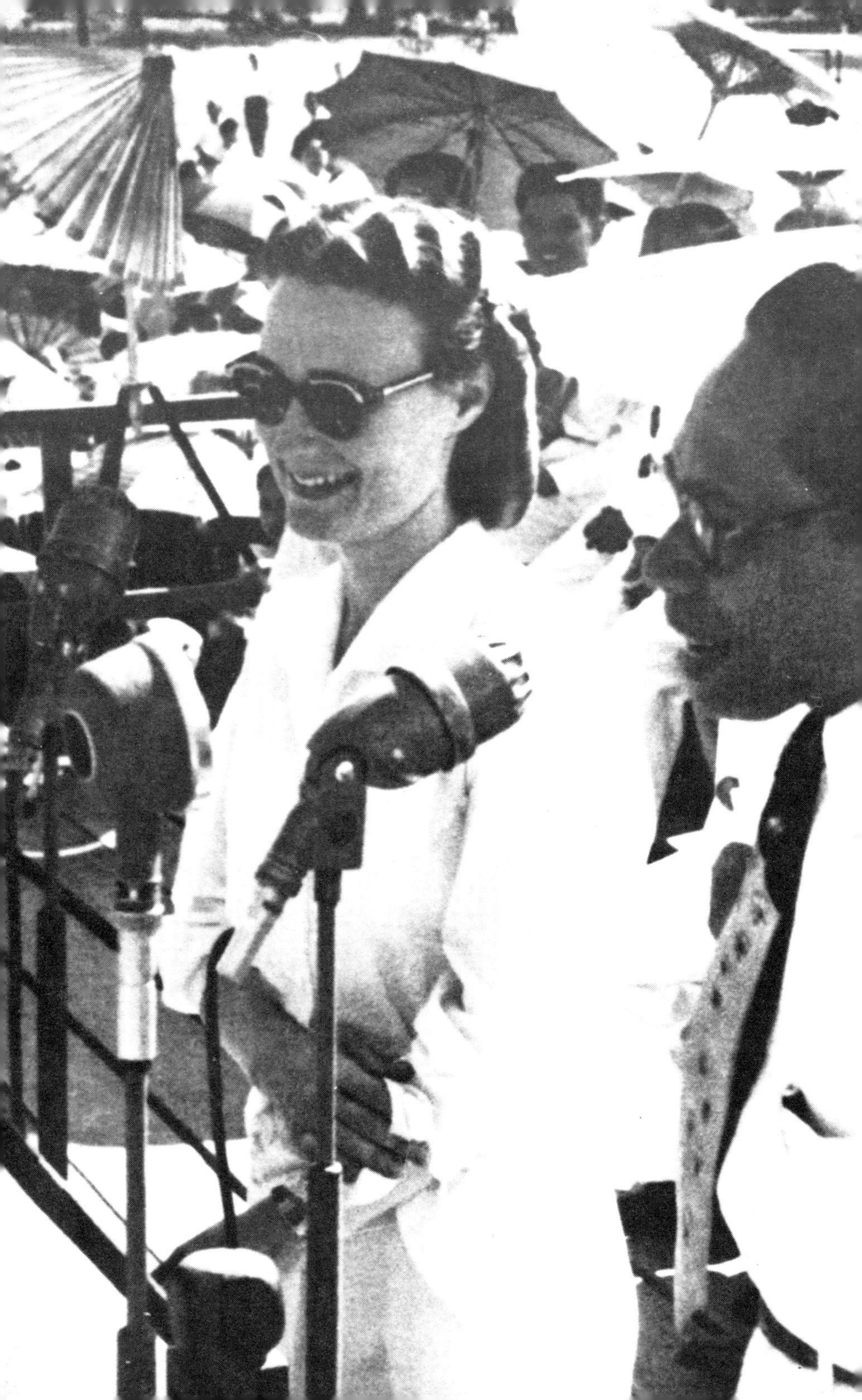

Evangelist Daisy Osborn preaches the good news to tens of thousands of Indonesians in Java.

"Lepers are being healed, blind are seeing, and cripples are walking at the airfield!" This is what I heard in the streets and in the market place as I edged around the people so as not to be noticed, because I WAS A LEPER!

Four years I had been tortured with the shame of being unclean. My nose, my ears, my upper lip and gradually my feet, hands, and arms became dreadfully infected. Running sores covered my feet and hands. In this condition I sought out the place where such unbelievable reports were coming from.

As I approached the grounds I saw other lepers, and all manner of sick people, some being carried, some being led, and others, as myself, staying on the edge of the multitude and all alone.

The very first night I attended, I was instantly and perfectly healed. The sores dried up, all swelling and deadness left and I was clean and whole.

This has made me, a former Mohammedan, know that Jesus is the Son of God and that He is alive just as the Bible declares. Thank God the Osborns came to Java!

PART 20
RETURN TO INDIA

T.L.: After the great Java crusades, we preached all over the world. But finally our dream came true.

DAISY: We returned to India.

T.L.: We went back to the same city where we had talked to those Moslems and Hindus and had not been able to prove whether the **Koran** of the Moslems, or whether the **Bible** was God's word.

This time it was different. We leased a big open field by the great stadium in the university city of

Lucknow. We set up our platform and invited the public to come.

50,000 to 60,000 people attended the crusade. We proclaimed to the masses in India that Jesus is the Son of God, risen from the dead.

DAISY: This time we knew how to prove to the people that Jesus Christ is alive.

T.L.: What a difference living faith makes!

DAISY: Those people had not changed. The situation had not changed. But **WE had changed.** Our thinking had been changed. Our lives had been changed. We knew God would fulfill His word.

T.L.: Fourteen years earlier, we had returned from India to the USA. We had said, "There is no use for us to stay here if we cannot prove to these people that Jesus is alive."

DAISY: We were ineffective as gospel ministers, if we could not prove what we preached.

T.L.: There was no reason for us to stay. So we had gone home. **But now we were back again,** and I do not think that we had ever seen greater miracles than we saw in that crusade.

The Osborns returned to India to proclaim the gospel with the evidence of miracles to prove that Jesus Christ is alive. 14 years earlier, they had left India because they could not give proof of God's word.

Crippled by polio when he was a lad, this man could never move about except by scooting on his hips. He was called the "frog man" beggar, and was instantly healed during the Osborn Crusade in India.

OSBORN CRUSADE

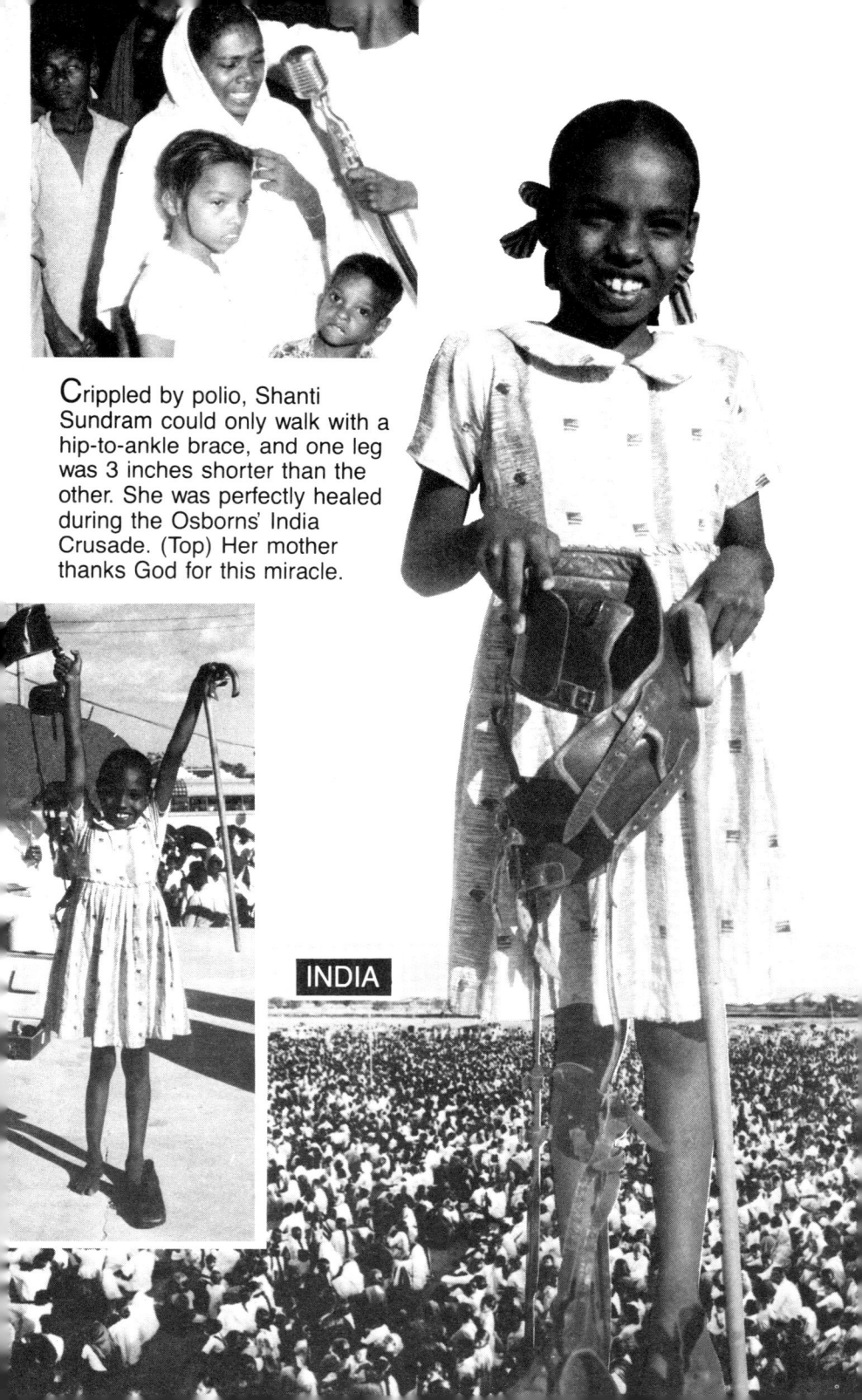

Crippled by polio, Shanti Sundram could only walk with a hip-to-ankle brace, and one leg was 3 inches shorter than the other. She was perfectly healed during the Osborns' India Crusade. (Top) Her mother thanks God for this miracle.

INDIA

DAISY: There was such great faith among those masses in our India crusades.

T.L.: There was tremendous faith. There was a man whom they called the frog man.

DAISY: Yes, he could only walk in a squatting position — like a frog.

T.L.: He was instantly healed and we almost lost control of the multitude when the people saw him walking and running like anyone else. Thousands of people knew him.

Hundreds of people were miraculously healed in that powerful meeting.

For 11 years he was crippled with arthritis. During the message, T.L. pointed at him and told him to believe on the Lord and he could be made whole. He was miraculously healed that same night during the Lucknow, India, crusade.

PART 21
THE HINDU WHO SAW JESUS

T.L.: I will never forget one night during that great crusade in Lucknow, India. Far to the edge of the crowd, there was a young student from the university — an agnostic — who hated everything that we were saying about Jesus Christ.

He was a member of the religious political party of India that had vowed to drive Christianity from their shores. He was a real fanatic.

He stood there with his arms folded across his chest, in a defiant mood. Then as we preached about Jesus, suddenly the Lord appeared right in front of him.

He opened His hands where the man could see His scars, and stretched them out toward the man. Then Jesus spoke these words, **"Behold my hands! I** am Jesus!"

That arrogant young student fell to the ground, in the dust, weeping and crying.

After he regained control of himself, he came running to the platform and grabbed the microphone with trembling hands, and appealed to the multitude: **"Accept this Jesus! What this man is telling us is true! I saw Him! I saw the scars in His hands! He is alive!"** Thousands of people that night believed on Jesus Christ.

Blind people, lepers, deaf mutes, cripples, invalids carried on cots, and all kinds of sicknesses were healed in that overwhelming crusade.

"I saw the scars in His hands. He is alive!"

PART 22

100 PEOPLE SAW THE LORD

T.L.: Daisy and I felt that if we would share these experiences with you, that Christ would visit your house like He visited ours. I believe He wants to do that TODAY.

We have gone all over the world and in practically every crusade we have ever conducted, Christ Himself has appeared, alive — at least once and in some crusades, several times.

One night in Thailand we were preaching to a great crowd of Buddhists and **over 100 people saw the Lord in that meeting.**

It began when a man looked up and saw the Lord above the people. He cried out in alarm: **"Who is that man in white there in the sky?"** And over 100 people saw the Lord's appearance in that meeting.

In Buddhist Thailand, while T.L. was preaching, over 100 people saw the Lord. It began when a man cried in alarm: "Who is that man in white there in the sky?"

(This photo was taken of a cloud formation during a storm near the Osborns' office building, amazing all who have seen it.)

T.L. Osborn, with his interpreter, Sook Pongsnoi, praying for the Thai people who have believed the gospel of Christ.

The next day we spent the entire afternoon listening to the people tell what they saw the night before — those who had seen "that man in white walking above the multitude."

With typical village gestures, they each told their story. As the interpreter translated their words, **it was an overwhelming experience to hear over 100 village people, who had not believed in Jesus before, all confirm the same miraculous visitation.**

Jesus Christ wants to come to you today. **Whoever** you are, **wherever** you are listening to or reading this testimony, the Lord wants to come to you and to show Himself alive to you. I believe that if you will draw near to Him, He will come to you right now.

DAISY: Jesus promised to do that. He said, in John 14:21, *If you love me, you will be loved of my Father, and I will love you, and **I will manifest myself to you.***

PART 23
WHY NOT AT YOUR HOUSE?

T.L.: This has been an unusual testimony. We have shared some great experiences — some that are very dear to us — which produced the turning point in our lives.

DAISY: When we were so very young, we went to India to help people know about Jesus, but we could not convince them that He is God's Son or that He is risen from the dead. So we returned to the USA. But we were in turmoil. For one year, we searched for the answer.

T.L.: Thank God He gave us the answer, and thank God He said, **"If you ever see Jesus, you will never be the same again."**

That is as true for **you** as it was for us.

I do not mean to suggest that you must see Him physically with your eyes, like I looked on Him. Certainly that COULD happen to you.

But I **do** mean to say that **Jesus Christ wants to show Himself to you.** As Daisy pointed out, Jesus promised to MANIFEST (show) Himself to you. Then He added: *My Father will love you and we will come to you and will live with you.* (Jn.14:21,23)

The Bible says, *He showed himself alive* ***by many infallible proofs.*** (Ac.1:3) He has **many ways** to reveal Himself to you. He has done it all over the world. **Why not at your house?**

He came to **us!** He will come to **you!**

I can assure you of this: Even though you may not see Him with your eyes, **He will show Himself to you in a way that you will know that He is alive and that He loves you.**

Will you accept Him now? Will you receive Him into your house — into your life? Will you let Him make a visit to your home?

PART 24

PRAYER

T.L.: Draw near to God. Daisy and I are going to pray that the Lord will, in some miraculous way, do something at **your** house — in **your** life NOW — as you listen to or read this testimony right now.

Let us bow our heads in prayer.

O LORD JESUS: You promised in Your word that if we would follow You and love You, You would love us and that You would come and MANIFEST Yourself to us.

That is what You did after You were risen from the dead. The disciples preached, and You *showed yourself alive by many infallible proofs.*

You want the world today to know that You are alive and real. Lord, come now and show Yourself in a way that the person listening to or reading this right now will KNOW that You are real.

Either appear to them, or come to them through the scriptures or in a dream or in a vision or let them sense Your presence.

In Jesus' name, come now. Touch this person now. And whatever the need is, if it is a spiritual or a material or a physical miracle, let something happen in this life TODAY.

Most of all, if this person does not know Jesus Christ, reveal Yourself right now.

Oh, Jesus Christ, come now and make Your presence real.

Let this person hear You say, "Your sins are forgiven you." Let them believe it now. Let them look up to You now, in Jesus' name.

Let them believe now that Christ who was lifted up on the cross, who shed His blood and gave up His life for them, that the same Christ is real now, and that the blood of Jesus Christ cleanses us now from all sins.

Thank You, Jesus. You are doing it now. Peace is coming now to this house. Thank You, Lord.

If there is sickness in this life, let it be cured now.

In the name of Jesus, God's Son who is risen from the dead, who is the Savior of the world, in *that name above every name,* I adjure the spirit of sickness and depression and suffering to leave the body of the person who is reading this right now.

Leave now, in the name of Jesus Christ, and enter this person no more. May the sickness be cursed at its roots and die — right now!

Wonderful!

Thank You, Lord!

It is done — now — as a sign and as a wonder that You are alive — as proof of the resurrection of our Lord.

Thank You, Lord!

And now Lord, move into this home. You are the Lord of this household now. From today You are Jesus. You are Lord. Manifest Your presence.

If there are material needs, supply them. You are God who made the material world. All that exists in our world that is material, was made by You. So You do touch our world materially.

If there is a need, if there are bills that cannot

be met, if there is a financial crisis, meet it, Lord. In some mysterious way take this burden upon Your shoulders, and bring to pass an answer that will be evidence that You took a hand in this life and that You did a miracle.

Wonderful, Lord. It is wonderful that You have heard us. We thank You for this visitation.

Thank You that You came to our home, and now we thank You that You are coming now to this home.

You are real. You are alive. You are *the same yesterday and today and forever.*

AMEN!

PART 25
ACCOUNTS OF JESUS — ALIVE

T.L.: During the decades of our world ministry to the masses in over 70 nations, I have kept a diary.

DAISY: I try to jot notes as the people crowd to the platform to give public witness of the miracles they have received. Then T.L. often refers to my notes when he writes in his journal.

T.L.: The Bible says: *Make known God's deeds among the people.* (Ps.105:1) Peter said: *We are His witnesses.* (Ac.2:32) And in Acts 4:20 he added: *We* *speak the things which we have seen and heard.* That expresses the purpose for which these **Accounts of Jesus — Alive** are included in this book.

DAISY: We have shared with you how Jesus Christ visited us and how our lives were enriched by the knowledge of His living presence with us to confirm His word wherever we preached or taught it.

T.L.: Now we include some of the wonders, signs and miracles which we have witnessed around the world. These accounts are very scanty and incomplete. They were written in haste, when we were sometimes too weary to hold a pen in hand, late at night, after the long meetings were ended.

These accounts are only **representative** of what has taken place night after night, in great mass meetings around the world.

We have only been able to include **a few days**, to give you **an idea** of the wonders of Jesus Christ at work, confirming His word, week after week. (We've included only **one day,** per crusade.)

DAISY: The most appropriate scripture I can think of is John 20:30-31.

And many other signs truly did Jesus in the presence of His disciples, which are not written in this book.

But these are written, that you might believe that Jesus is the Christ, the Son of God. And that believing, you might have life through His name.

T.L.: We offer no medical documentation or other evidence or proof of what we have recorded.

For years we accumulated x-rays, physicians' statements, photostats of hospital records and all kinds of documents to verify personal testimonies of miracles received. We cannot name one person who ever became **a believer in Jesus Christ** through that evidence. So, no valuable space is used to include it here.

We believe the Bible, and that Christ does today what He did in Bible days. What we have heard and seen is proof enough for us, and we hope that your faith will be encouraged by what we have published.

We witness as John and others did, of *what we have heard, what we have seen and looked upon, and what our hands handled.* (1 Jn. 1:1-2) *We speak the truth in Christ, and lie not.* (1 Ti. 2:7) *We are His witnesses.* (Ac. 5:32)

KINGSTON, JAMAICA
23rd meeting

People gathered from 3 p.m. to get into the auditorium. **The press of people could hardly be controlled by the police.**

We prayed for about 600 people in a collective prayer out in the street, before going into the auditorium. **There was no hope of their getting inside,** so we ministered to them there in the street, and marvelous things were done. Then we inched our way through the crowd to get inside and after preaching, over 300 accepted Christ as Savior.

One deaf-mute was healed. Two blind people were healed; they could see my hand and count my fingers. Many stroke victims and lame and sick folks were healed. **It was marvelous!**

As we left the auditorium, we met a blind woman in the street. She heard our voices and begged us to pray for her. We did, and she was completely and instantly healed. **She could count my fingers out in**

the dark, could see the stars in the heavens, and walked away in the night unaided, praising God for such a great miracle ... evidence that Jesus Christ is indeed **ALIVE!**

Howie Tullock attended the Osborn Crusade being conducted in the Presbyterian Church at Port Marie. After Howie watched a few of the miracles, he ran home to tell his mother that if he could only get to that man, he knew that he would be healed.

His right arm had always been drawn almost double, and his hand paralyzed. His right leg was also crooked and his foot never set straight.

His mother explained that since he had been born that way, he could not expect such a great miracle. But this did not shake Howie's faith. He went to the crusade on the following night, and when commanded to "stretch forth your hand in the name of Jesus Christ," he did so and was instantly healed.

All Port Marie knows about little Howie's great faith and marvelous deliverance. He is a testimony of God's miracle power today in Jamaica.

OSBORN TOUCHED HIS EAR AND WILBERFORCE HEARS AGAIN

The Kingston, Jamaica, newspaper, THE EXPRESS, confirms healing of deaf-mute.

Seventeen-year-old Wilberforce Morris had been deaf and dumb since he recovered from a typhoid fever attack when he was nine years old. In February last, a man told him about two American evangelists who were preaching nightly at East Street. News had spread around the city that they possessed healing powers. Hundreds flocked to their meetings.

Young Wilberforce went one night. The place was crowded with cripples, mutes and others suffering from nearly every form of infirmity.

He knelt at the feet of Rev. T.L. Osborn, the evangelist. He knew he laid his hands on his head and placed his fingers at his ears. He could hear nothing. Then the evangelist motioned for him to rise. He heard the sound of singing, praying, voices for the first time in eight years.

Yesterday morning he called at The Express to tell this story.

He said he could hear perfectly. He could answer any question but he could only speak in a whisper. He went on with his story.

He spoke of his life as a mute. During his years of speechless silence, he communicated with others by writing on a pad he carried around. When anyone wished to say anything to him, it was written on the paper. He still carried a pencil. "After so many years it became a habit," he explained. He did not find this mode of communication difficult, as he could read and write fairly well before his illness.

Before his father died, he taught him to play the clarinet, so Wilberforce, despite his illness, continued to study music. He visited the Junior Centre regularly and gained the interest of Mr. Robert Verity, the supervisor. He continued to read and learn. Then came the miracle at East Street.

Telling of his first reaction to his cure, Wilberforce said: "It sounded strange to me after so long. I was excited and happy. I could not speak then but my voice came the next day. I went to see a doctor soon after and he, too, thought it was a miracle."

It was exciting, his return to the world of sound ... music, laughter, voices; but this new happiness brought its attendant difficulties. He wants a job and cannot find one. Wilberforce said he does not want the kind woman who has been taking care of him to go on supporting him now that he can hear and speak.

Armed with a recommendation from Mr. Roberts Verity, he has been on the job-hunt since his cure but he has not yet been able to find employment.

He is bright and intelligent. Can anyone help? He lives at No. 2 Wellington Street, Denham Town.

PONCE, PUERTO RICO
9th meeting

Today the radio station offered us 45 minutes free of charge, to help the thousands of people who are unable to get to the crusade. **Policemen were sent to guard the radio station** from being invaded by the people during our broadcasts.

A man reported that a woman next door to him was healed of paralysis. Her leg and arm had been drawn up for many years. In a moment, she was made whole! She is going everywhere testifying of her marvelous healing.

A man from a city 90 miles from here brought an old woman to the crusade tonight in order to let her testify. She was healed of total blindness this afternoon during the broadcast. At least 50 miracles have already been reported since the broadcast today.

At least 10 totally blind people were wonderfully healed tonight. It was almost unbelievable!

75 partially blind persons had their sight restored.

Seeing the paralytics restored was a sight to cause the hardest heart to rejoice. Two little girls, with braces to their hips, were instantly restored. They took off their braces and walked all over the platform unaided.

A little boy, with one foot twisted straight in crossways and with the ankle stiff so that he could only stand on his toes, was perfectly healed. The foot was made exactly straight and could be placed flat on the floor like the other. Several other paralytics were marvelously healed.

I think the greatest miracle of the night was that of a poor woman who had, for six years, walked with her hands, dragging and swinging her body between her hands on the ground, with both legs doubled to her side, totally stiff. They were rough like a board on one side. The skin was calloused like leather where she had dragged the weight of her body for six years since an operation.

She testified: **"I had been believing for 20 minutes after Mr. Osborn prayed that God was healing me. I kept feeling my knees, and I suddenly noticed a slight movement of one of my knee caps. I knew God was healing me. I began to get up and was perfectly and completely healed."**

She came to the platform, shouting and walking as perfectly as any person. She showed the audience how the sides of her legs were like leather, then demonstrated how she used to drag on the ground between her hands. Then she stood up, jumped and walked about as perfect as I can.

Another amazing miracle tonight was that of a raving insane woman who was brought to the meeting by her friends. She was suddenly and instantly healed and began begging them to let her go to the platform and testify. She gave the most amazing testimony of how she had been insane, of how horrible it was to be out of her mind, and how suddenly she knew all things clearly. She wept for joy, and so did the audience.

I cannot take time to record but a small fraction of what occurred tonight. No wonder John said that *if all were recorded which Jesus did, the world would not contain the books.* (Jn. 21:25) Over 2,000 accepted Christ tonight. When people discover that Jesus is **ALIVE** — and able to do the same miracles He did in Bible days — they gladly believe on Him and receive Him! I believe it has been the greatest night in my life. Undoubtedly, the future holds yet greater things.

Julia Flores had walked with her hands, dragging her paralyzed legs on the ground. She said: "I knew God was healing me ... I began to get up, and I was perfectly healed!"

OSBORN CRUSADE

PONCE, PUERTO RICO

CAMAGUEY, CUBA
27th meeting

The service was attended by great throngs of people. After the message, over 1,500 accepted Christ. Then the mass prayer was offered for the healing of the sick, and God surely answered from heaven.

One man who was blind from birth was led to the meeting, and as he listened to the message, he **fell to the ground, having seen the Lord Jesus ALIVE in a vision.** He lay there for some time, and those around him thought he had died. Suddenly, he regained consciousness and stood to his feet with an expression of joy on his face, declaring: **"I have seen the Lord, and now I see! I was blind, but now I see!"** His sight was restored; he could see fine print. The multitude was hysterical with joy when they heard this report.

Six deaf-mutes were healed during the service, one of which was 55 years of age and had been born in this condition.

One young man, who was going to commit suicide, was gloriously converted. Several hernias, growths, and various classes of sickness and paralysis were instantly healed. Again, Jesus has shown His power — **ALIVE!** To God be all the praise!

HIP JOINT CREATED

All my life I have had a calcium deficiency, and almost two years ago my left hip joint began slipping out. It continued to get worse until my hip was always out, and I suffered much.

Ten months ago, the doctor operated, and completely removed the joint of my left hip. After spending five months in bed, the doctors put me on crutches on which I would have to walk the rest of my life. It was impossible for me to walk without them.

But I am so happy, I can hardly give my testimony for weeping. Evangelist Osborn prayed a mass prayer for all who were crippled, and he commanded the cripples and paralytics to walk in Jesus' name.

I laid my crutches aside and stepped out by faith to walk as the evangelist commanded. It may seem impossible to believe, but I was instantly and perfectly healed. Something happened to my hip. I can walk as perfect as any person.

I took my crutches and went to the platform and gave my testimony to the newspaper reporter, and left my crutches, walking away as perfect as I ever walked before the illness.

OSBORN CRUSADE

POLIO HEALED

This young girl had been a victim of polio. Both legs were in steel braces to her knees. She removed the braces and shoes, walked back and forth on the platform, perfectly healed. She walked as soundly as anyone could. She joyfully testified, looking down at her feet. "Oh, my feet and legs feel just like they used to feel before I was sick." She was a great demonstration of God's power to heal polio.

OSBORN CRUSADE

CAMAGUEY, CUBA

My right leg has been three inches shorter than my left for the past 11 years. My hip was broken, and this resulted. Now, I can testify that both legs are the same length, and both of them are normal. I am grateful to God for this miracle. I can never forget the wonders of God's power which I witnessed during the Osborn Crusade here at Camaguey.

SANTIAGO, CUBA

PONCE, PUERTO RICO
1st meeting

I started to preach early, but after greeting the audience, was told that Juan Santos was present. He had been healed here in our last crusade the night I preached on the **"Healing of the Cripple"** from Mark 2. So we asked him to give the testimony of his miraculous healing. He testified for about 30 minutes. **There are few cases in the Bible as dramatic and marvelous as this case.**

He had been shot through the spine, destroying his spinal column and the nerves below the waist. It left him totally paralyzed in both legs. For **15 years** he was crippled. Both legs were dead, drawn double, and withered. They were just skin and bones and were completely stiff, drawn in a double position. One arm hung paralyzed at his side. The other shook constantly, so that he could hardly feed himself.

His head also shook because **he had attempted suicide** by hitting himself with a club; but the blow only caused the palsy. He could hardly talk because his tongue and throat were partially paralyzed. He dragged himself on the ground with his hands, his drawn and withered legs resting in the dirt between each swing of his arms. He was losing his mind.

He was instantly healed and is now **as perfect as any man could be.** His testimony is known by thousands in Puerto Rico as an undeniable miracle of God's power. He has become a radiant Christian witness.

When Mr. Santos finished his heart-moving testimony, which was more convincing than a thousand sermons, an old lady had mounted the platform, anxious to tell what God did for her in our last crusade. She had been healed of total blindness. This is what she told the people:

"Friends told me about a man who was performing miracles. I tried to get someone to take me to the meeting, but no one would guide me. I decided to go myself. I finally found my way there. They told me the service began at 5 p.m., so I went there at 12 noon. I listened, but was not healed that night.

"Then I tried to get home in the dark. I got lost. I took a box of matches out of my pocket and struck some and cried, 'Ciego!' (Blind!) A man heard me and came to help me, but I became fearful of him that he was leading me astray in the night, so I told

THE JUAN SANTOS MIRACLE

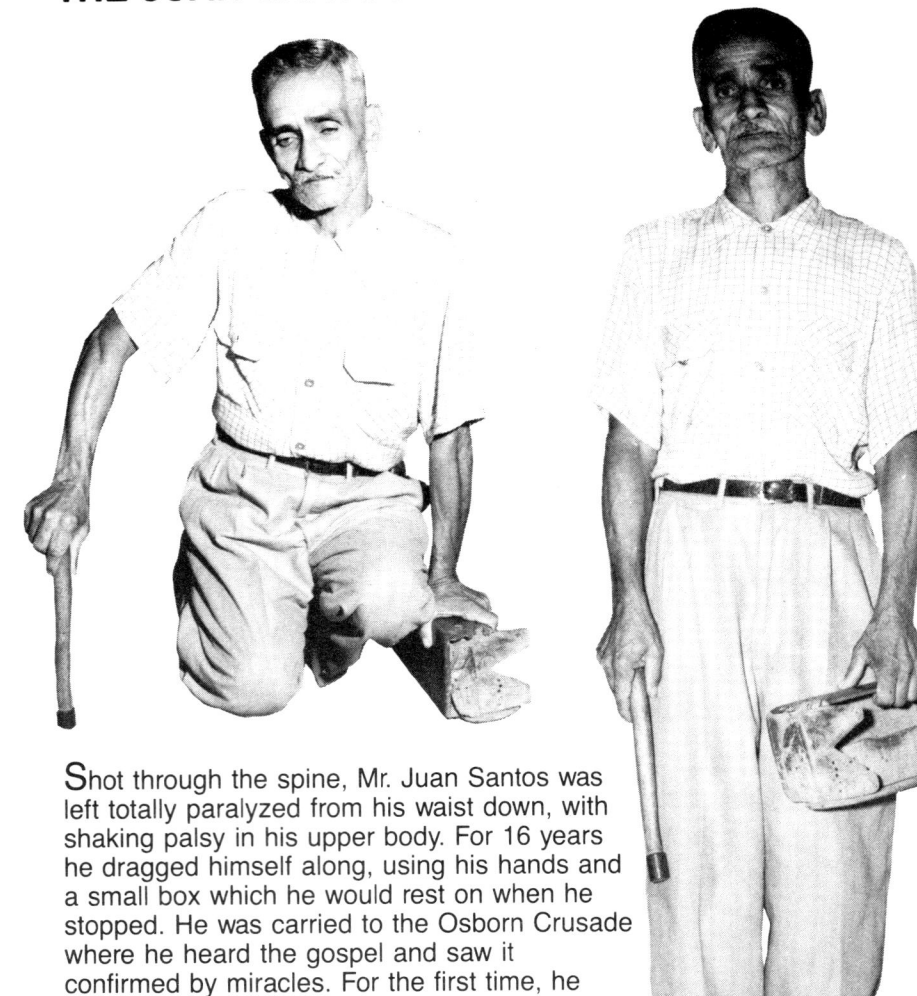

Shot through the spine, Mr. Juan Santos was left totally paralyzed from his waist down, with shaking palsy in his upper body. For 16 years he dragged himself along, using his hands and a small box which he would rest on when he stopped. He was carried to the Osborn Crusade where he heard the gospel and saw it confirmed by miracles. For the first time, he learned that what Jesus did in Bible days, He will do today.

OSBORN CRUSAD

He believed on the Lord and was instantly and totally healed. The entire city was astounded by this notable miracle. Mr. Santos became a living witness for Christ by going from town to town and showing how the Lord miraculously healed him. Thousands believed the gospel because of this **living proof of God's power.**

PONCE, PUERTO RICO

him to leave me and that I would stay there by the road and sleep that night. He left me, and I was alone again. I finally found my way home at 4 in the morning.

"The next day I went again and got near the platform and purposed if I could touch the evangelist's trouser legs, I would be healed.

"I listened closely to the message; and when the prayer was offered, I believed. The people all around me were standing tightly together. I finally managed to get some space to move a bit, and I reached out my hand around the edge of the platform, trying to touch the man of God. After a long time, I was begging God to help me touch His servant; and, finally, I heard him moving near my side of the platform. I reached for him and found his legs and grabbed his trousers.

"Then my eyes came open and I could see every thing clearly. I shouted, 'Hallelujah! Hallelujah! I can see! I can see!' It was a very great miracle. I can see you people tonight! I go about telling of God's miracle on my poor blind eyes. I am so happy and thankful to God."

(It was not the trouser legs that healed this woman's eyes, anymore than it was the garment of

Jesus that healed the woman in the Bible. It was the woman's faith.)

After these two testimonies, I exhorted the audience about ten minutes, as I did not need to preach. These two testimonies were sermon enough. Then we led the audience in a prayer. Hundreds accepted Christ as their Savior, then the people began receiving their healing.

A totally blind man came to the platform so happy. He could see, as he said, "Very clear! Very clear!" A paralyzed man was restored and stomped his feet for joy. Many others were set free. The crowd rejoiced as miracle after miracle was reported for almost two hours.

PUNTO FIJO, VENEZUELA
3rd meeting

Here we have a large open field that is surrounded by a wall. The road was jammed all the way from town to the location of the meeting. There were hundreds of cars and buses. The meeting was thrilling, as over 2,000 accepted Christ.

The miracles were amazing tonight. An old man who had been blind for years was partly healed the other night, and tonight God finished the job; his eyes were completely healed tonight. He was so happy.

Another old man totally blind for six years was healed tonight, too. It is impossible to record the weeping and rejoicing of those so miraculously healed! A girl who was born badly cross-eyed was completely healed, her eyes becoming straight and normal. A boy with one deaf ear was healed and could hear a watch with that ear. Scores of others were healed who could not possibly get to the platform to testify.

SAN JOSE, COSTA RICA
5th meeting

We arrived at the Mendoza Stadium and found **thousands of people jammed in the street** in front of the place, unable to get inside because of the multitude in the arena. Some people who arrived when we did asked, **"Are they not going to open the gates tonight and let the people in?"** The answer came, **"The gates were opened. The place is packed with thousands inside, and now no more can enter."**

We had to struggle to get in, and finally made it. The owner was angry, and pastors feared the authorities would stop us on the basis of public safety.

The crowd finally completely broke down one big door and flowed in like a river until the audience just swayed like a field of grain in the breeze. **We announced that we would move to the huge "Bull Ring" tomorrow.**

At least 2,500 accepted Christ as Savior after the

message. Then we prayed for the sick, and it seemed like all heaven opened up on us as miracle after miracle was reported for nearly two hours.

A boy, who was dying with tuberculosis of the spine and could not bend his back or even move his head, was healed. The mother was in tears as the boy walked normally. At least eight deaf-mutes were healed. The father of one of them was so happy that he was reeling to and fro like a drunk man, with his face bathed in tears, telling the people to look at his boy. We checked the boy every way, and he was perfect.

A lady, who had been totally blind for two years, was led to the service and received her sight. A woman was healed of a tumor. A businessman was healed of a big rupture. He had been to the hospitals, but received no help. Tonight he was healed!

At least 200 more raised their hands in the audience, signifying that they too were miraculously healed, but that **it was impossible to get through the pressed crowd** to testify. My words fail to describe the glory of this great meeting tonight. The presence of the **LIVING JESUS** literally filled the place!

SAN JOSE, COSTA RICA

GUATEMALA CITY, GUATEMALA
5th meeting

After the meeting last night, a woman who had been sitting in a car, crippled and unable to walk for over five years due to a broken spine, continued praying and suddenly felt that she should walk. She got out of her car and was made whole! Many witnessed the miracle.

OSBORN CRUSADE

Many thousands were present in the hot afternoon service. At least 2,500 accepted Christ in tears. Then I prayed for all who were sick. **The miracle power of God filled the hillside.**

The first woman to testify had not walked in 15 years without two crutches. She was made whole and left her crutches. Then a lady of 18 years was healed. She had tuberculosis in her hip, could not bend it, and had to walk with a crutch. She was completely healed and testified weeping.

GUATEMALA

Then a young doctor came to the microphone to confirm her testimony, saying: **"I know her; she was incurable. We treated her; she could not walk. It is true! We can only say, truly God heals!"**

Then a child who had polio was healed. An old man who had walked with a cane was restored, after

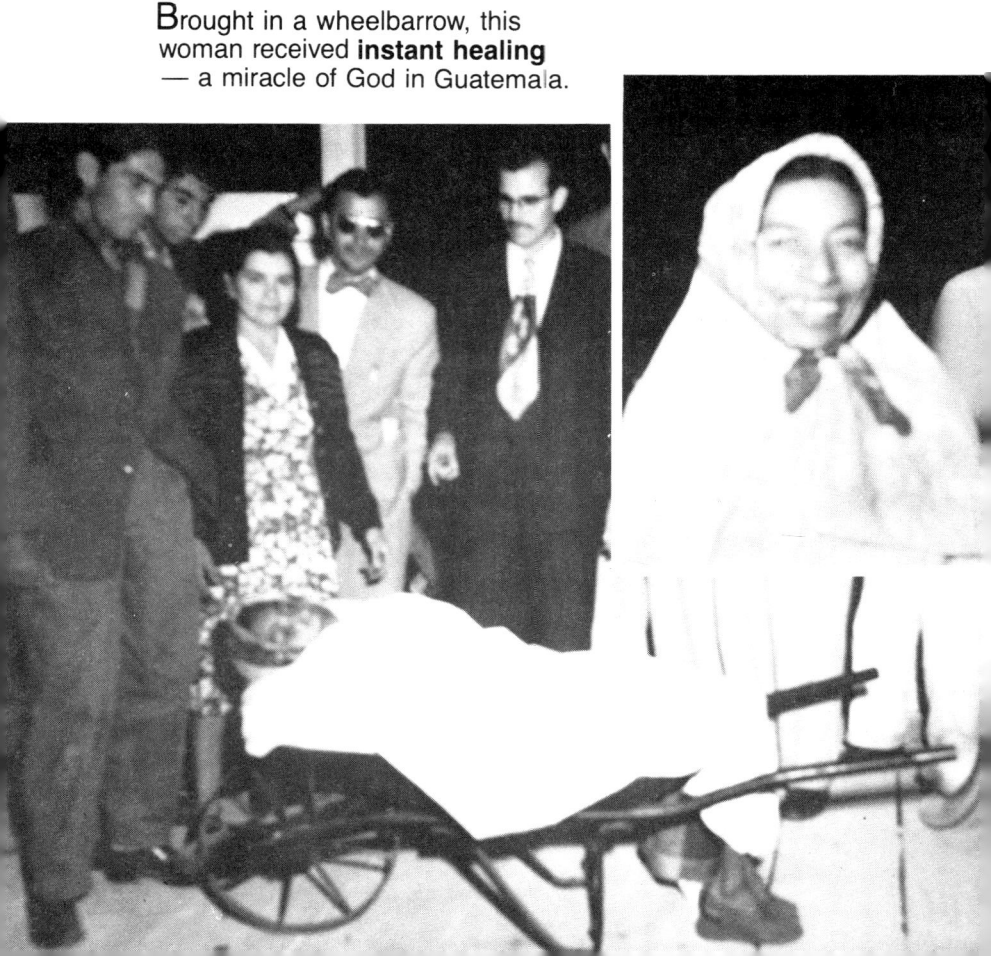

Brought in a wheelbarrow, this woman received **instant healing** — a miracle of God in Guatemala.

having suffered for 20 years. A woman whose foot was wrapped in cloth because of a cancerous ulcer was healed. The leg had been badly swollen and she walked on crutches, but she was totally and miraculously restored. **It was great!**

A wealthy lady and her son came running, extremely excited. He fell on my neck weeping,

DRAGGED HERSELF ON GROUND 52 YEARS

Maria Luisa Gutierres had smallpox and other serious fevers when she was a child. She was left paralyzed from the waist down.

For 52 years she hadn't stood or walked. Her legs and hips were calloused from dragging her body on the ground with her hands.

She was carried to the crusade in Guatemala City, and when the paralytics were commanded to rise and walk in Jesus' name, her son (who had never seen his mother walk), lifted her up, and SHE WAS HEALED.

As she walked across the platform, the multitude was amazed and glorified God, because many present knew her!

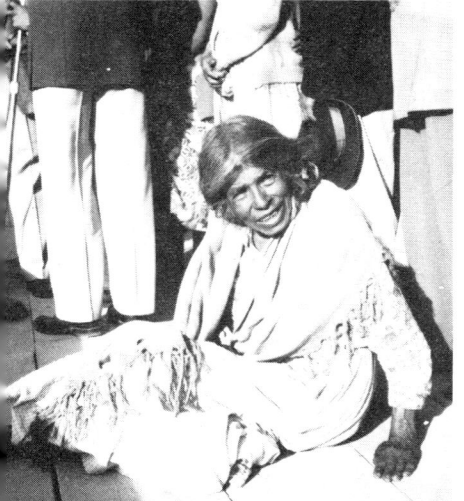

crying out: **"Oh, Mr. Osborn, here is my mother; she has been deaf since my birth. She has never heard in 23 years. Now she is healed! She hears! Oh, Jesus is so good!"** Many people knew her. She testified in tears of joy.

Next was an old medical doctor who had not been able to walk for several years; he was restored. A woman who had a rupture for 20 years was healed. A policeman was healed. An old woman who was carried in arms to the meeting was made whole. A man who was brought in a wheelchair arose and walked, healed by God's power. A woman also was healed from her wheelchair.

Afterwards, over **1,000 people remained in the audience who declared that they were healed;** but we did not have time for their testimonies.

The night service was twice as large, and thousands more received Christ, after seeing proof that He is **ALIVE** today! Among a great host of miracles of healing was a boy who had been cross-eyed from birth. He was perfectly healed.

A fine educated young football player from Honduras was healed of epilepsy. For 12 years he had suffered convulsions, but tonight he received Christ. He said that when the prayer for healing was prayed, he actually **felt the strange evil power leave him** like a whirling wind; then peace and freedom came to him. He wept and wept as he testified.

BLIND BEGGAR HEALED

This man, a beggar in Guatemala, had diabetes, which resulted in total blindness. After the diabetes had destroyed his eyesight, it affected his mind, and he became insane. In addition to this, one side of his body was paralyzed and he hobbled along on the streets with an old cane, crazy, blind, and paralyzed, begging for a living.

One day a man told the old beggar about the Osborn Crusade, and urged him to attend. Jose Antonio Solorzano, the beggar, replied that he did not know the way to the crusade, and that it was impossible for him to go.

The friend offered to carry him to the meeting, so he came and carried Jose to the crusade on his back. He set him down on the ground where he could listen to the message, and that was the last time Jose ever heard of his friend. (continued)

Jose Solorzano

BLIND BEGGAR HEALED (continued)

The beggar listened to the message and when the prayer was offered for healing, God had evidently seen his desperate condition and instantly and completely healed his body from his head to his feet.

He was one of the most touching testimonies that I have ever heard in all my life.

After he testified and explained to the people his deplorable condition, and expressed the shame that he felt for having been a beggar, we asked the people to raise their hand if they knew him, and knew his testimony to be true. Many hands raised signifying that they not only knew him, but had given bits of money to him on the street.

You should have seen the

Esteban Crispin

A man was brought to the crusade who had been tormented by demons for more than 25 years. They would throw him on the ground, and literally pound his head and chest on the ground. That night the demons tormented this man, and he would cry out with loud voices until he greatly disturbed the meeting. People pressed around him to see him in this condition. Not at all coincidental was the fact that that night we were preaching on demon possession, and it seemed that Satan had come to challenge the truths which we were proclaiming.

I told the audience to believe with me and to be reverent in God's presence; to ignore Satan's demonstration, and to give attention to the word of God; that Satan would not be able to stand before the authority of God's word. They

reaction of the audience when this man humbly thanked the audience for having helped him in that way.

Jose Solorzano continued to attend the crusade and several times he gave his testimony to the people.

It was a thrill to hear him repeat the wonderful story of how Jesus Christ had come into his heart and life.

Before his sickness, he had been employed by the government as an architect. In less than two weeks after his healing, he had his old job back again, and had completed three plans for government buildings in the city.

Certainly God has been glorified in this miracle, and thousands have been convinced of His power to heal today.

---

all joined with me in their faith and did as I told them to do.

As I was preaching on Christ's power over demons, and of the power of His name today, this man shouted, "I'm an enemy of Jesus! I fight with Him! He cannot overcome me!" etc. All sorts of blasphemous words flowed from this man's heart. But when the mass prayer was prayed and the people with one accord joined in faith, the demons could not resist the truth. In one last desperate attempt on his life, they threw him to the ground, and literally pounded his head on the earth, and then with a loud scream, left him, and he was delivered in peace.

Just a few moments later, the man came up the steps, with tears in his eyes, and gave the testimony of his deliverance. How the audience rejoiced, and how we all gave praise to God as we heard this man tell how the demons had tormented him, but how they had gone from him, and how Jesus Christ had come into his heart bringing peace and satisfaction.

An elderly gentleman was on the platform ready to testify, and he told the audience that when he came on the grounds, he saw this man who was completely crazy. He admitted frankly that he feared the man, and had gone to the opposite side of the audience, because he was afraid that some danger might result from this man in his insane condition. This gentleman wept as he expressed his gratitude to God for setting this captive free.

Esteban Crispin, one-time insane and possessed of demons, is now a faithful member of a church in Guatemala.

SANTIAGO, CHILE
35th day

After five glorious weeks in this great capital city of Chile, today was the closing parade. **It was the greatest evangelical demonstration in the history of Chile.**

At 2 p.m. we arrived at the plaza where the parade was forming, and people were pouring together like rivers. Thousands were carrying signs and testimonies on everything from poles and sticks to broom-handles. Scores of trucks, wagons, carts and every kind of animal-drawn vehicle were taking their place. Over 600 musicians were there from one church alone. There were over a thousand bicycles.

OSBORN CRUSADE

A huge Salvation Army unit was beautiful. A whole unit of policemen assisted.

The parade packed a street extending over **35 blocks.** Standing at one point, it took over an hour for it to pass. In all, it took over four hours from the time the parade started moving until the last of the parade reached the park.

The big evening newspaper bore the headlines: **"300,000 Evangelicals March in Osborn Parade".** Then the entire centerspread of the paper was a huge picture of the audience, together with other pictures and articles about the parade, stretching across both pages.

The whole city is talking about the crusade, the miracles and the celebrations.

SANTIAGO, CHILE

DJAKARTA, JAVA, INDONESIA
7th meeting

Many thousands of people were jammed together on the "Lapangan Banteng" grounds in the capital city. I preached on **"The Gospel for Everyone,"** stressing John 3:16 and Psalm 103:3. The people are so hungry and eager to learn. Actually, it exceeds what we saw in Latin America. Fully 8,000 people raised eager hands to accept Jesus Christ into their hearts and pledged their lives to Him. This sounds fantastic, but to **see** it is even more awesome, especially realizing that Java is 95 percent Moslem.

When we prayed for the sick, truly Christ showed Himself **ALIVE** — just like Bible days.

A boy, who had been blind in both eyes, was wonderfully healed and could see everything. A woman, who had been blind in one eye for nine years, was healed. A Chinese woman, who had been crippled for 12 years and who could only hobble on two canes, was miraculously healed.

A woman, who had been severely paralyzed on one side, became perfect. She was so bad that her left side had been hard and stiff and drawn. Her arm had been drawn to her side, and her leg drawn and stiff. For eight years, she had not walked. Every part of her body was healed. Another woman, who had been paralyzed on one side for nine years, was completely restored.

Four men testified of how they had been cripples and were healed. One had not walked in over four years. At least eight to ten totally deaf people were healed. A woman, whose shoulder had been broken and who had been unable to raise her arm for years, was healed.

A little girl who had been the victim of a disease (probably polio) which had destroyed the strength and muscles in her legs, received a great miracle. Her little legs and hips were just skin and bones, limp and useless. For over two years, the child had not taken a step.

The father brought her and laid her in a rickshaw during our sermon, and she fell asleep. As I prayed for the sick, the father laid his hands on his child and prayed earnestly. The child awoke and cried out: **"Papa, I am healed!"** She was instantly made perfect. She walked and ran, perfectly normal. One could hardly believe she had ever been crippled, but many witnesses knew her. How we thanked God for His mercy!

Two lepers were cleansed; one had been a leper for five years and the other for 12 years. Both testified that every feeling was returned to the previously dead parts of their flesh. Oh, how they wept as they told what Jesus had done for them, and they promised to follow Him.

DJAKARTA, JAVA

LAPANGAN BANTENG

"The Lepers are Cleansed." Mt.11:5

18 years ago, I went to the doctor for an examination. I had a white spot on my right shoulder. When he saw it, he sent me to a leprosy specialist who, after taking many tests, told me that I had leprosy. Immediately, my family put me in a separate room. From then, I could only talk to them at a distance, and I had to eat, sleep and live alone.

During the next year, my hands became swollen. I could not shut them. Bumps began to appear all over my body, and then my face began to swell. My eyes were nearly swollen shut, and my ears were several times their normal size, and hung down at least an inch longer than usual. They were about as thick as your finger. They were terribly swollen and infected, but numb.

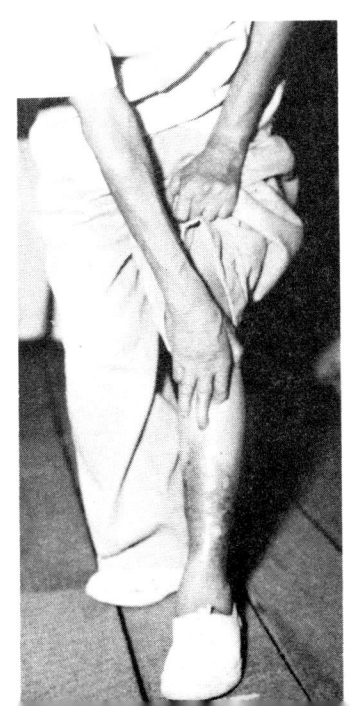

During the next few years my hands were so badly infected that I lost the first joints of my forefinger and little finger on my right hand. Then, five years ago, a big ugly sore started on my left shin near the ankle. It increased until it must have been more than 12 inches long and nearly encircled my leg. My leg was terribly swollen, and it drained continually. By that time I had bumps and sores all over my body, and the odor was stifling.

I was persuaded to attend the Osborn Crusade in Djakarta, where it was said that many people were being cured.

After attending for three nights and witnessing what was being done for others, I began to believe that I too could be helped. I decided to do as the evangelist said, and I accepted Jesus Christ and purposed to follow Him.

While I was following in the prayer being led by Mr. Osborn, I suddenly felt something in my hands. I found that I could open and shut them — this I had not done for years!

Then I realized that I was being healed. In one week I was perfectly whole. My skin is clean! The ulcer is dried up. Life has returned to all of my body, and I am clean within and without!

None of us were Christians, and never planned to be Christians, but we had never seen His power to cleanse lepers before. Oh, it is wonderful! My wife and I are reunited now, and can eat at the same table, and live together as husband and wife should.

All of my family have accepted Christ, and we are all following Him, and shall serve Him all the days of our lives.

SURABAJA, JAVA, INDONESIA
40th meeting

Today the meeting was heavenly. Christ proved to the Moslems that He is the Son of God and **ALIVE** by performing the same miracles that He performed before they killed Him.

Over 4,000 people accepted Christ as their Savior after I preached on the **"Healing of Blind Bartimaeus."**

Two totally blind women were healed and could see everything; one of them had been blind for 12 years. A totally deaf lady was healed. At least 15 other totally deaf people were restored. A woman, who had been so bad with tuberculosis that she had no voice, was instantly healed; and her voice was restored.

OSBORN CRUSADE

A Moslem woman stood listening to our message. Then, suddenly, **she saw a great ball of light appear behind me on the podium. It burst and then a huge open hand appeared behind me with blood dripping from it.** She believed on the Lord Jesus Christ and was healed also.

Another person **saw a great light cover the field of people and a huge cross appeared. Then two pierced and bleeding hands appeared so large that they covered the people. Blood ran from them over the audience. Everyone who was engulfed in the flowing blood appeared to be immediately healed and made whole.** But others feared the blood and fled from it, dragging their poor, crippled, racked, and diseased bodies in a frantic escape to destruction.

Signs and wonders like these and others caused tens of thousands to believe on Jesus Christ and to trust His word for salvation.

SURABAJA, JAVA

> "Daughter, your faith has made you whole; go in peace."
> Luke 8:48

I had a high fever and my feet swelled as big as they could without bursting, and when the sickness left, I could not walk. My legs were useless. The only way I could get around was to scoot myself along on the ground with my hands.

I attended the Osborn Crusade in Surabaja, arriving about 2:00 in the afternoon so that I could be close to the platform for the service.

The third meeting I attended, I was instantly healed. My legs became strong again, and I got up on my feet and walked as well as I ever could. I was restored and normal again. I thank the Lord Jesus Christ for healing me so that I can now walk again. I want to serve Him.

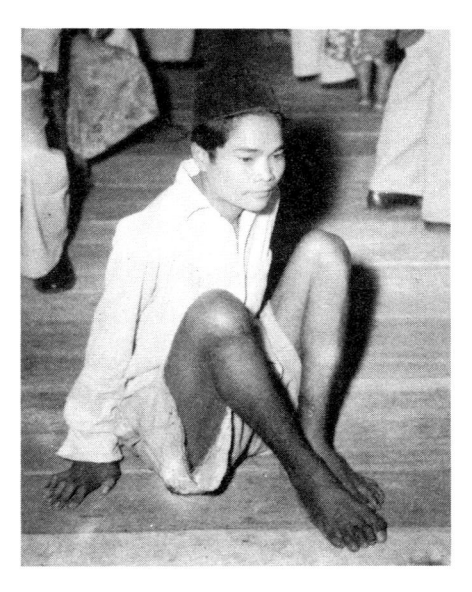

"And all the people saw him walking and praising God."
Acts 3:9

I had a high fever for four days and was sick in bed for a month, suffering awful agony in my body, especially in my legs. I would just lay in bed and cry with pain in my legs.

Then after that sickness and fever left me, I found I could not stand up and walk. When I tried, my legs would not straighten out or hold me up. From that time, the only way I could move about was to use my hands and scoot along in a sitting position. I continued to suffer much pain.

Then I heard of the Osborn Crusade in Surabaja, and I went there. I listened to the gospel, and when prayer was made for the sick, I believed what I heard, and was instantly healed.

I have been a Moslem all my life, but now I have accepted Jesus Christ as my Savior and I will serve Him always. I am perfectly healed and can walk as good as I ever could before I was sick. I am very thankful for this miracle by Jesus Christ.

Daisy Osborn ministers the gospel to the multitudes in the Djakarta and Surabaja Crusades.

BANGKOK, THAILAND
12th meeting

As we arrived at the gate where the great crusade was being conducted, I found my Thai interpreter talking to a woman who had been healed. For nine years she had tuberculosis of the spine and was bent over. She had suffered terrifying pain. She had been attending the crusade and had accepted Christ as her Savior. This morning when she got out of bed, she was completely healed. Oh, she was thrilled!

Neighbors asked her: **"What happened? What medicine did you take? Who healed you?"** She told them how she had believed in Jesus and had been healed by Him. They said: "It is better that you remain bent down and die than to give up your Buddhist religion." She told them: **"You have your heart; I have mine. I accepted Jesus and He healed me."** All day she had testified. She told how one of her neighbors, who was unable to raise her arm, had come and was healed too.

After the sermon, hundreds received Christ as Savior. We then prayed for the sick. A leprous woman was healed. The leprosy had affected her hands until they were just clenched fingers, welded tight, with no movement; and they were numb and dead. Her feet were the same. Sores had erupted on her legs and hands. She said: **"I was alone. I had no job. My parents died from leprosy. No one would talk to me or come near me or visit me. I was lonesome. But now I have a friend. I am not alone. Jesus loves me. He is not ashamed to come to my hut. He is not afraid of me. I am healed. I will always follow Him."**

Many others told of tremendous miracles. It was a great meeting among the Buddhists, and Christ really proved Himself to be **ALIVE.**

MIRACLES IN BUDDHIST THAILAND

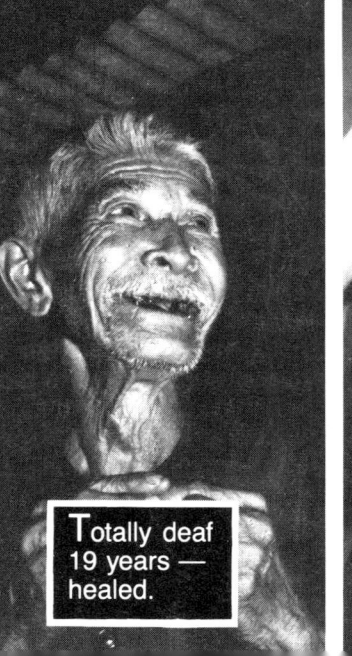

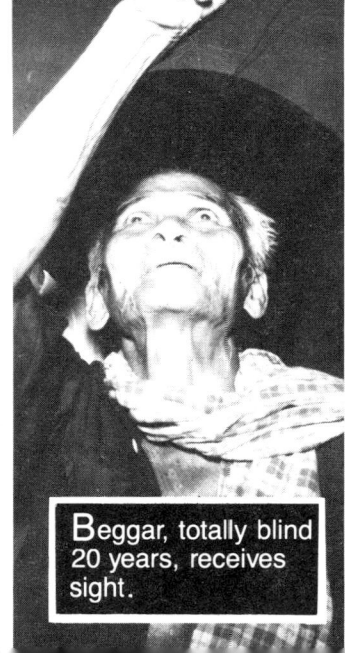

Totally deaf 19 years — healed.

Beggar, totally blind 20 years, receives sight.

Buddhist nun, 74 years old, receives Christ.

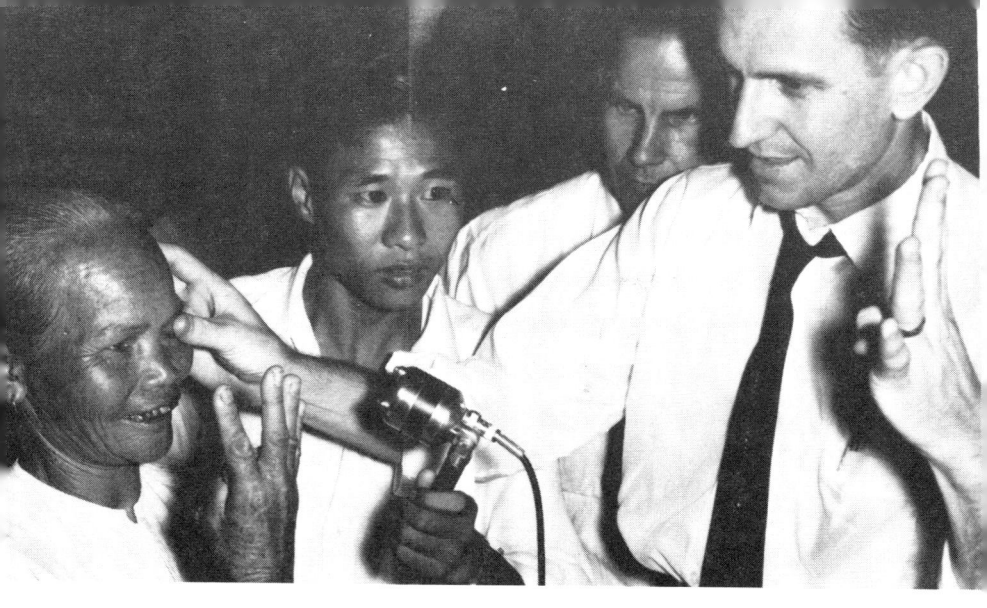

TOP: Blind 28 years; instantly healed.
BOTTOM LEFT: Eight years old, had never walked without crutches; healed.
BOTTOM RIGHT: Eight years a leper; restored.

Osborn Ministries has provided tons of gospel literature and equipment for Christian workers in Thailand.

The Osborns conduct seminars for Christian workers around the world, like this one in Bangkok, Thailand. (Photos — Top: United in prayer after a teaching session. Bottom: Final day of seminar. Center and opposite page: Equipped to share God's big love plan with their nation.)

TOP: This traditional old Japanese woman was instantly healed of total blindness in one of her eyes.

RIGHT: This 70-year-old man had been crippled for seven years. Both hips were broken. He accepted Christ and was perfectly healed.

KYOTO, JAPAN
5th meeting

Kyoto is the great seat of Shintoism. It is a city of magnificent temples. We are seeing great throngs gather on an open field to hear the gospel. Tonight was a tremendous meeting, one of those truly great visitations of our Lord to the Shintoists of Japan.

I preached on **"Good News for Everyone."** Hundreds accepted Christ. Then I prayed for the sick **en masse.** People literally ran to the podium to testify. The platform was filled in 15 minutes.

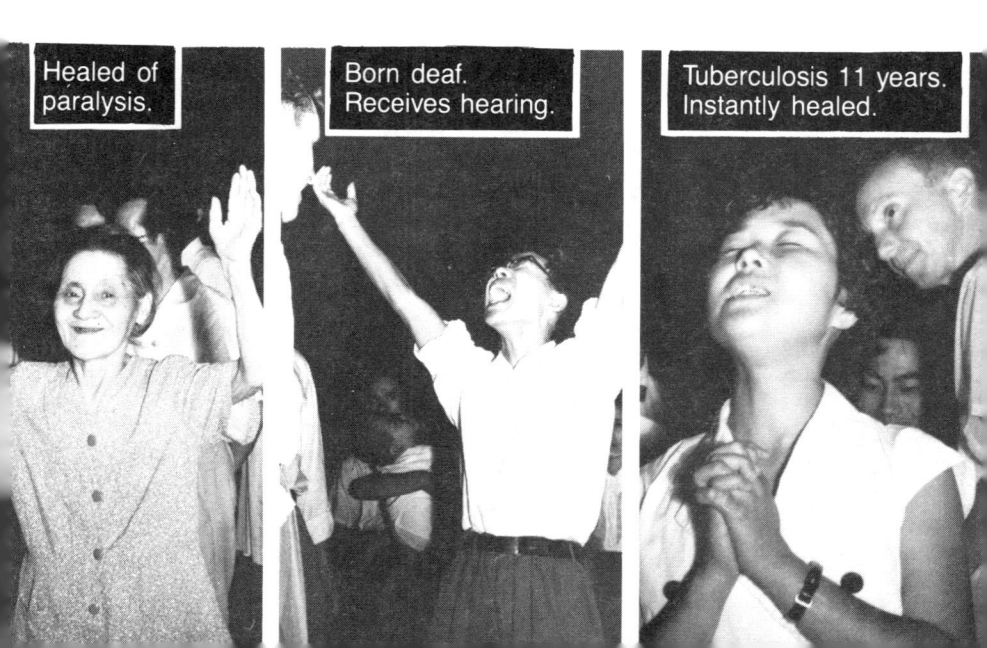

Healed of paralysis.

Born deaf. Receives hearing.

Tuberculosis 11 years. Instantly healed.

MIRACLES IN JAPAN

LEFT: Paralyzed for 5 years. Instantly healed. TOP: Blind in one eye. Sight restored.

BOTTOM LEFT: Pastor had crossed eyes since birth. Perfectly healed.

BOTTOM RIGHT: Born deaf and dumb. Healed marvelously and weeps with joy at being able to hear and talk.

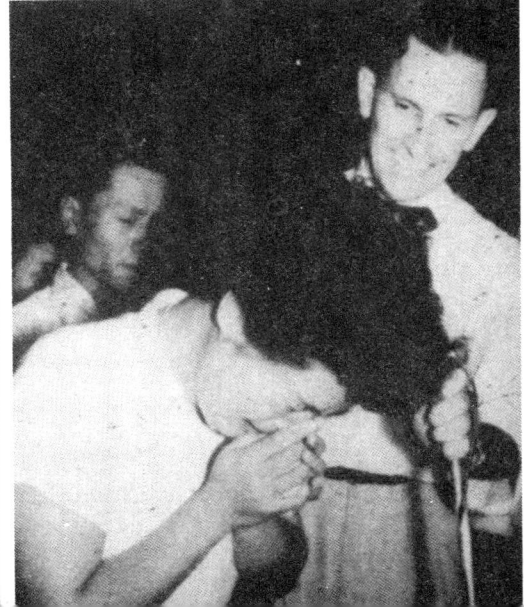

He had never heard of Christ, and was a terrible drunkard all of his life. When he accepted Christ he was instantly healed. He wept like a baby as he told how Christ had saved him.

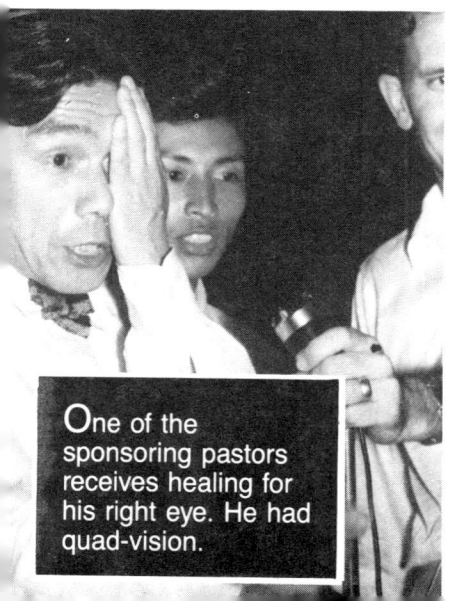

One of the sponsoring pastors receives healing for his right eye. He had quad-vision.

Japanese father praised God for healing his child of total deafness. The child is learning to talk.

A man who had been blind, carrying a white cane, was healed so perfectly that he could even read the Bible to the audience. It was amazing! Seven deaf-mutes were healed. It was absolutely tremendous to see them weep on one another's shoulders.

I do not think we have ever seen people so emotionally stirred. A man with an itch all over his body was cured instantly. A woman was healed of cancer and coughed it up during the meeting. She was well. Three or four were healed of tuberculosis. A woman, lying on a pallet, arose and was made whole. A boy with paralysis and epilepsy was restored instantly. A woman with one leg that had been paralyzed for several years was healed.

A boy was healed of crossed eyes; they became perfectly straight. Another lad was healed of a rupture. It was gone. A man, whose finger was stiff because the leaders had been cut, is now perfect; and he was so excited to show how his hand is now normal. Many other great miracles took place, but I do not have the time to record them. What a visitation of Jesus to the Shintoists of Japan!

ACCRA, GHANA
12th meeting

What a sight to see a field of people waving their arms and swaying in rhythm, singing about the power of Jesus Christ.

Tonight I preached on **"Why Jesus Came."** Hundreds (maybe thousands) accepted Christ. Then we prayed for the sick. Almost immediately so many jammed the platform to tell of the miracles they had received, that the floor of the platform broke through.

Several insane people were restored. A woman who had not walked since she was a child, was perfectly healed of the polio effects which had paralyzed her legs. She could walk, run and jump normally. Six or eight people with large tumors were healed.

Many epileptics, blind, deaf and lame people were made whole. God's glory filled the huge field and covered the people.

OSBORN CRUSADE

OSBORN CRUSADE

OLD POLO GROUNDS — ACCRA

JAMES TOWN MANTSE PARK, GHANA

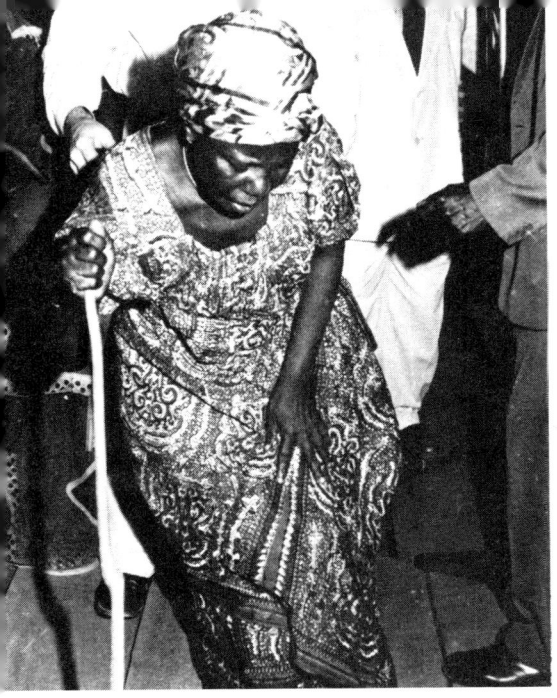

ABOVE: The only way she could walk was bent over, aided by a stick. While cutting weeds in the sun, she collapsed and this paralytic condition resulted.

AFTER: Another *daughter of Abraham* was loosed, straightened up, discarded her stick and was made whole.

BELOW: David Kwame had been totally blind for four years. His mother brought him on an old truck loaded with people for over 75 miles, to the Osborn Crusade in Accra.

AFTER: David was perfectly healed and his mother rejoices with him for the great miracle her son received.

IBADAN, NIGERIA
3rd meeting

Oh, what a meeting today! It was amazing! This is **the largest all-African city on the continent.** I preached on **"Why Jesus Came."** A vast company of people believed on Christ as their Savior. Then we prayed for the sick. It was amazing what took place. The multitude gave great praise and glorified God!

First to testify was a man who had been blind for 15 years. His eyes were totally healed. He could see everything clearly. Next was a man who had been paralyzed and unable to walk for over five years; he was made completely whole. Then there was a woman who had hobbled about on two crutches. Her family had helped her to the crusade. She was totally healed and paraded back and forth, hoisting her crutches in the air. Thousands glorified God!

Then all of heaven broke loose when a man, who had dragged his body on the ground with his hands for over 30 years, was healed and made whole. He tied old rubber pads on his knees to protect them and used blocks in his hands to help him move about. His legs looked like poles; but as he walked, they grew! He had been a beggar in the streets, and he was a Moslem. Everyone knew him, and the field of people went wild with joy when they saw him walk! He gave a powerful testimony saying: **"If Jesus is dead, how could He heal me? You know me. I have accepted this Jesus because I know He is ALIVE!"**

We have never seen a miracle so shake a city. The king knows him, as well as every business owner. It took over an hour to quiet the multitude after hearing and seeing this miracle. While the crowd glorified God, hundreds of others were healed and decided for Christ.

Suddenly, a woman rushed up to testify. She had been a hopeless hunchback. They said she was so disfigured, it looked like she had a child on her back. She was made straight in a second, and the people around her were frightened by the power of God as it straightened her back. She was so crippled that sometimes she scooted on the ground rather than to try to stand up enough to walk. The woman was completely restored. Oh, it was glorious!

A woman who had been blind for eight years received her sight. She cried out, **"I am not blind any longer. I can see!"** Several deaf persons were restored, and so many scores of miracles took place that it would take a book to contain them! How great God is!

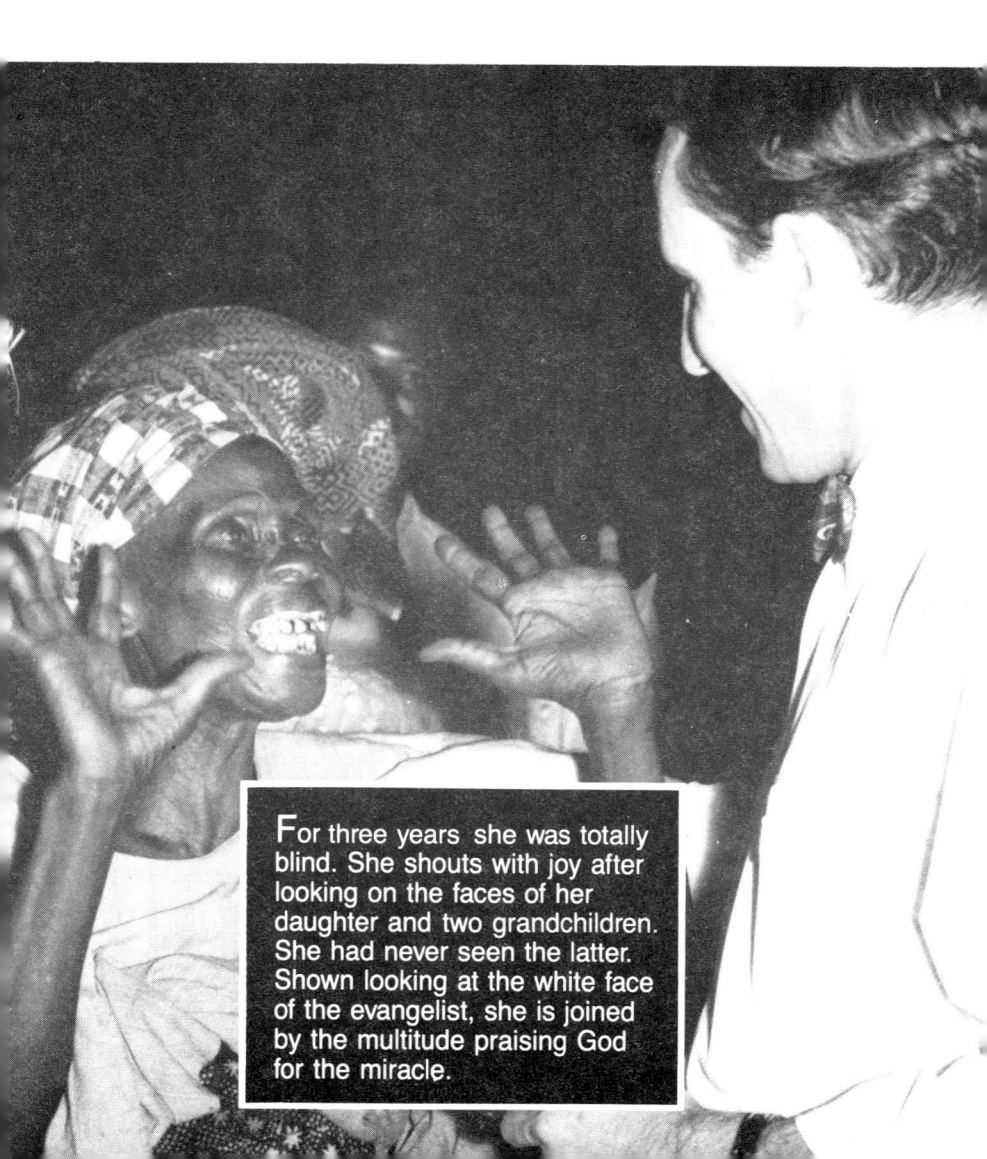

For three years she was totally blind. She shouts with joy after looking on the faces of her daughter and two grandchildren. She had never seen the latter. Shown looking at the white face of the evangelist, she is joined by the multitude praising God for the miracle.

MOSLEM BEGGAR CRAWLED

"I am no longer a Moslem. I will follow Jesus Christ who is alive. He proved it by healing me!"

OSBORN CRUSADE

FOR 30 YRS.

This man crawled on the ground, from village to village in West Africa, begging for his living.

Then he became a notable walking miracle of God for the thousands who knew his condition.

He was miraculously healed during the Osborn Crusade in Ibadan. His testimony of healing is known throughout Nigeria — proof that Jesus Christ is ALIVE! "I went many places with my wife and child, telling what God did for me. Some nights I never slept, so many wanted to talk to me."

NIGERIA

"Many of the men were rejoicing with me, holding my arms up in praise, looking at my legs and shouting."

"During the prayer, something lifted me up from the ground so that I did not feel that I was sitting as before. It was such that I opened my eyes to see if someone was lifting me up but no one was. It was so real that I next thought I was sitting up on something that was holding me up in the air. I felt and there was nothing at all. It was such a strange feeling. A power was actually lifting me up and holding me."

"Then another thing happened. I felt ghosts or spirits going out of my body. I saw these ghosts leaving me and I knew they were going.

"I began to be overcome with joy. As I kept trying to walk, these spirits came back to me, then left again. Once more they returned, but I began walking faster and better with faith in the living Jesus, then I saw those beings go away from me, and they never came back again.

"I am determined to follow Jesus with all my heart. I will attend church meetings to learn all I can about Jesus so I can know how to obey Him and please Him. As fast as I learn more, then I will preach that too, so others can know.

"If you come to Africa, you will find me preaching for Jesus as I have seen the revivalist do. You will find me following Jesus and learning all I can about His way so I can teach it to others."
... Cornelius

"A LARGE CROWD GATHERED. I TESTIFIED ABOUT MY HEALING."

RENNES, FRANCE
17th meeting

We have just come in from one of the greatest days we have witnessed in France. **Thousands of people with signs and banners and their conveyances formed a great parade and came singing and marching through the city to the campaign grounds.** It was impressive and very large. After the people gathered on the grounds, I preached on water baptism and led them in a great prayer for salvation as many received Christ and were born again.

Then the baptismal service began. Our daughter, LaDonna, was the first to be baptized by a Gypsy pastor (see photo, opposite page). Then followed the others. Many could be seen going down into the water weeping and coming up praising God!

Then a Moslem from Algeria came confessing that he wanted to be baptized since he had believed on Jesus Christ and had accepted Him in the crusade. He was baptized, and we all rejoiced. He went to the microphone and gave his testimony of faith in Jesus

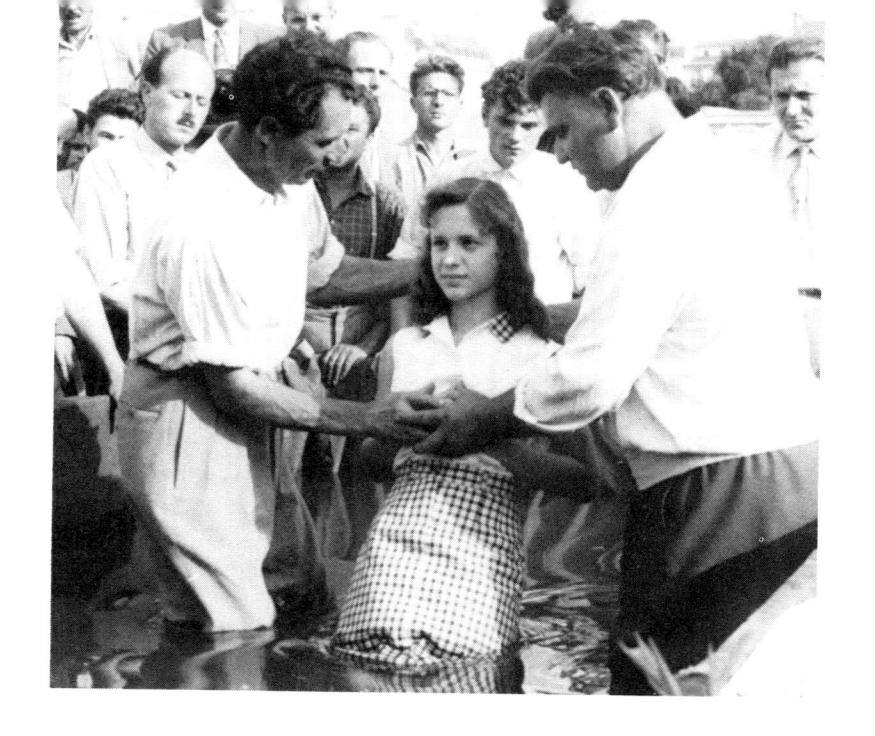

Christ, declaring that his entire life was now dedicated to Jesus.

Then a man, who is an outstanding Gypsy nightclub singer, came and testified that he, too, had been saved today and must be baptized. He had on a beautiful suit. He had run to nearby shops to see if he could buy clothes to be baptized in, but could not, so he returned quickly to keep from missing his opportunity. He confessed that he had been a very unclean and terrible man, but now he is completely changed and so happy. His wife was by his side in tears, and together they were baptized. It was wonderful!

Many others came and testified and were baptized, too. I was particularly impressed by two outstanding Gypsy violinists who had played in the Gypsy orchestra. They came to be baptized. One is old — very witty, lively, an excellent musician. The other one is **considered to be the best Gypsy violinist alive.** He was converted a few days ago. Both of these great musicians went into the water together.

Before they were baptized, I asked the orchestra to play a beautiful Gypsy hymn as these two great Gypsy musicians were buried with Christ in the waters of baptism. Hundreds of people wept as the

Acclaimed the best living Gypsy violinist, this man was saved and baptized during the Rennes Crusade.

Skilled Gypsy violinist who played for President Woodrow Wilson in America. He was baptized during the Rennes Crusade.

RENNES, FRANCE

orchestra played like angels. When they arose from the water, the crowd rejoiced and glorified God. Hundreds were baptized. Only God knows the glory of this occasion today. This great city of Rennes will never be the same. I thank God we were there!

SPINE MIRACULOUSLY RE-CREATED

A father brought his ten-year-old son who had suffered with tuberculosis of the spine. His bones were virtually "rotten" and easily breakable, so he wore a heavy cast from his waist up. He could not stand or bend.

The father took the boy from his hospital ward to the Osborn Crusade.

When the mass prayer was prayed, they believed that the miracle had taken place.

Standing behind the platform, the man cut away the cast, then they came to testify of what God had done.

Many in the audience knew the boy's condition and marveled as they saw him standing there, erect and well. He could bend, twist, walk, jump or run as well as any normal lad.

Many believed on Christ because of this miracle in the Osborn French Crusade.

T.L. Osborn holds aloft the large body cast which had been cut off the lad's body after the mass prayer.

THE HAGUE, HOLLAND
5th meeting

This Holland Crusade is truly historic — **the greatest crowds ever in Europe's history** to receive the gospel face to face. Police claimed that from 120,000 to 150,000 were gathered on the Malieveld grounds tonight. There were at least a hundred policemen present. I do not know how many scores of Red Cross nurses and staffmen, stretchers, and trucks were on duty. To watch them was like watching an ambulance corps on a battlefield, serving the wounded and helpless.

The **papers, radio,** and **TV** are all favorable in their news coverage.

The crusade committee has been uneasy about the Chief of Police who has been quite demanding on us. They thought he might be looking for technical reasons to curtail the crusade. But today, the committee secretary was summoned to the office of the Chief of Police who had also gathered together a large number of his top men. Before them all, he told his men how he believed that this was of God, that he was very

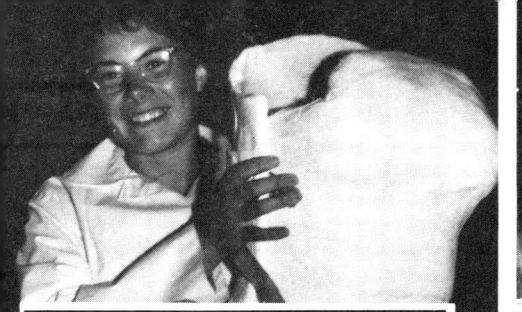

Nine months bedfast after accident in which her back was broken. Instantly healed in Holland crusade. Removed 13 lb. cast. Is perfect.

She is 26 years old, and was born with crossed eyes. She was healed in the Holland crusade, and her eyes are 100 percent straight.

OSBORN CRUSADE — THE HAGUE, HOLLAND

OSBORN CRUSADE

For 15 years he suffered with glaucoma. His left eye was blind; the right almost blind. His sight was restored during T.L.'s mass prayer at The Hague. Now he can even read.

GRONINGEN, HOLLAND

very thankful that such a meeting and such wonders of God could take place in his city — Holland's capital.

It seems almost unprecedented to me, the way this nation is doing everything possible to make the crusade a great success. Tonight I preached on John 3:16,17. Never have we seen a mass of people more attentive. Literally thousands accepted Jesus Christ as their Savior and were born again when we invited them to decide for Christ.

Then we prayed for the great mass of people, and miracles of healing were everywhere. There is no way I could convey the glory of this meeting. A girl who was 90 percent blind was completely healed. A man, who had a severe back injury, a cancer on his nose, and a double rupture, was perfectly healed. The cancer simply vanished. No sign of it remained. His back was as free as a child's, and both ruptures disappeared.

A woman who had been in a wheelchair for 21 long years was perfectly healed. During the message, she just got up and began to walk and was made entirely whole. Then she ran to the platform to show everyone how she could run, and even jump.

A lad took off the steel braces from legs which

had been paralyzed by polio. He walked back and forth on the platform to show that his legs were perfectly healed. A man on two crutches was marvelously healed and came across the platform, carrying his crutches. Another man, who could only walk with the aid of two canes, was healed. He, too, came rejoicing, carrying and waving his canes. A woman in a wheelchair got up and was healed. She was so very happy. A lady was healed of cancer in her breast. It was gone. Another lady was healed of a hernia. A man was healed of asthma.

Evangelist Daisy Osborn preaches good news to Hollanders, building up their faith in God's promises.

An old woman, totally blind, was brought to the crusade in a wheelchair. That dear old lady was completely healed! She really raised a shout in the camp when her blind eyes came open, and then she got out of her wheelchair and began to walk normally! She could see everything clearly and could walk as good as ever. It was really amazing!

Oh, there were scores of other marvelous miracles; and, as usual, hundreds raised their hands in the audience, saying that they were healed but could not get to the platform. **Holland can never forget this day and can never be the same again!** Jesus has shown Himself **ALIVE** by many infallible proofs!

"A great multitude followed Him because they saw His miracles which He did on them that were diseased." John 6:2

"With one accord they gave heed unto those things which Philip spake." Acts 8:6 — So it was also in Holland.

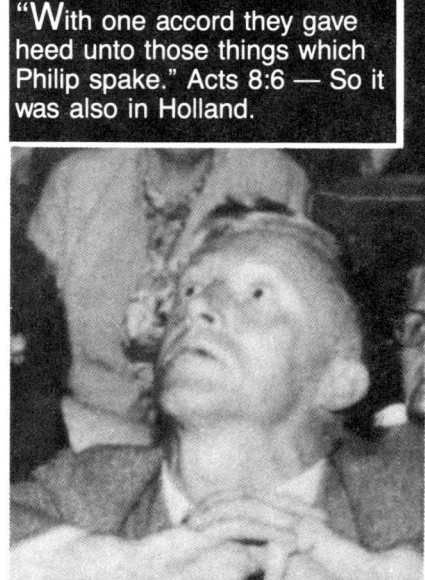

LOME, TOGO
11th meeting

Tonight I feel more amazed over this campaign than ever before. **It is among the greatest.** Such **power!** Such **conversions!** Such **miracles!** Every day more and greater miracles are taking place. And as far as conversions, there never seems to be anyone who refuses to accept Christ. **It is mass conversion and mass healing.**

Tonight I preached on **"Acting Faith."** Four lepers claimed complete healing already. Two of them had sores all over their hands and feet; in a few days all of those sores have dried up. One of them had the type of leprosy where all his flesh burned like fire. Now his flesh never burns, and he feels well. The other had the painful type, and she is free of all pain.

An old lady who was totally blind for over five years was healed and could count fingers of people in the audience. Then there was a girl who was **carried by her father from a far-away village.** For some years she had not walked a step. Tonight she could run and jump like any girl!

A young man was carried by his father to the meeting from a distant area. He had been unable to walk for about six years. He **had tried all of the native fetishes** and **witch doctors,** but to no avail. Then he heard about the campaign, and his father carried him here. He was completely healed tonight, and just smiled and wept and rejoiced as he testified.

Another young man was healed who had been bedfast for three years. From far away in his village, **he heard about the campaign. He said that he heard that the Son of God had come down to earth and was healing the people.** I told him that was right; but that I was not the Son of God, that His name is **Jesus.** He understood and was marvelously converted.

A poor man had been vomiting blood as often as 20 times a day. He was dying of tuberculosis. Over a hundred miles up in the interior, he had heard of the miracles. He had been bedfast for three years and could not walk. He had no voice. His parents were so poor that they only had enough money to pay the truck-bus driver to carry him to Lome. They knew if he was not healed, he would die. If he was healed, **he could walk home.**

They carried him to the old truck, paid the fare, and put him in the care of the driver who helped him during the trip. On arriving in Lome, the truck driver carried him and laid him on the ground under a tree near the platform. He had a few precious coins with which he bought some rice from a woman who occasionally went to the grounds. **Three days he had lain there, and tonight he was healed.** As he testified, his voice grew stronger. He was one of the happiest persons I have ever seen!

The Lord's mercy is unfailing! We feel so awed to think that He has allowed **us** to be His instruments to bring the gospel to these dear people. **Over 50 towns and villages have already sent invitations begging us to come preach the gospel to them** or send someone in our place. It is so touching to hear different people testify of coming from afar, then to hear them begging us to come or to send a preacher to them. Another chief has sent a letter and is even here in the audience, begging us to send preachers to his people, so they can hear the gospel and be saved.

LEFT: Mr. Adzon carried his 12-year-old daughter to the Togo Crusade. Due to syphilis, the child had not walked since she was two years old. She was completely healed.

ABOVE: Mr. Adzon with his daughter and sister, Dora, who had been insane for three years. Dora was kept chained to a tree. She tore her clothes from her body. Every demon fled during the mass prayer, and she was perfectly healed in the Lome Crusade.

BEFORE: For ten years Comola had not walked due to paralysis. His father and friend carried him to the campaign.

During the mass prayer, he was healed instantly. His old father said: "I am going to tell all the country about this Christ who has healed my son."

Osborn campaign in Lome, Togo, drew thousands to hear the gospel from the very first service.

LUCKNOW, INDIA
2nd meeting

I take up my pen to try to set down what my eyes have beheld on this second night of the Lucknow, India Crusade. Words are inadequate to record the glory of the meeting.

Early in the afternoon the people were crowding onto the grounds near the stadium. By 6 p.m. when I arrived, the multitude was packed tight and stretched far out across the field, past our large light installation, out into the darkness. Officials estimated 50,000 to 75,000 people present. They were so reverent and orderly; not once did we have any difficulty controlling the multitude.

No one could imagine the looks on the people's faces. Some of the strange characters present were beyond description. For example, right in front of the platform, not three feet from me, there stood an old Hindu holy man in an old robe. His long dingy white beard and his dishevelled hair shrouded a desperate and pitiful face. He was standing erect. In his right hand was a large "Father Neptune" spear with three rusty prongs, which he kept poised before his face. It was his staff. He stood right in front of me as I preached.

What a joy to give the gospel to that dear man! **How marvelous to see the power of Christ dominate,** not only that man with his weird staff, but to the multitude of others who had come, by the tens of thousands from north India, in their search for God and truth!

I preached on Mark 9:23, urging them to **"Only Believe."** Thousands **did** believe; and when I finished my message, we called on them to accept Christ. It looked as though everyone raised their hands into the air to receive the Savior. It was overwhelming — a sea of hands, **a tidal wave response!** As in the Bible, *multitudes were added to the Lord.*

Then we prayed for all the sick. When finished, we have **seldom seen anything like it:** Literally hundreds were miraculously healed and began trying to reach the platform.

The first one up the steps was an old Hindu man, carrying two crutches above his head. He was beaming! His long hair and beard were flowing. For five years he had been crippled. Now he paraded back and forth, so happy. By that time, another old man with a large red turban came bounding across the platform. He, too, was healed completely. A man whose foot and leg were crippled was perfectly healed. He had walked on one side of his foot, which was turned directly inward with the ankle twisted over. Both feet were perfectly healed and completely

The first miracle of the Lucknow Crusade: A devout, high-caste Hindu merchant, healed of total deafness in his right ear, which had been deaf for 30 years.

A serious fever during childhood left both of his ears totally deaf. The first night he was in the crusade, he was perfectly healed and could hear the tick of a watch from either ear.

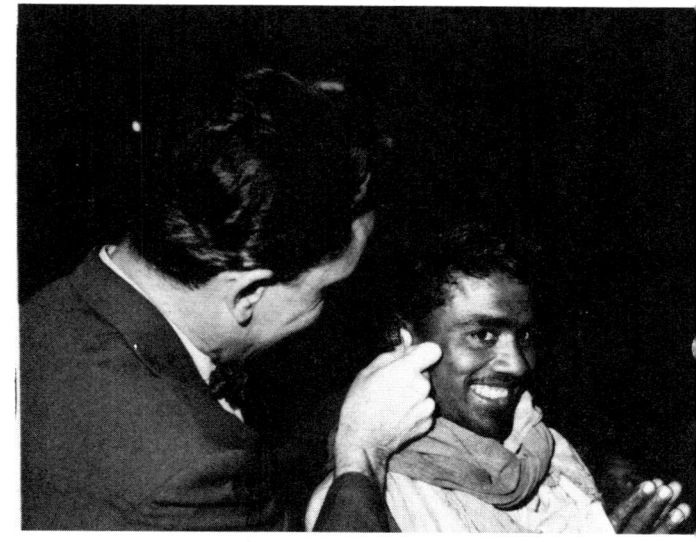

He was crippled from paralysis and also suffered from a large rupture. Both were instantly healed and he hastened to testify to what Christ did for him.

straight. He ran and jumped as the people glorified God!

Two men who were blind came to the crusade together. Both of them were healed. Their eyes were so bright and clear that one could hardly believe they had been blind. Oh, they were both so happy! A child with one arm bent double, so that he never had been able to stretch it out, was perfectly healed. He was very happy. Two boys who were brothers — **both of them totally blind** — came and were healed. **It was a most wonderful sight to see them look at each other and rub each other in admiration.**

Then a girl was healed of blindness and could see everything. A 70-year-old woman, who had been nearly blind for seven years, was healed and could see clearly.

A most touching thing: A little old woman, clad in a dirty filthy garb, testified in tears. She would praise Jesus, then place her open palms together and bow to me in Hindu fashion. Then she would bow to my feet and touch them, then repeat it again and again. **She had been a beggar and had no one to help her.** Her children and her husband were dead. She was left alone in life to beg.

Being a Moslem woman, she could not lift her veil in the presence of men, but she secretly showed the evangelist's wife her eyes which were badly crossed. They were perfectly straight, healed by a miracle. Also, her child was healed of a withered leg and her servant was healed of dumbness.

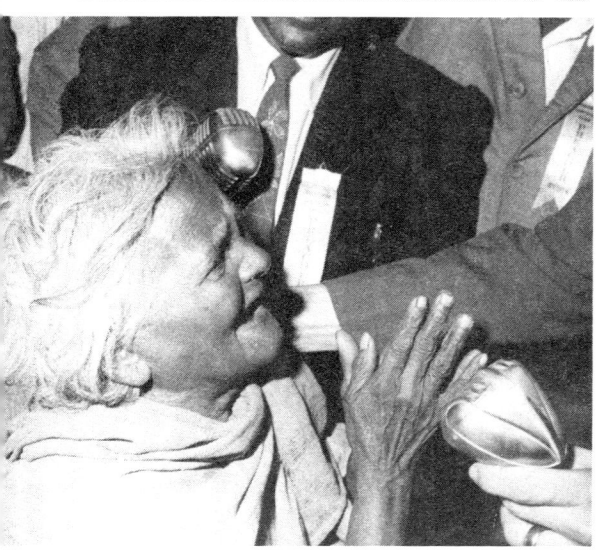

All of her children died in infancy. Old and dejected, she begged for food to stay alive. Disease-ridden, she became too ill to beg, and surrendered to die. Then news of the crusade brought her hope. Miraculously healed, she worshipped the Lord and exclaimed: "Now I can manage for myself."

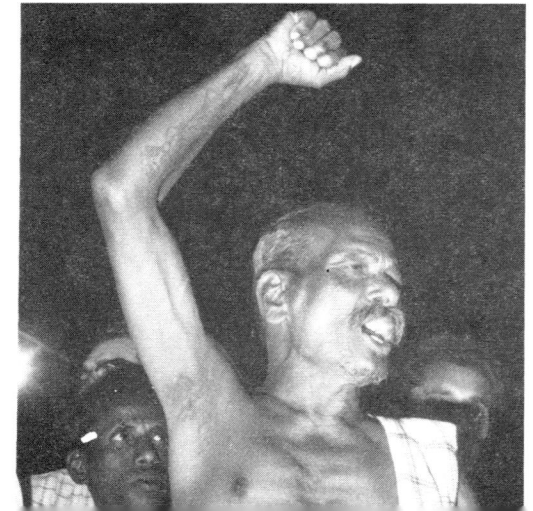

Totally blind, this man was led to the services by his son. Instantly healed, he shouted his testimony before the multitude in the Osborn Crusade in India.

She said that she had become terribly sick until she was too weak to beg. Each day that she could not beg, she had no way to get a bit of rice, so she became sicker and hungrier and weaker.

Then she would cry and touch my feet again to say how thankful she was that she was not lying in the bushes anymore, sick and hungry. Someone had found her in her dying state and had told her about Jesus and about this crusade. Somehow she had managed to come, and she was healed. She said, **"Now I can go back on the street and beg, because I am not sick and weak. I can talk loud enough to ask for alms and get a few pisas a day to eat."** Oh, it was touching!

How thankful we are to have come to India — **just for her.** There were at least 20 blind people healed tonight. Daisy counted six people healed of crossed eyes. Numerous cripples and lame people walked. Several deaf-mutes were healed. All praise to the Lord Jesus Christ!

MANILA, PHILIPPINES
2nd meeting

Tonight was a very wonderful service. The multitude was large. I preached on **"Four Steps to Healing,"** closing with great emphasis on the fact that **salvation includes healing and that to receive healing, one must receive the Healer.** The Lord surely confirmed His word to the people as they cried out to God for salvation.

Then we prayed for the sick and God really confirmed His word. A man who had been deaf for over 30 years was healed. A woman who was deaf for ten years was healed completely. A girl, healed of polio, took off her steel leg-brace and shoe and walked perfectly. A lady was healed of a large goiter. A woman with one leg two inches shorter than the other felt God's power go through her, and both legs were perfectly equal. Another woman was healed of a goiter and a blood disease. It was an outstanding case.

A man carried both of his crutches above his head as he came to the platform and testified. He can walk as well as anyone. A man, who had a cancerous

OSBORN CRUSADE

OSBORN CRUSADE

CABANATUAN, PHILLIPINES

BATANGAS, PHILIPPINES

growth on the side of his neck the size of two fists, was perfectly healed. They had sent him home from the hospital to die. Nurses were afraid to touch him. **The huge growth simply disappeared.** It was astounding! He walked back and forth, pounding the side of his neck, shouting: **"Look! It's gone! It's gone! The cancer is gone!"** One of the missionaries knew the case and was amazed. A pastor grabbed me and, in tears, said, **"He is staying in our church. We know how he was. The cancer is gone! It was as big as two fists and was an open, odorous sore. It is gone! It is amazing!"**

What a tremendous meeting. Scores of great miracles took place. The multitude will never forget what they saw tonight.

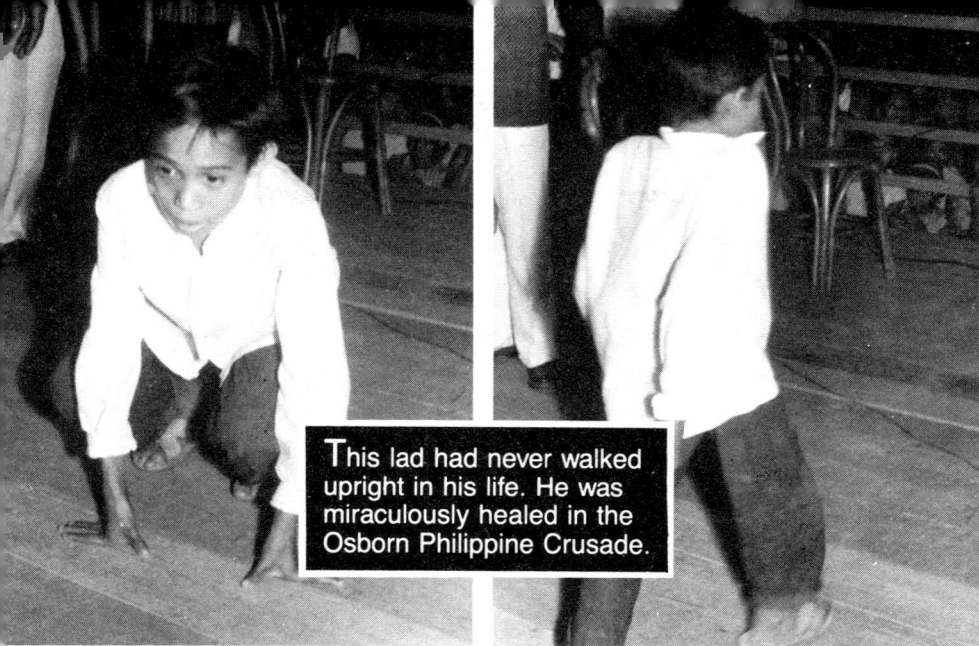

This lad had never walked upright in his life. He was miraculously healed in the Osborn Philippine Crusade.

Polio at the age of one destroyed the use of her left leg. She was fitted to a steel brace. The God of miracles passed her way and the child was completed healed in the Osborn Crusade.

She was totally blind. Healed by a miracle in the Osborn Crusade at Manila, she weeps as she tells the multitude how Jesus restored her sight.

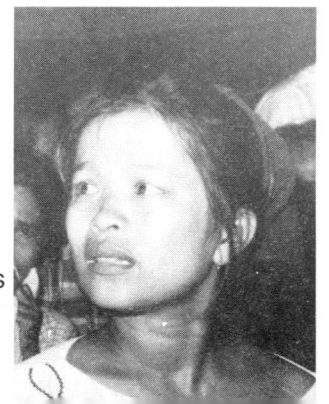

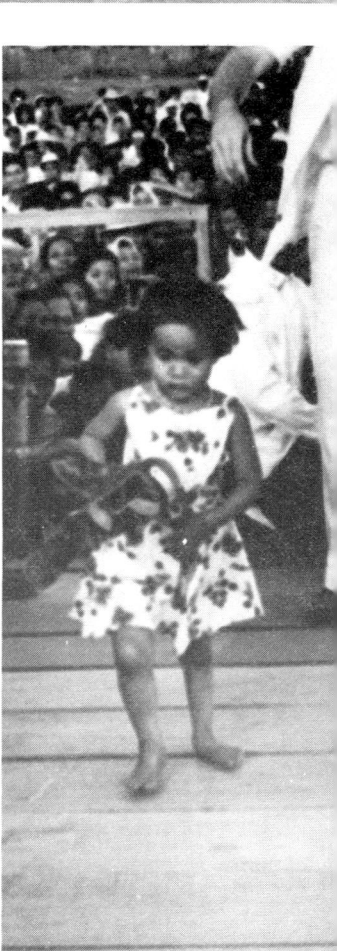

Evangelist Daisy Osborn proclaims Christ's teachings in the Osborn Crusade at Cabanatuan, Luzon.

SAN FERNANDO, TRINIDAD
10th meeting

The crusade here in San Fernando, Trinidad, has been one of the greatest we have ever seen in our lives. **Literally, the entire city has been attracted to hear the gospel.** Upwards of 50,000 to 75,000 people, perhaps even 100,000, have poured onto the great crusade grounds at the edge of the city from all over the island-nation.

Tonight I preached on **"What Jesus Did For Every Individual At The Cross."** I emphasized His substitutionary work for each one and stressed Romans 1:16 — that *the gospel is the power of God to everyone that believes.* When I finished the message and gave an invitation to accept Christ, at least 5,000 people raised their hands to believe on Jesus Christ and to receive Him as their Savior. Then we prayed for the sick, and there was an avalanche of miracles. All over the crowd rejoicing could be heard, and one could see people here and there being healed.

At the edge of the crowd, **groups were running after different ones who had received miraculous**

healing. Before we knew it, the platform was being inundated with people who wanted to testify of what God had done for them. They were shouting and praising God. Some were jumping; others were crying.

A young man was weeping and rubbing his eyes. His left eye had been badly crossed, and he was nearly blind. Twice he had undergone surgery to straighten the crossed eye and to restore his sight, but both operations failed. Tonight his blind, crossed eye was completely restored.

Then an old woman touched me on the arm, wanting to testify. For over three years her right eye had been totally blind. She was completely healed. A 13-year-old lad, who had been born deaf, was healed. His ears were perfect. A little baby, which had been born crippled, was brought in the arms of its mother. There was **no sign of knees or kneecaps.** Both legs were rigid and doubled flat against its chest. Doctors forced the stiff legs down and bound them in casts. The mother attended the crusade and believed for a miracle. The next morning both legs were normal! Pain was gone, and the child's knees were perfect. Those who knew the child's condition were astonished at this creative miracle.

A dear man was healed of a paralytic stroke which had left him dumb and helpless. His wife had to feed and dress him. But in the meeting tonight he was completely restored! **He could walk, jump, run, and talk normally.** It was a great miracle! A lad was healed of a totally deaf ear. There was a large scar behind his ear that showed where **a radical mastoid operation had been performed in which his hearing faculties had been removed.** God performed a **creative** miracle. Now, he can hear the faintest whisper.

A little boy whose left eye was totally blind after being hit in the eye with a stone, was completely healed. He had also been bitten by a serpent, and his right leg was swollen and painful. But it also was made whole.

There was a girl who walked very awkwardly because her left leg was curved in and her foot was twisted. But tonight the bones in her leg and foot became perfectly normal and straight. A dear old woman who was totally blind and deaf was healed. Those around her were delighted that her sight had been miraculously restored.

A man who had come to the crusade hobbling on crutches was made whole. He had prayed to God for his miracle and had been completely restored.

Another man was carried to the crusade on a bed because he was paralyzed and unable to move his legs. He was instantly healed! He got up from his bed and began to walk, swinging his arms and moving his hands. **He was perfect.** An old woman, who had been totally blind for several years, was led to the great campaign. She listened intently to the message of the gospel and believed on Jesus Christ. During the healing prayer, she placed her hands on her blind eyes, then **acted her faith.** Her sight was restored, and she was overwhelmed at being able to see clearly again.

There was a woman who had been totally deaf for 32 years. During the prayer, her ears popped open, and she could hear the faintest whisper! A beautiful lad about 12 years old was healed in his legs. One leg was twisted inward, and the foot was malformed. Some might call it a club foot. He walked on the

OSBORN CRUSADE

side of his foot, and the knee was twisted inward. With childlike faith, this lad asked God to heal him as we prayed for the mass of people; and he received a **creative** bone miracle. The club foot was straightened out, and his leg that had been twisted was also made perfectly whole.

Perhaps the greatest miracle of all was the healing of Harold Khan, who was a Moslem lad, reared in a Moslem home. When he was only 12 years old, he was injured while playing football. His right leg was damaged so that all growth stopped abruptly. An incurable bone disease resulted, affecting his left leg, too.

Since the accident, his body has grown as any robust youth, except for his right leg which never developed after the injury. It had already become **five inches shorter** than the left one and was much smaller. **Harold walked with the aid of a special**

TRINIDAD

shoe for his dwarfed right leg, elevated on a five-inch platform. His left leg was bound in a steel hip-to-heel brace because of the bone disease affecting it.

News reached the Khan home of the crusade. Mrs. Khan wanted to take Harold, but was forbidden by the staunch Moslem father. But while he was away, **she took her son at the risk of family disfavor** and attended the great meeting. Both she and her son believed on the Lord Jesus Christ tonight as we expounded the simple dynamic message on the meaning of the gospel.

Before we prayed for the sick, Harold believed that God was healing him, and he wept before the Lord as he listened to the message. As we were praying, he took off the elevated shoe from his right leg and the steel hip-to-heel brace from his left leg and accepted Jesus Christ into his heart. Then this awesome miracle came to pass. **His short leg became normal as the Lord passed his way!**

Harold and his mother came weeping to the platform, carrying the steel brace and elevated shoe. When Harold mounted the stairs with this strange elevated shoe in his hand, holding the big leg brace above his head, he was weeping. I presumed that he had come to tell us about someone else who had been healed. I looked at him and his legs were perfectly normal. I could see no reason for **him** to have needed this elevated shoe and the big leg brace, so I asked him: **"Who has been healed?"**

He was sobbing convulsively. He finally said, **"It's me! I have been healed! These are the things I have taken off my legs!"** It was incredible to behold!

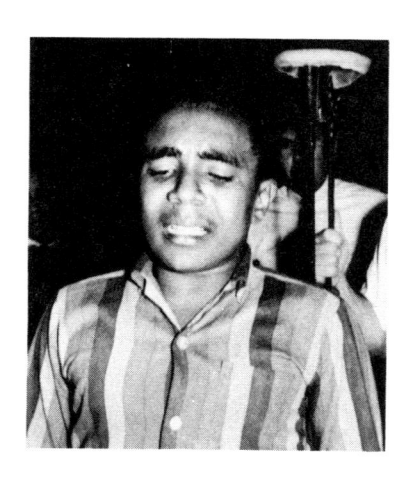

Harold came weeping to the platform. He demonstrated that both legs had become perfect — and equal.

Pondering that pair of perfectly equal legs, one could but wonder at the awesome power of God to do the utterly impossible! He walked back and forth on the platform, and both of his legs were perfectly equal. It absolutely astounded the multitude of people!

THE HAROLD KHAN MIRACLE

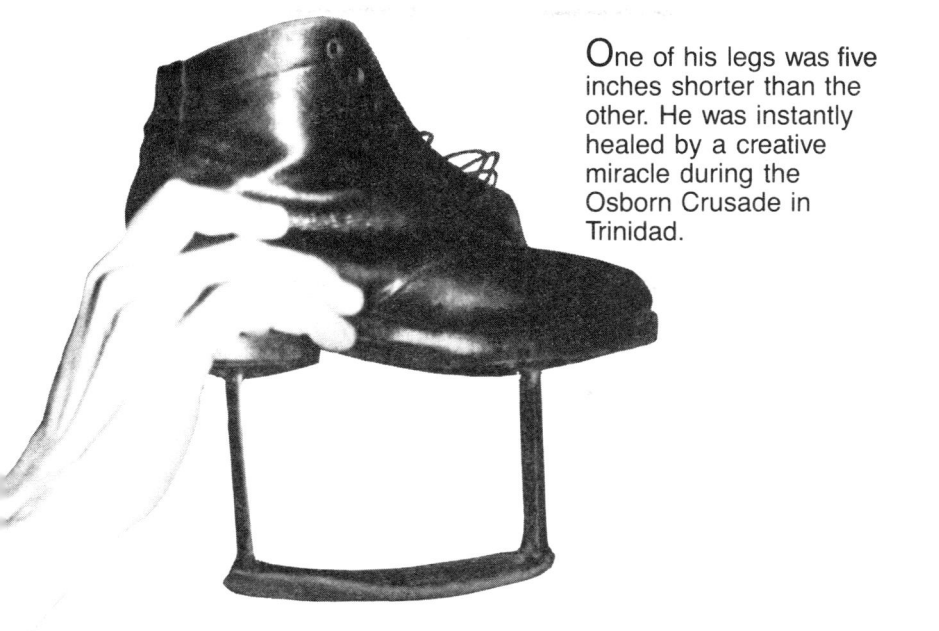

One of his legs was five inches shorter than the other. He was instantly healed by a creative miracle during the Osborn Crusade in Trinidad.

Harold's mother and father, both Moslems, accepted Jesus Christ as their Savior.

The picture at left shows how this lad's left leg was twisted, and how he had to walk. He was brought to the Osborn Crusade in Trinidad where he learned about Christ's power to heal. With his child-like faith, this lad *asked and received* a miracle from Christ and his left leg was made perfectly normal, as the picture on the right shows.

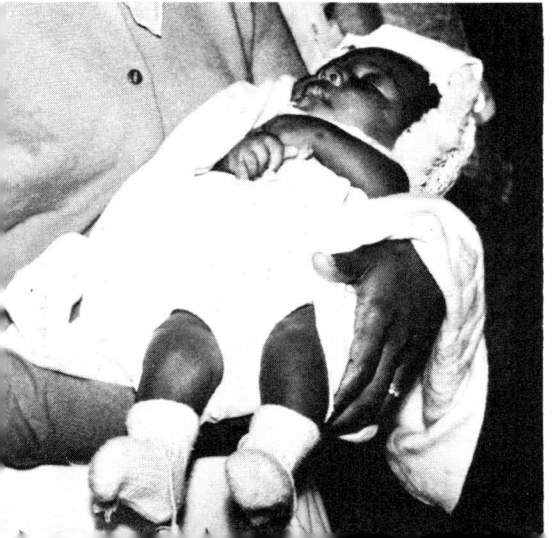

This baby was born crippled. Its legs had no signs of knees or kneecaps; both were rigid and doubled flat against its chest. Doctors forced the stiff legs down and bound them in casts. The mother attended the Osborn Crusade and believed for a miracle. The next morning, both legs were normal, pain was gone and the knees were perfect. She brought the child to show the people how its legs were healed. Those who knew the child's condition were astonished at this creative miracle.

KINSHASA, ZAIRE
13th meeting

When I take up my pen to record a day like today, I feel helpless to express the glory and wonder of it all. **A great multitude heard the word** as I preached on Psalm 103:3. The people scarcely moved. **They just riveted their attention to each word.** When we prayed the prayer of repentance, everyone prayed. There seems to be **no opposition. No one refuses.** It is overwhelming to witness!

After the prayer for healing, an avalanche of testimonies converged onto the platform. It was so thrilling. There is no way to record them. **It was the same as in Bible days.** The **dumb** and **deaf** and **blind** and **lame** and **crazy** and **sick** were all healed. The people cried and laughed and were amazed.

As we were closing the meeting tonight, a mother placed two of her children up on the platform with a bucket. I have never seen anything so precious. Those two children reached up to tell me to look. Then they set the bucket on the platform, took off the lid, and pointed. There was a spotless white cloth covering a clean pan with a lid on it. They lifted it out, removed the lid, and **there were eight clean white fresh eggs.** The children smiled sweetly and wanted me to take them. **I took my hat and squatted down as the kids placed each egg in the hat,** smiled, then replaced their pan in the bucket and put the lid back on. Then they got up and the larger one (about four years old) reached out to shake my hand, then went back to the edge of the platform to their mother. It was truly a **love gift,** and a tremendous expression of affection.

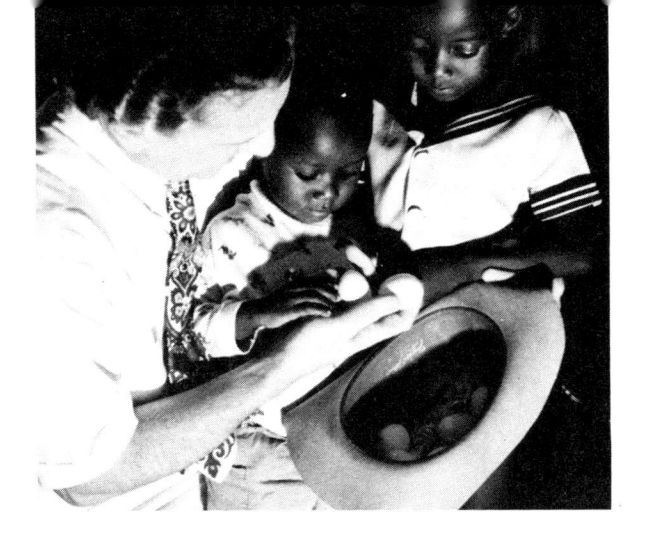

OSBORN CRUSADE

I thank God that we can be among these people. It is a tremendous experience. We quickly ate a roll of bread in the car and drank some fruit drink, then went to the large hall where 1,200 preachers were waiting for us to share with them the secrets of evangelism.

Rushing directly from the crusade services to the late-night ministers' meetings, there was no time to return home for supper. Bread and cheese, washed down with a fruit drink, carried us over until the next day's breakfast.

KINSHASA, ZAIRE

PHOTO BELOW: During the Osborn Crusade in Kinshasa, night after night, following the prayer of faith, dozens of people swarmed the platform, waving crutches and braces, jumping, weeping, hearing or seeing again. Seldom have we ever witnessed such an avalanche of miracles.

"The power of the Lord was present to heal." Luke 5:17

"What's that thing?" someone cried. A paralyzed woman had been healed and was out of her wheelchair. The crowd passed her discarded chair over their heads to the platform. The woman (in striped dress, walking) never returned to claim it.

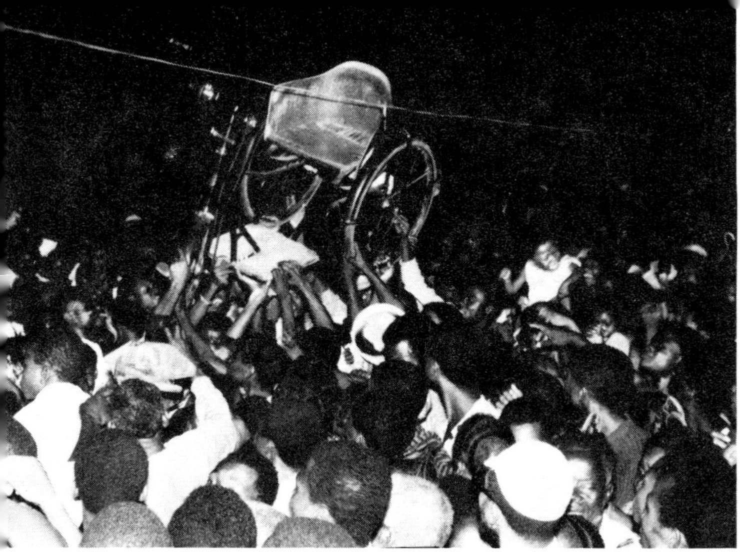

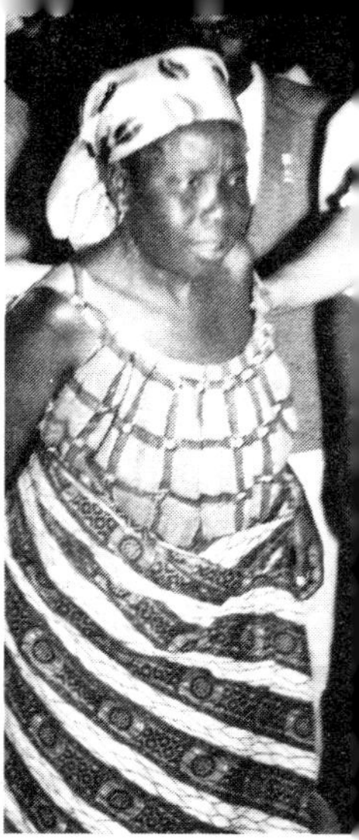

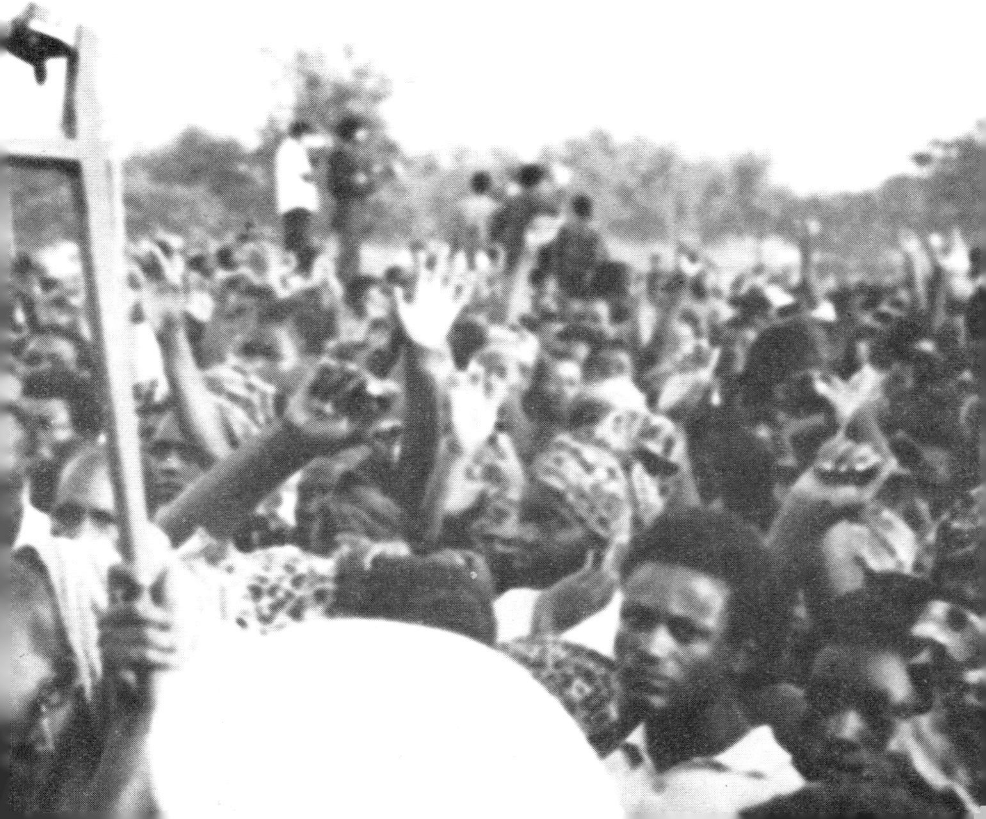

BENIN CITY, NIGERIA
3rd meeting

This is an enormous crusade in this city whose **history is so steeped in pagan culture and primitive superstition.** Tens of thousands are attending.

Tonight I preached on Romans 1:16 — **"The Gospel."** I was able to really convey the message of the good news and was under an unusual anointing as I told them at the finale: **"My government in heaven has authorized me, as an ambassador in Christ's name, to announce to every sinner, who believes in what Christ did at the cross, that you will never be condemned by your sins; that you are FORGIVEN now. I am authorized to pronounce that every captive is FREE, to announce to all sick people that you are HEALED and that Satan no longer reigns with authority in your lives, if you believe on Jesus Christ. I am sent from God with a special proclamation, and I have been ordered to tell all captives of sin, disease, and devils, that the term of your captivity is ended and that you may now walk out of bondage, as free persons — SAVED and HEALED by Jesus

Christ, God's Son."

Needless to say, hundreds **did** walk out of bondage. In all directions, spontaneous outbursts of praise and excitement could be seen as **cripples suddenly began to walk** and as people began to realize they were healed. Great glory was given to God, and all believed that Jesus truly was among them!

The message was clearly grasped, and a great wave of reverence gripped the people as they repented of sins and received Jesus Christ. It was a powerful night, and the many thousands present could easily witness the great signs and wonders which God did among them to confirm His word.

The platform was simply inundated by hundreds, pushing and crying and rejoicing, wanting to tell what God had done for them.

There is no way that I could record the scores and scores of great testimonies. A girl who was born with no vaginal opening was brought last night and was healed. Today they came and told us that she is now normal. It is a very unusual case.

A boy wept as he confessed that he was a thief. Now he says he will never steal again. A lad testified whose right heel had never touched the ground

T.L. and Daisy Osborn arrive at Benin City to begin their mass evangelism crusade.

OSBORN CRUSADE

Rev. Daisy Osborn ministers God's word to the vast crusade crowds and (left) meets with the Police Chief of Bendel State to assure order during the meetings.

BENIN CITY

because his knee was bent; he had to walk on tiptoe. He was perfectly healed. His leg became straight, and the foot was flat on the floor.

Then a boy came who had one leg quite a bit shorter than the other. He, too, was absolutely perfect and walked with a true, even stride. It amazed everyone.

A woman threw away two canes with which she had staggered along for 17 years. Also, for over seven years, she had vomited nearly all her food. Tonight she was totally restored. She walked perfectly, and her stomach was completely healed.

A man came carrying two heavy sticks. For years he had only been able to stagger along, by bracing himself with these two canes. Now he tossed those heavy sticks away and walked as well as anyone.

An old blind woman was healed. She could see everything and was so happy. A young woman with one blind eye was completely recovered. At least three deaf-mutes were healed, and many who were deaf in one or two ears were restored.

We examined so many that we finally had to say, "Praise the Lord!" and pass them on. **It is impossible to tell how great God's presence and power was.** We just give Him the glory!

OSBORN·CRUSADE — BENIN CITY

He had been totally blind for five years. He is shown on the platform weeping and thanking God for answering his prayer at the Osborn Crusade.

This man who came to the crusade on crutches, carries them up the steps to tell the multitude of Christ's miracle in his body. He is typical of thousands who experience the unspeakable joy of newfound salvation and healing when they confessed Jesus Christ as Lord.

UYO, NIGERIA
7th meeting

Tonight we have beheld the glory of God in a way seldom seen. The newspaper estimated that at least 200,000 were present. How like our God it is to descend among these dear people and perform such wonders for them!

I preached on the **"Healing of the Leper"** in a narrative style, expounding as I read the story. Each time I emphasized a point, the multitude would break out in clapping. All of this area seems to be receptive to the crusade. As usual, we directed them in a prayer for salvation, accepting Jesus Christ and confessing faith in Him. Hundreds wept freely. **It is very touching to see them and to hear them pray. You could see different ones smiting themselves on the breast, as the sinner did in the Bible.** God must be moved with great compassion when He sees a multitude like this crying out to Him for mercy.

After a long period of prayer and thanksgiving, I began to announce to them that it was time to accept the answer by FAITH and to put FAITH INTO

OSBORN CRUSADE — UYO

ACTION. Some most remarkable miracles took place. A handsome lad, about 15 years old, had been deaf since he was two years old when he had a bad fever. Tonight he could hear the faintest whisper from either ear.

Suddenly, a dear man mounted the stage, looking so happy. He had crawled on his hands and feet in a pitiful way. His knees had been stiff. It seems that a deadening, stiffening paralysis, mixed with perhaps arthritis, had crippled him. His hands had been twisted and gnarled. To show us how he had managed to move about, **he bent over and walked across the platform on his hands and feet.** It was really sad. But then he rose to his feet and raised both arms heavenward and praised the Lord in such a precious way that hundreds of us wept for joy! He could now walk, bending his legs, and could do anything in a normal way. He was really made whole — a wonder of God! The multitude cheered and clapped for joy.

The next one who testified was quite an old man, who for the past eight years had only been able to move about by scooting on his haunches with his hands at his side. He pushed himself along in a most painful way. He showed us on the platform how he did it. Then the dear old man rose to his feet and showed everyone how he can now walk **upright,** which he had not done for eight years. Oh, he was so grateful!

Then a dear woman bounded up on the other side of the platform, crying: **"Look at me! I was a leper! See my feet! Now I am healed. Look at me walk. Look! My feet are healed. I can feel them. They are well. I am healed!"** It was a marvel of God. She stomped her feet. Some of her toes were gone. There had been angry open sores on them, but they were clearly drying up and closing. She was overjoyed! She left, crying out: **"I am healed! My feet are healed! I can feel them. They are not dead. They are alive."** No one could doubt what God had done for her.

Then a man came who had been totally blind for several years. He was able to see everything. Next, a woman who had been blind came rejoicing because she could see everything clearly. She had been led to the crusade. Now she rejoiced, as she pointed out all the people. **She could count the fingers of anyone who raised his hand out in the audience.** It was marvelous!

A dear mother brought her child which had one side paralyzed by polio. She was crying and thanking God because the child was healed and could run and jump and walk perfectly. Then an older man, who had been a witchdoctor, came up the steps. **He was ashamed of the curses he had put on people and the deaths he had caused. Now he wanted to receive Jesus so that he would never be a witchdoctor again.** I commanded the evil spirits of witchcraft to leave him and to never torment or possess him again. **The people were astonished;** and then, as though someone had defeated a great enemy, they cried out in joy and clapped for a long time. It was touching. The old man was clearly delivered, and everyone marveled!

Suddenly, Daisy brought up a young man about 25-28 years old. He was completely bald. For eight years, he had been a raving maniac. It took four men to bring him and to control him during the meeting. He had been in the university at Lagos, studying medical science. Then one day **he suddenly began to lose his mind and became totally insane.** A growth began to develop in his throat and neck area; it was large like a mango seed and extremely painful.

Tonight during the mass prayer, he began to be calm, returned to his absolute normal mind, and every trace of the growth in his throat disappeared.

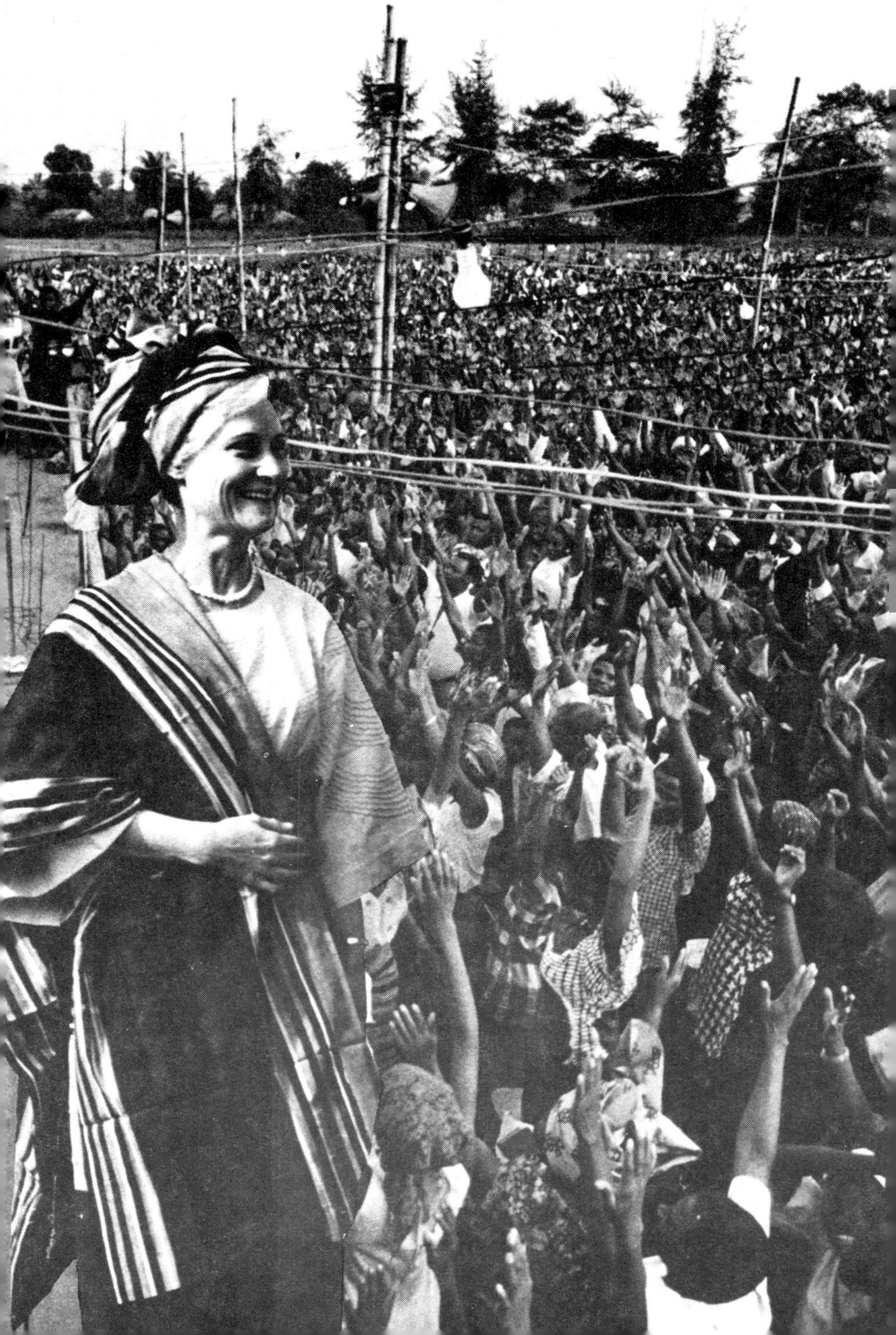

T.L. Osborn and Daisy Osborn (opposite page), minister the good news of Jesus Christ to throngs of people in Nigeria.

Another man on the platform verified his story. We were all amazed. He spoke good English and was a brilliant young man. He gave the most moving testimony, explaining how he fell into terror and confusion of mind and began to be compelled to rave and rage and to try to hurt people. Nothing made sense to him any more, and he felt that everyone was seeking to harm him. He became mad. Now he says everything is clear and normal. He is amazed that **all of the terror that had tormented his mind is gone.** He thanked Jesus and pledged to serve Him always. Really, the case was marvelous, and we glorified God!

Then I turned to see a man coming up the steps who had been a leper. **He was overwhelmed that the deadness from his feet and hands was gone.** His hands had become motionless, drawn to a clenched position and stiff. But now he could open and close them well. Every finger was free. He could feel with his feet and his hands. He was amazed and overjoyed and kept on praising God.

An elderly man came up the steps with a long staff. He was surprised and so happy. He said that he had been operated on for his back and hip and had never walked since the operation six years ago. He was helped to the crusade by friends, but got there late, just as we began the prayer. When the prayer was finished, he could stand up and walk with no trouble and with no pain. He was overwhelmed. All were thankful to see how God's mercy reached out to this dear man.

A young man about 20 years of age came and said: **"I was mad. I was crazy. But now, I am healed."** We were all amazed by his words. He looked so nice. We wondered if his story was true, so I asked for his name. He announced his name over the loudspeaker. Then I asked if anyone knew him. Suddenly, some hands raised. I asked them to come to the platform. A fellow came and said: **"I know him. It is true. He was crazy, and we had to hold him at times. He has been like that for several years."** They marveled. He was absolutely sane, normal, radiant and sensible looking. He talked calmly and coherently. One simply stood amazed at the mercy of God!

An old woman who had been crippled in her back for many years came to testify. She had not been able to stand upright, always walking humped over, supporting her back by bracing her hands above her knees. Now she stood perfectly erect, reared back, forward, and sideways; then she waved her arms. She was healed by a perfect miracle. A middle-aged woman who had been blind was led to the meeting, and now she has received clear sight. She could obviously see everything.

Suddenly a man about 40-45 years of age came to testify. As he talked, **I heard gasps in the audience and expressions of wonder.** My interpreter was so awestricken that he quit interpreting. I nudged him to keep translating for me. He said: **"Wait, wait! What is this!"** He was amazed. I had to insist that he tell me what the man was saying. Then the man stretched out his arms with wrists upturned, placing them close together, and **I saw big scars and tough calluses on his wrists.** Then he showed the people his ankles; they were the same. I asked my interpreter: **"What is this? Tell me!"** He said: **"Oh, this cannot be true! This cannot be true!"**

Then he explained that for 11 years the man had been crazy and possessed by demons. **They had to keep his feet and his hands in iron bands with chains. They had kept him locked in a mud hut.** He would fight and try to kill people. They could not get near him, so he had to be kept in iron bands.

Again, a preacher said: **"This cannot be so!"** I asked: **"Then why are these scars on his wrists? And look at his ankles!"** They were worse. Deep calluses circled his ankles and told the awful story. The dear man looked and seemed so normal that it was difficult to believe he had been insane; so I asked for someone in the multitude who knew him. Promptly, a woman came through the crowd, excited and crying. She was shouting: **"I know him. I live by the place where they kept him chained and locked up. He screamed. He was dangerous. He tried to kill people. To change his clothes or to feed him, they had to fight with him."**

Then the man interrupted the woman and opened his mouth wide, pointing at his teeth. Some of them were gone. He said: **"They beat me and kicked out my teeth."** It was sad, yet it was glorious to behold. The man was so normal that it was hard to believe he had been a dangerous, raving maniac. The woman kept talking and thanking God for the wonder of his healing. The man was truly delivered. Obviously, **the tormenting demons had gone out of him as we had preached the word and prayed for the multitude, and he was healed.**

Who could doubt the glory and mercy of God after witnessing such an avalanche of miracles, signs, and wonders? I could write for hours and not recount what happened tonight. **The stories are endless.** People were healed everywhere. The platform was

OSBORN CRUSADE — UYO

full of people who had been healed. All across the crowd, hundreds of people raised their hands to signify that they were healed but could not get through the pressed multitude to testify. It is truly amazing as it was in Bible days when *Jesus saw the multitude and was moved with compassion toward them and healed their sick* (Mt.14:14). **He is ALIVE!** And He is truly *the same yesterday and today and forever* (He.13:8) for those who will have simple child-like faith. Thank God for His word!

OSBORN CRUSADE

ENUGU, W. AFRICA

NAKURU, KENYA
3rd meeting

Amazing things are taking place in this city. The whole town is talking.

We are hearing of amazing things that took place last night. At the far edge of the crowd, a woman who was born blind and had never seen in her life was suddenly healed. As she began to see, she became so frightened that she screamed aloud and started to run. Then she saw a car moving. It horrified her, and she became frantic. She was just a poor village woman who **had never seen in her life.**

NAKURU, KENYA

EMBU, KENYA

EMBU, KENYA

Seeing masses of people moving about, she was horrified. Her husband called to her to calm her. **She knew his voice and turned to him, but seeing him coming toward her, she screamed and turned and ran.** They finally caught her and held her until they could help her overcome the shock of new eyesight. Zacharia Gichohi, a leading Christian businessman, saw it all.

One of the hotel men came and said to Daisy's interpreter: **"I must go today and get my wife from the village. I was standing in the meeting last night, and my own eyes witnessed a great miracle. A woman, who was born blind, suddenly received her sight. She screamed and tried to run from everyone and from everything that moved, and they had to catch her and hold her. I saw it with my own eyes! Oh, I never thought I would ever see something so wonderful as this!"** (It was the same woman I described above.)

Then another blind woman was sitting in a car at the edge of the multitude. The husband was standing by the rear of the car. His wife was totally blind. When the prayer was finished, the woman opened her eyes and her blindness was absolutely gone. She was so shocked and overwhelmed that she shouted, almost fearfully, and jumped out of the car and called

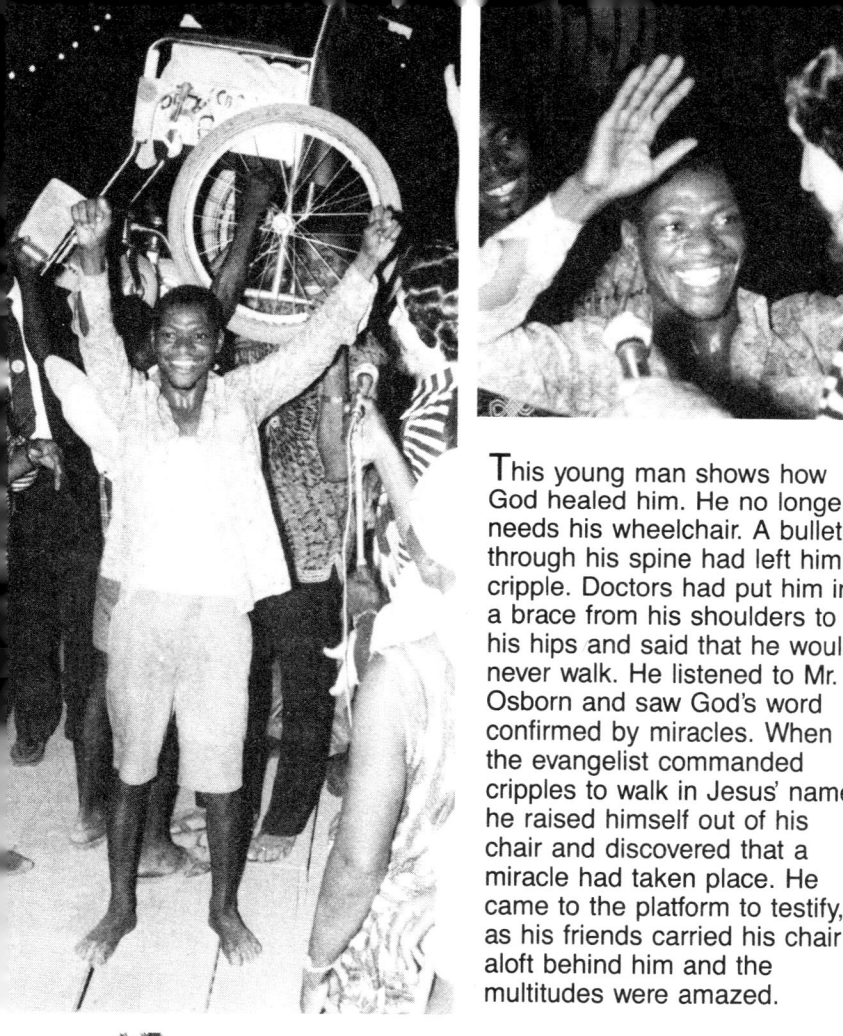

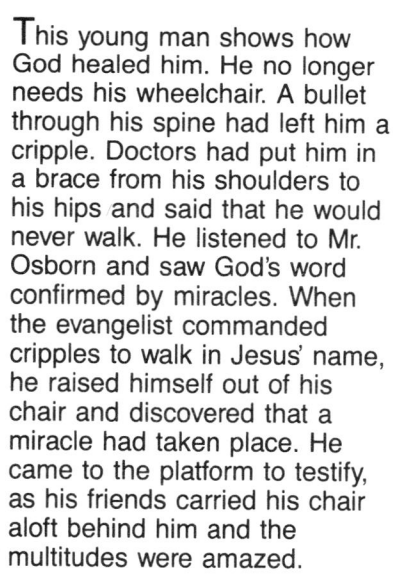

This young man shows how God healed him. He no longer needs his wheelchair. A bullet through his spine had left him a cripple. Doctors had put him in a brace from his shoulders to his hips and said that he would never walk. He listened to Mr. Osborn and saw God's word confirmed by miracles. When the evangelist commanded cripples to walk in Jesus' name, he raised himself out of his chair and discovered that a miracle had taken place. He came to the platform to testify, as his friends carried his chair aloft behind him and the multitudes were amazed.

for her husband. **When he rushed to her and saw what had happened, he fell on his face on the ground, weeping and crying out loud.**

One of the main ushers, and many local people saw it and verified it as she came to testify.

Then over at another area, Ismael, **who operates one of the Mobile Evangelism Units we have placed in Kenya,** had been watching a lad with terribly crippled feet. They turned up so that he walked on the sides of his ankles. All of a sudden, after the prayer, the boy's feet straightened out and he could stand upright on them. Both feet were flat, and he was healed! Ismael took him and **tried for over an hour to get the lad to the platform,** but could not even get near, so great was the press of the multitude. The boy will come today and testify.

Pastors have been coming to our room all day with new reports of miracles that are taking place. The Finnish missionary here, with two of our interpreters, came into our room, almost out of breath. They said that over on Kolingen Street, **the police are having to forcibly open a way through the crowd in the streets so the cars can pass.** A four-year-old child, who was born totally blind, received sight last night and the street is jammed by people who are amazed. The mother has the child there, showing everyone. What is overwhelming to the people is that many of them know the child and confirm the mother's words — that it **was born with a white film on its eyes, so thick that it seemed like a skin.** Now that film has disappeared, and the child **is clearly seeing everything.**

While I have been writing this, they brought the child to the hotel for us to see, and it is absolutely amazing what is happening to that boy's eyes. It is a **creative** miracle.

Then one of the missionaries pointed out of the hotel window to a woman who was sitting on the wall by the road. A group was with her. We just received word of her miracle last night. She had been crippled in both legs and could barely move about. Her knees were bent and turned inward so that they had to be forced around each other. She could scarcely walk at all. She had to shuffle herself by moving her legs below her knees, balancing her weight with a heavy stick. Last night the woman was healed. **God literally straightened her bones!** They brought her to the hotel to show us the miracle. It is absolutely awesome. Her legs are well. It was a marvel to see the woman showing the crowd that gathered around the hotel what God had done for her. Her legs are restored; they are normal.

The first miracle that reached the platform last night was a lad with crutches and steel leg braces. He and his mother came to the hotel today and gave us the most wonderful testimony. The boy was a healthy 11-year-old lad, who went to school. Then he was in a car accident. His right leg was broken above the knee. After the cast was removed, he fell and broke it again and broke the left leg, too. They put both legs in casts up to his waist. Then they discovered that he had a bone disease which made them brittle and weak.

For three months the lad lay flat in bed. In boarding school, he was finally able to walk again by using two crutches. Then he fell and broke his right leg again. One more time he spent three months in a cast. This time, **the feeling in his leg was gone, and it seemed to be dead.** A creeping paralysis had set in, and there seemed to be no life in his legs. Again, he was put on crutches; but both legs had to be fitted with steel braces. Even so, he could hardly swing his legs along. Without the supports, he could not bear weight or take a step. **But last night he took off his braces and handed his crutches to his mother** who gave them to me. Then the lad walked all over the platform, back and forth, while the multitude marveled. Oh, how happy he was! Today his joy is even greater as every hour he is gaining strength. Praise the Lord! **We are really seeing Bible days.** I wonder what else we will hear about before the day is over.

By the time we arrived at the crusade field around 4:30 p.m., it was filling up with people. By the time I began preaching, there must have been 40,000 to 60,000 people present. **Every road leading toward us was a literal river of human beings pouring**

Mary Kioko is left holding her son's discarded apparatus. They are evidence that Jesus, the Son of God, is alive today!

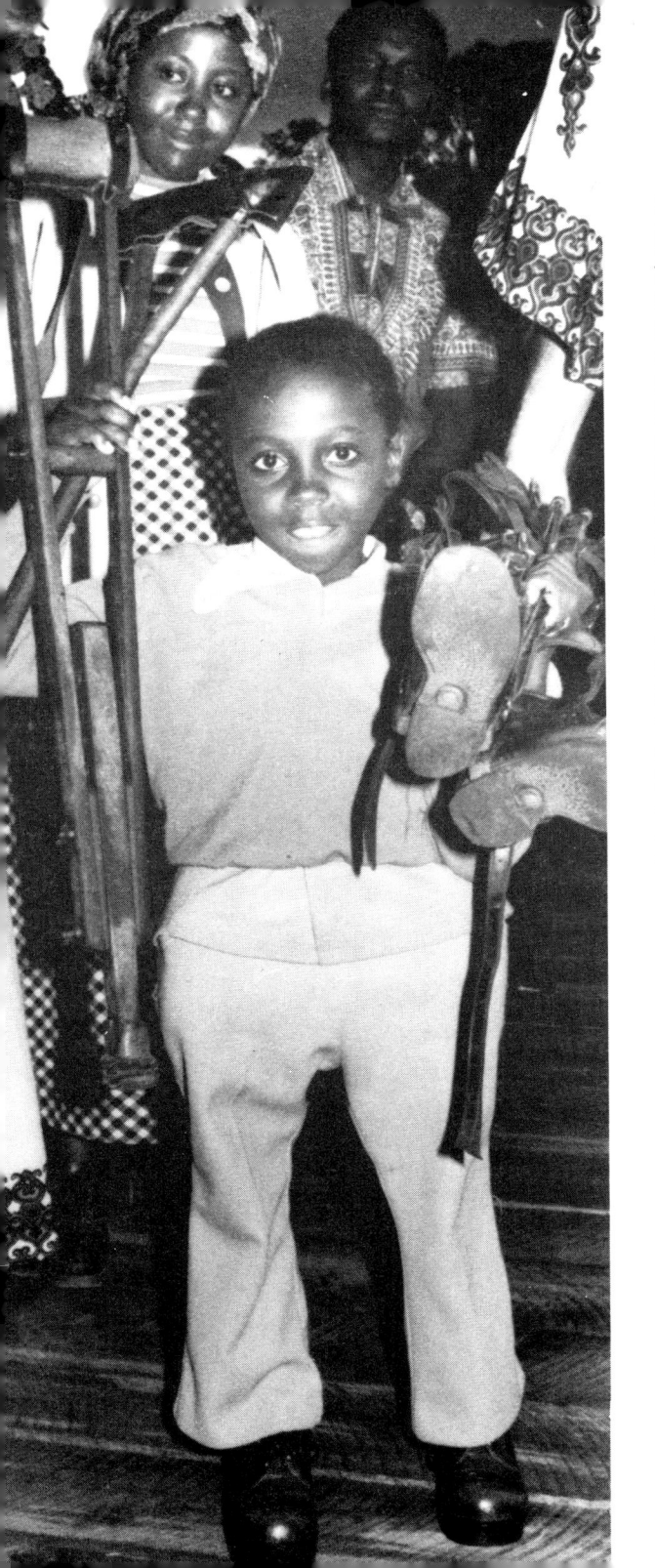

Mary Kioko's son, George, at the tender age of seven was lifted from the scene of a terrifying accident and taken to the nearest hospital. Due to multiple fractures, he lay encased in a cast, from his ribs to his heels, for three torturous months. After agonizing years of bone fractures, casts, crutches and finally braces as well, he could only walk with the aid of crutches, steel braces and special shoes. In this condition, George was brought to the Osborn Crusade in Nakuru. It was a special miracle the young lad and his mother came expecting, and they were not disappointed. In just moments after Mr. Osborn prayed, **George was made whole.** What was correctly tagged by professionals as "impossible," became **possible** through simple child-like faith.

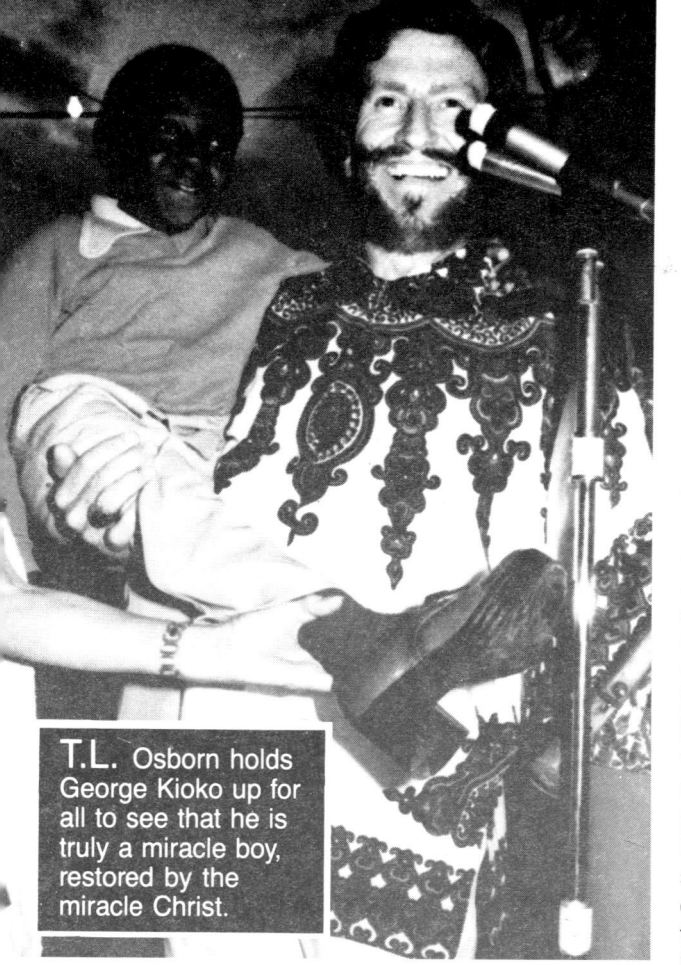

T.L. Osborn holds George Kioko up for all to see that he is truly a miracle boy, restored by the miracle Christ.

After disburdening himself of the heavy, awkward braces, George handed them to Mary, his mother. The evangelist was saying, "If you couldn't walk, rise and walk in the name of Jesus. Don't be afraid. **Only believe.**" At that very moment, George rose up and, as he began to walk, a beautiful smile spread over his handsome face. Others were weeping but George's tears had been replaced with radiant joy. His miracle created a predicament for him. He had no normal shoes and he certainly couldn't put the braces back on. His brother fitted him out with a pair of his own, but we felt that George should have new ones. Our team took him shopping the next day for a new pair of shoes, like other teenage boys were wearing. What a lot of fun they had watching this miracle boy try on shoes. That evening George walked back and forth across the platform.

into the grounds.

I preached on **"Blind Bartimaeus,"** then dealt thoroughly with the multitude about salvation and receiving Jesus Christ. What an experience to lead such a multitude in prayer to be saved! **I wish the whole world could experience what we saw today — and what we have seen for over three decades in nearly 70 nations.**

No words can describe the sacred and powerful atmosphere and presence of Jesus when He shows Himself **ALIVE** through miracles, as a great multitude cries out to Him for salvation.

Literally thousands and thousands were absolutely converted today. And there was such joy in the city! It was like Bible days when Philip preached in the city of Samaria. There is just no way to tell the wonder of it all.

After urging them to follow Jesus, we instructed them about healing and prayed for them to be healed. Then we led them in a thorough confession of **thanks,** of **faith,** and of **acceptance** of healing.

Then we asked them to put their FAITH INTO ACTION, to begin to do what they could not do before the prayer. **I must here testify that I do not** believe we have seen the equal before — at least not often.

It seemed that the healing power of God literally exploded across the field and, in every section of the multitude, groups at the far edges started running, following cripples who had been healed or who had taken off braces or tossed crutches aside and had begun to walk and run. The field was an explosion of joy! It was one of the most heavenly scenes we have ever witnessed.

Just about the time I was getting ready to ask them to come to the platform, a lad burst up the ramp, carrying two crutches in one hand and two braces with shoes on them in the other. That dear lad was so marvelously healed!

Just as I was trying to calm the audience to explain the case, a girl about 15 years old bounded up the ramp, past the excited photographers, carrying two large braces and walking almost perfectly normal. **There I was with two crutches and four big braces and shoes trying to get the audience quieted down enough to explain these miracles. Then I saw them handing braces and crutches over the heads of the people, passing them toward the platform in four places at once.**

About that time, the multitude realized what was happening and things went **wild!** They rushed a woman up the right side of the platform, carrying two crutches and one brace above her head. She had been healed, too, and was weeping for joy. Then someone yelled: **"Look here!"** A woman, whose eyes seemed wild with excitement, came yelling and crying, carrying two hip-to-foot braces with shoes on them, and we tried to have her testify. She kept looking about wildly and, finally, she said, **"It's not me; it's my daughter! She was healed! She took off these braces and began to run and I have lost her! Can you help me find her?"** And she began calling for her daughter. It was pandemonium everywhere as you could see people with crutches, canes, and braces, waving them in the air in no less than a dozen places at a time. **Groups could be seen breaking out of the press, running,** as someone was healed on the edge of the crowd.

The platform, by this time, was overrun with miracles — and yet it kept increasing. A pastor pressed through frantically, with two crutches above his head. He saw a man throw them down and turn around and start running as the people opened up a way before him. The pastor had not been able to get on the platform, and this had happened when he was standing out in the audience. We called for the man, but could not get things quieted enough to find him.

A youth bounded up the ramp, among the crowd of healed cripples. He had been born deaf and dumb, and the lad could repeat every word I pronounced. When the crowd realized it, it was amazing. I was trying to explain it all when a mother, carrying two crutches high above her head, came rushing up the ramp and across the platform, walking as well as I can.

Then a lady who was deaf and dumb and who had spastic paralysis came, looking almost **wild with excitement.** Some pastors knew her. Now she was completely healed. She could clearly repeat every word I pronounced; and by the time we finished checking her, her twisted contortive muscles were relaxed. Her eyes were filled with amazement as she discovered that she could move her arms and hands up and down, double and straighten them, with no more spasms.

It was an awesome wonder to behold! By this time, there was such hilarious joy and boundless happiness that **we simply could no longer control things.** All ramps — both sides and back — were jammed with miracles! When I asked how many more out in the field were healed, but could not come forward, probably 2,000 hands were raised and

Another miracle takes place. A girl crippled by polio has been healed out in the audience and has been passed over the heads of the pressed multitude, from one to another, until she is handed up to the platform where the astonished thousands can see her and hear what God has done. She stood, walked, then ran across the platform to prove her miracle. She would never need the heavy steel brace again. Jesus is alive!

waved as they praised the Lord to affirm that they were healed.

It would take a great book to begin to recount the wonders God did this night! Witnessing this day, I can only say: **To God be the glory!** I thank Him again for letting Daisy and me experience yet another such wondrous day, after over 30 years of it! Amen!

Two lads, crippled by polio, miraculously healed. They could each walk normally as they paraded across the platform to show the multitude what God had done.

MONTERREY, MEXICO
5th meeting

So much is happening so fast in this historic crusade that **one can only record a small percentage** of what is reported. News keeps coming in about more miracles. **Tens of thousands of people are talking about it.** A group from Veracruz came by plane. One of them had paralysis and was unable to walk. He is up now, feels strong, and walks erect. He walked up to me as I was preaching and wanted to testify.

A woman from Saltillo, with a broken leg and a fractured disc in her spine (an accident victim) was perfectly restored. One man who had been paralyzed for 27 years, hobbling on a cane, was completely healed. Another man, paralyzed since an accident 20 years ago, was healed. He said: **"I came for a miracle, and I got it!"**

Almost everyone that comes here to our room tells of someone else who has been healed. **The city is being stirred.** Only God knows what will happen this week. We are living a miracle! Why the government has allowed this is still a marvel to us, and we stand in awe before the fact that when God wants to give a witness to a city, or to a nation, the hearts of the leaders are in His hand.

Today the meeting was formidable. Such a multitude came. Such hunger for the Word! The poor people are so overwhelmed and are so appreciative, seeming to realize that **God is giving a special witness** and blessing to them. There are many on stretchers, dozens in wheelchairs; others are carried on beds.

Tonight I preached on the **"Healing of Bartimaeus."** I stressed the point that God still heals the blind today. I emphasized what an **opportunity it is when Jesus passes our way.** How **Bartimaeus himself prayed.** How he **prayed the right prayer — for mercy.** How **all forces unite to keep one from asking** for a miracle — to keep quiet and humble— but how he **prayed more** and how Jesus **heard his call.** How **he was healed** and how **he followed Jesus.**

I was never able to finish my sermon. **Four times during the message I was interrupted by miracles taking place in the crowd.** It was amazing how the power of the Lord was present to heal! Early in the message, clapping and rejoicing broke out as someone was healed. Far to the edge of the multitude, we heard another group rejoicing and crying out about a miracle. I got them quieted, then continued preaching.

After a few moments, I heard rejoicing far out to my right. It was like a rustle in the crowd. I saw it moving slowly toward the right. I kept preaching; but as it came within range of the powerful mercury vapor floodlights, everyone saw it. **Two steel leg braces were being held up in the air, and the crowd was opening as the group advanced.** I lost control of the multitude and had to stop preaching and wait.

Up the steps came a girl, walking marvelously and absolutely steady. This dear child's bones had a disease that caused them to crumble and break. It was impossible to bear her weight, as her knees would slip out of joint. Her ankles were brittle, and it caused excruciating pain. That child was healed. **She never looked up, only straight ahead, and marched triumphantly across the full length of the 60-foot-wide platform, then back, three times!** The people wept and rejoiced as the girl walked. It was truly a wonder to behold! There was nothing to do but rejoice with the child and her mother.

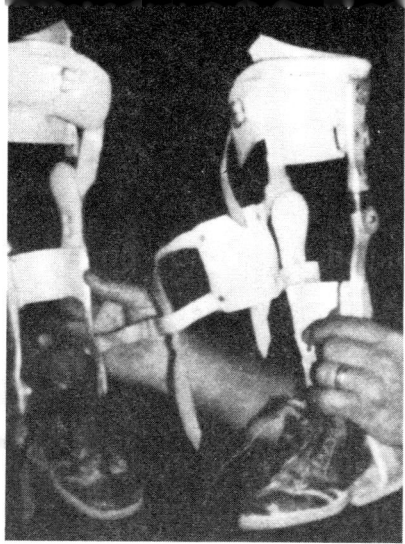

This eight-year-old girl could not walk without leg braces and special shoes. During the message, her mother removed the shoes and braces and the child could walk. She came to the platform and walked its full length without faltering. Mrs. Osborn holds the girl up for the audience to see while the mother explains the miracle. As soon as her feet touched the platform, she was gone again — from one end to the other — while the people glorified God. Nothing is too hard for the Lord.

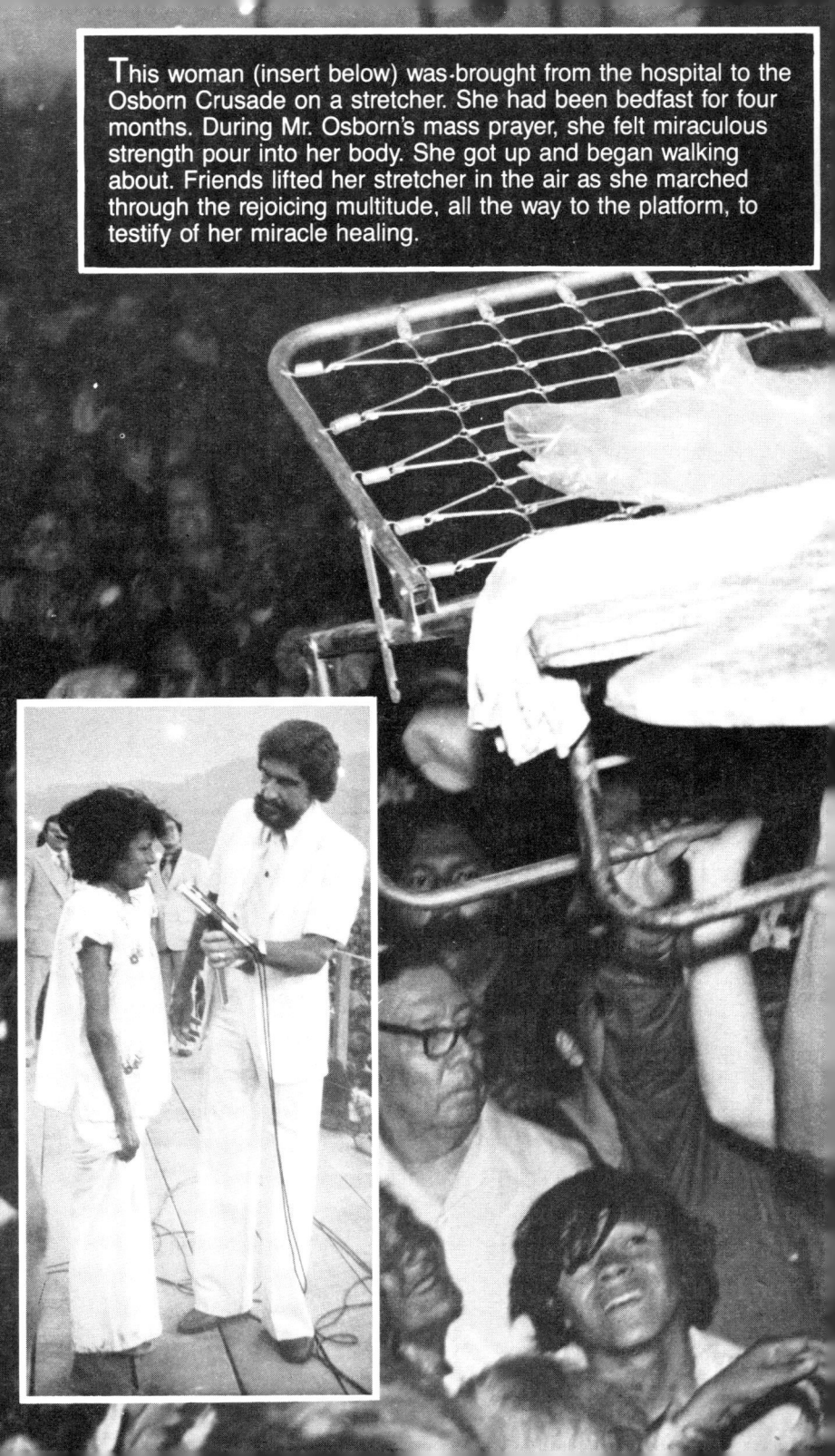

This woman (insert below) was brought from the hospital to the Osborn Crusade on a stretcher. She had been bedfast for four months. During Mr. Osborn's mass prayer, she felt miraculous strength pour into her body. She got up and began walking about. Friends lifted her stretcher in the air as she marched through the rejoicing multitude, all the way to the platform, to testify of her miracle healing.

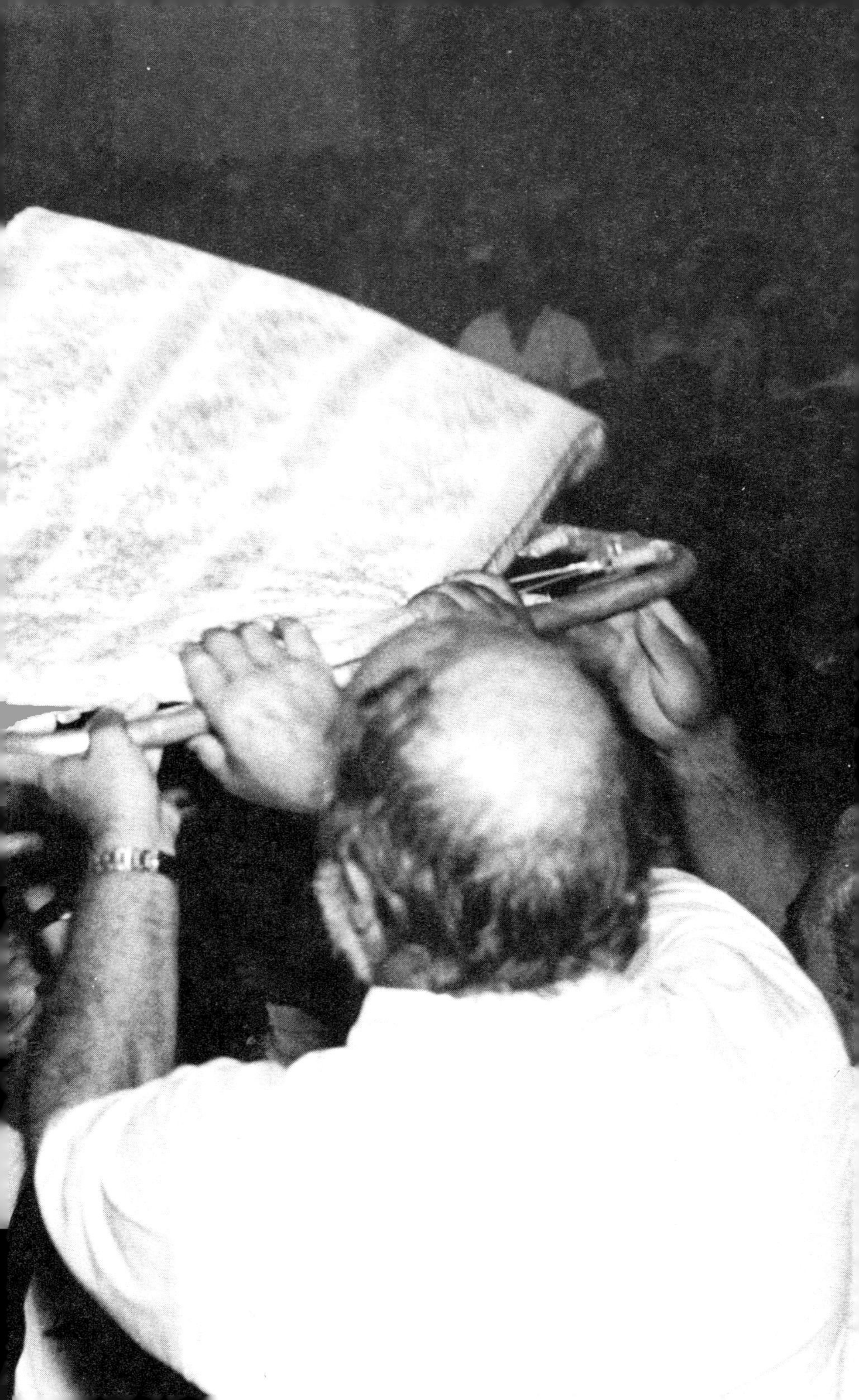

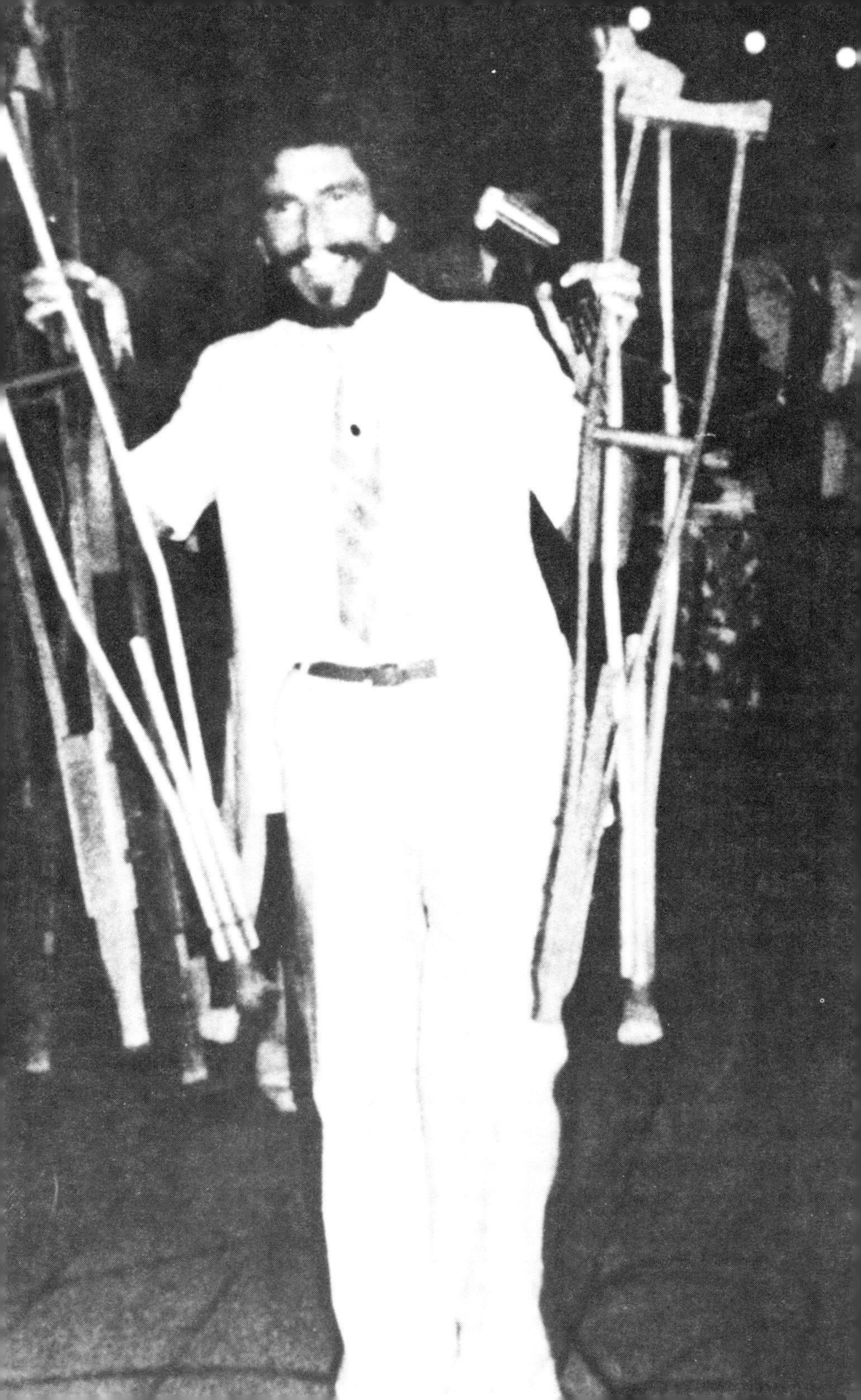

Mr. Osborn seldom preached a message during the Monterrey Crusade without being interrupted by someone in the audience who received a miracle and hoisted crutches or canes or braces as they came pressing through the throng, toward the platform, to give public testimony of what God had done for them.

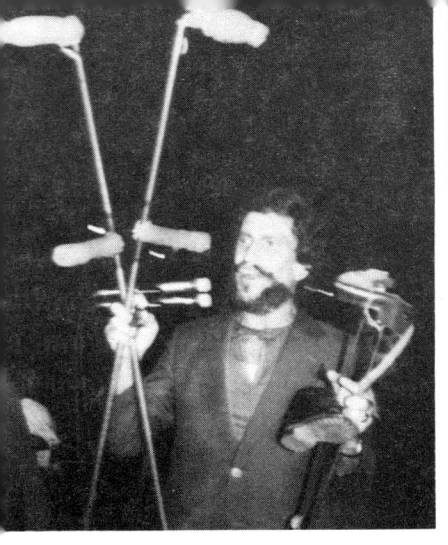

T.L. Osborn holds aloft the crutches and braces of a miraculously healed polio victim, as he affirms: "This Jesus of the Bible is unchanged. He never cripples, wounds or destroys. He lifts the fallen, forgives sinners, heals the crippled."

"I stood there amidst the press of people on the platform, with eleven crutches in my arms. An assistant held up two big braces. Two pastors were holding up an ambulance cot and two others a wheelchair — evidence of Christ's presence at work."

"Some nights, even before we could pray, people would get converted and healed and changed. They would interrupt the sermon to tell what had happened to them. One night, this happened three times — so mighty was the Lord's presence to save and to heal.

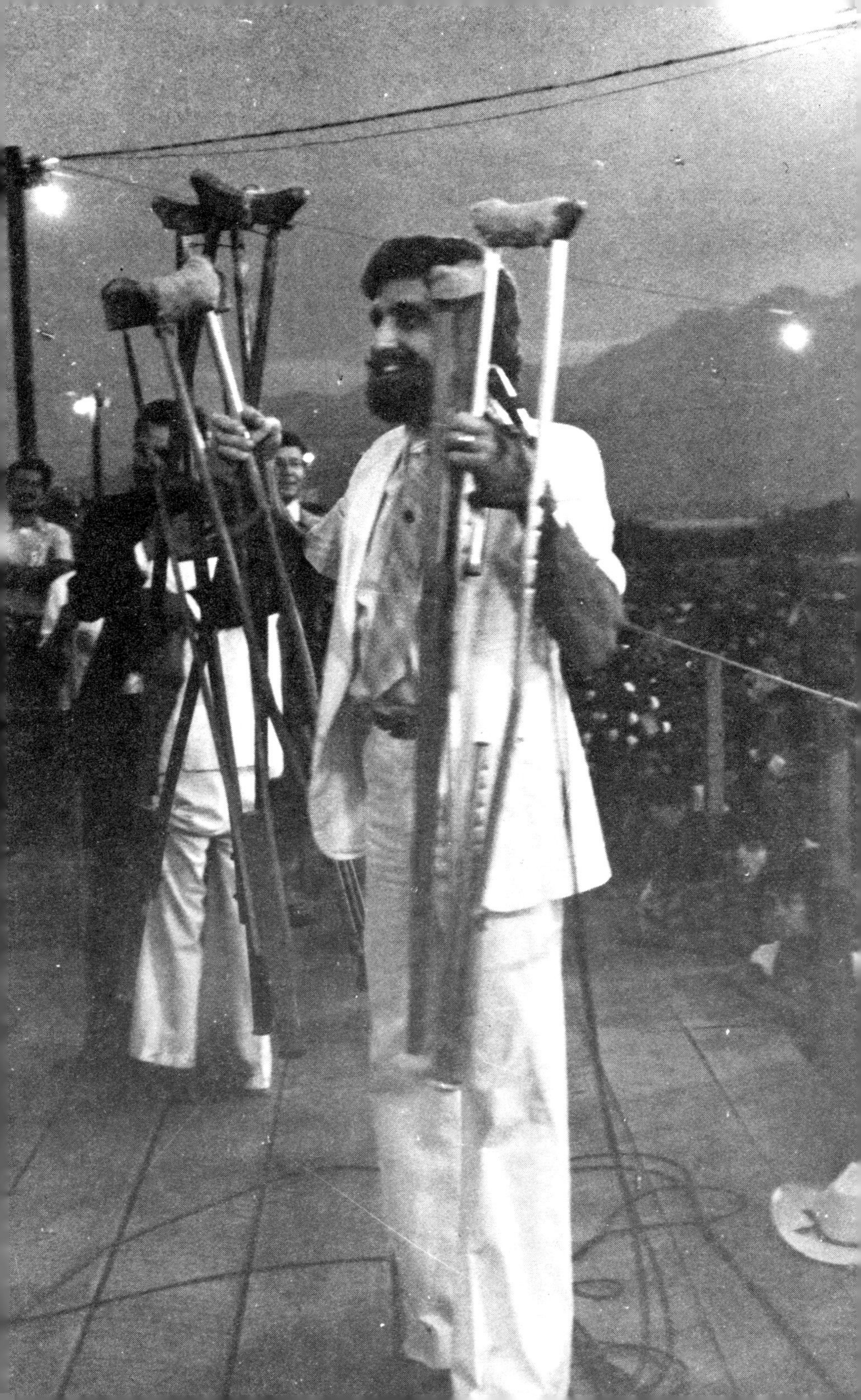

For 12 years this woman suffered from rheumatoid arthritis. Crippled and unable to walk or use her arms, she was carried to the Osborn Crusade on her bed. She was instantly healed and got up and left her cot in the crowd, almost running to the platform, marching back and forth, jumping, waving her arms and weeping, to give public testimony of God's mercy to her.

OSBORN CRUSADE

Deformed feet with toes turned inward caused this lad to stumble as he walked. During the prayer, Jesus instantly and completely healed his feet. The bones were made straight and his feet became perfect. He could walk and even run **perfectly.** The mother and her son were overcome with joy and burst out in tears as they embraced each other and thanked God together for such a miracle.

MONTERREY, MEXICO

Finally we restored order and resumed preaching and had not preached more than 15 minutes when another **bigger** commotion broke out, and I could see what was happening. Someone far out in front of me had been healed and was moving toward the platform. As they came within range of the powerful floodlights, there was some kind of steel brace being waved over their heads, and someone was walking rather rapidly. I simply had to stop preaching as they triumphantly marched up the steps.

There was a boy about ten years old. **His father was carrying a big steel brace that had been strapped from the lad's waist, up around his chest, to support his neck.** The boy had a disease of the bones, which had twisted his body and neck severely, and only the brace could hold him straight. Now he was walking upright with his hands in the air, and his father was in tears. The lad was made whole!

Then others started rushing up to testify, and from both sides, miracles were happening. I saw that I would never be able to preach if I stopped. The power of the Lord was present to heal. We finally got the multitude calmed, resumed preaching, and had made several major points when it happened again — on both sides of the platform at once! I knew that this time we would never control them, so I refused to let them come up the steps, because **I felt it was important for the people to pray the prayer of repentance and to receive salvation.** I asked them to wait until I had finished; then I made a call to accept Christ and a **multitude** repented and cried and prayed for salvation.

As we were thanking God for His new life, they started getting healed again. Then I said: **"I have preached enough! There is no use trying to preach when God is healing so many people. Obviously He thinks I have preached enough. His miracles are more important than my preaching. So I am not going to try any more tonight. Come on up and tell of God's wonders, for His glory."**

And they started, from both sides, until the platform was full. What a sight and what a night to be remembered in this great city!

The first lady up the steps just walked past me and ignored me. She paraded to the end of the platform, then came back. I walked along by her side, and all she would say as she was weeping was: **"I'm healed. I can walk. I can walk. Look at me. I'm well!"** Back and forth she paraded steadily and perfectly, while the multitude clapped.

Then a lad was healed. The mother was weeping. She said: **"My son had meningitis when he was only three years old. He is ten now and has not walked since that attack. He has only lain in bed or sat in his chair. Now he is healed!"** None of the family wanted him to be brought, and they tried to discourage the mother from her "crazy" idea. The mother finally sneaked her son out of the house and carried him here, and the boy is **perfectly healed.** He walked as normal as any lad. It was wonderful!

A woman paraded about who had not walked normally for 20 years due to an operation. She was well. A 15-year-old youth, who had never walked without crutches, carried them above his head as he walked back and forth. A farmer, who had been a paralytic, gave a moving testimony. He had numerous gods in his house which he had trusted. He did not know about the **reality of Jesus.** He had been in an accident 13 years before and spent nine long years in the hospital because of a broken spine. For the last four years he has hobbled on crutches. Tonight he was healed and promised that his whole life was for Jesus now.

Then a lady came to testify who had not walked in 25 years. She had received a leaflet announcing the crusade, but she did not want to know anything about such a meeting. She had always gone to her own church and had prayed: "Why can't I walk?" Her family was faithful to carry her about. Finally, she consented to be brought to the crusade tonight, and the family was so happy because she was healed. She was overwhelmed!

A young lady, who had fallen twice and ruptured a disc in her spine, was unable to stand or walk. But during the prayer, she got up and walked and was healed. She was so happy as she cried: **"Look at me! Jesus has healed me!"**

A woman was healed of arthritis in all of her joints. Oh, she was thrilled! She said: **"The doctors are going to be amazed to see how I am healed."** One dear man's heart was healed. He was scheduled for surgery because he could not walk more than a few meters without gasping for breath. Now he had walked 30 blocks to the meeting and was well and breathing normally. He had no tired feeling. It was clearly a miracle!

A dear 78-year-old man was healed. He had been in a wheelchair for a long time and during the last eight months was bedfast. He trusted in God and told his family: **"Someday I will get healed!"** The campaign was his hope, and **he would not miss it.** Now he has been healed. He paraded back and forth and was clearly made whole. His daughter-in-law had brought him, and she was so happy.

A woman, who for seven years had eaten almost nothing because of a cancerous tumor, was brought to the meeting by her daughter and was healed. The mother of Daisy's interpreter has had a disease of deterioration of the bones. Tonight she was healed. An old woman shouted because she was healed of heart trouble. Oh, she was happy!

A lad about 13 years old was healed of crippled feet. They were turned in so badly that he could not walk without tripping, and he could not run at all. It was a glorious miracle! Both feet were perfect and absolutely straight. He ran back and forth. **I studied his feet, and they are perfect.** He fell into his mother's arms, and they both wept. It was really wonderful!

Dozens of others were made whole. It was a tremendous night. To God be the glory!

NJORO-MENENGAI, KENYA
4th meeting

Today was one of those historic never-to-be-forgotten crusade days. An enormous multitude of people was assembled to hear the message of God. **Daisy and I knelt as we prayed with the multitude for God to reach into the homes and lives of each of our Partners and bless them with the same miracle power that He is pouring out on this crusade here.**

Then I preached from Mark 2 on the **"Healing of the Lame Man"** who was carried to Jesus at Capernaum. I was able to get the message across by the anointing of the Holy Spirit and a great spiritual work was done among the people. I finished with a call for people to accept Jesus and **there was a great move of God among the multitude.** Thousands believed on Jesus. I led them in a confession of faith until it was clear that they had truly understood and received Christ.

They received Him in such a real way that **suddenly** they began being healed everywhere. I never did get to pray for the sick. **They knew Jesus had**

entered their lives, and His power began healing them everywhere. It was among the very great miracle nights of our whole ministry.

Among the first to mount the platform was a mother with her three children. **They had all been born deaf.** Each was healed and able to hear perfectly. What a miracle! What mercy from God!

Then a woman bounded across the platform, stomping her feet and waving her arms, carrying crutches above her head. She had been in a terrible accident, and many of her bones had been broken. **She had been dragged to the side of the road and left for dead** because they could only help those for whom there was some hope of saving their lives. Hours later, someone heard her groan and realized life was still in her. So they put her on an old truck and hauled her to the hospital. But she was so near death that her bones were never set.

Her recovery was very slow; and by the time she was out of danger, they would have had to **re-break the shoulder, rib, and pelvic bones to align her twisted body.** Since she was a poor village woman, she was left to heal as she was. She had to walk with crutches. Her left arm was twisted and could not be raised. Her shoulders were deformed, as were her legs and pelvic area. But tonight Jesus came to her and she was miraculously healed! **She bounded back and forth across the platform waving both crutches above her head,** raising her left arm, weeping aloud, praising God for His mercy to her. Really, it was marvelous!

Following her was a man about 22 years of age who had been crippled by polio when he was a child. He was unable to walk without crutches, but was healed wonderfully tonight. Walking well, he carried crutches above his head as he glorified God before the multitude.

Then a lad came to testify. He had an injection which had damaged the nerves in one leg. It never grew and was **three inches shorter than the other.** It had been paralyzed. Tonight he was healed, and the people were amazed.

A young fellow with a full leg brace and built-up shoe for the other foot came walking across the platform, carrying his shoes and the brace above his head. He was healed miraculously.

A lovely girl who had been born deaf and dumb was healed. She had come each night, and today at home, she began to talk. Her parents were

Convinced that God's promises in the Bible are true, this father unstrapped the steel brace from his daughter's leg (paralyzed by polio), hoisted her above the people and carried her to the platform where she walked back and forth, proving how Jesus had made her whole in the Osborn Crusade of Njoro-Menengai.

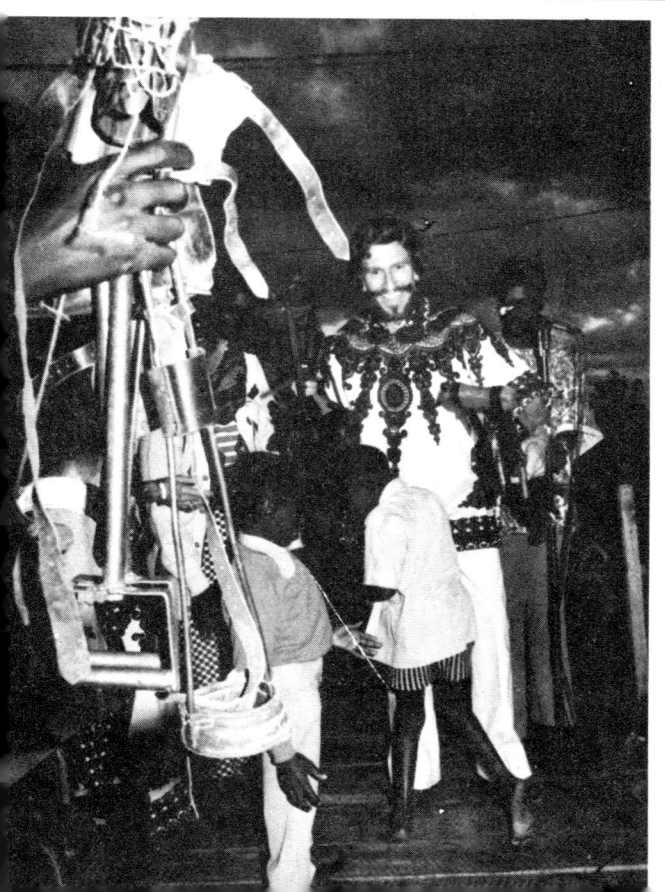

TOP: Another polio victim has been healed in the crowd. By faith the boy's steel brace was unbuckled and removed, and HE WALKED! Overwhelmed with joy, the father hoists the brace high and calls out: **"My son can walk!"** With his striped jacket removed (left), the lad walks back and forth — a perfect wonder of God!

Caught up by friends who saw him take his first miracle steps, the lad is hoisted above the shoulders of excited onlookers, and rushed through the crowd to the platform.

INSET: As the multitude looked with amazement, the young man, with steel brace and shoes lifted high, marched across the platform to show the miracle God had done for him.

astonished. Then tonight the full miracle took place, and **she could hear a fine whisper in either ear and repeat every word and phrase in a normal voice.** It was one of those awesome deaf-mute miracles.

A fine lad, deaf in one ear since he was born, was perfectly healed; and he gave the most wonderful testimony. He actually preached like a man. I was so touched. No doubt God will use him as a preacher as he grows up.

A woman who had never walked in her life was brought to the crusade **in a bed** by her friend. She was visited by the Lord tonight, and she got up and began to walk. It astonished her friends. The Finnish missionary knows her case. She walked back and forth across the platform to the amazement of all who were present.

Several people suffering with epilepsy were made whole. They really accepted Jesus, and demons left them.

We never prayed at all for the sick tonight. **The people just accepted Jesus Christ in their lives and understood that, when He comes in, sickness must leave.** They believed; they put their faith in

ACTION; and according to their faith, it was done to them.

One of the greatest miracles tonight was a young man who had polio when he was a baby and was unable to walk. He tried crutches and canes, but fell and broke his weak legs so often that he finally gave up hope. **To move about, he dragged himself backwards on his buttocks, with his hands.** He had lived like that for 23 years.

Three weeks ago **when our team began having film services in the villages, this fellow saw one of our films in his town, and he purposed to come to the crusade.**

He listened and received Jesus Christ in his heart and was wonderfully healed. He got up and walked alone, back and forth across the platform. **He showed us how he had to scoot along on the ground, then he jumped up and paraded his new miracle.** He literally preached a sermon as he testified for no less than 15 minutes. I was astounded at his words! He is handsome in the face, and has a sharp and sound mind. **He spoke for all of Africa, thanking us for coming and for giving his people a chance to hear the gospel of Christ and to see His power.**

He talked about others, more than of himself. He pled for his people. He felt that we had blessed his country by coming. He longed for all of Kenya to be present and to hear and to see what he had witnessed. **He vowed that he would never forget Jesus Christ, and he would always serve Him.**

Then God spoke to me and showed me His plan for the fellow's life, while he still poured out his heart to the multitude. I heard Africa speak through this man in the Njoro-Menengai crusade.

When he finished testifying, I told him that **Jesus Christ had chosen him and had set him apart to be a preacher to his nation,** that God would use him and that people would support him and be blessed and saved and healed wherever he would go. Everyone was amazed. I urged the pastors to help him learn and to assist him.

His miraculous healing was a great testimony to Kenya and to all present. God's presence was mighty!

Then a lad came, carrying a steel leg brace in one hand and a shoe in the other — another polio victim who was healed. He walked well, and again the multitude worshipped God.

The night he was saved and healed, Peter Amakanji stands with T.L. Osborn on the crusade platform in the provincial capital.

"Praise the Lord!" Peter is ecstatic with joy at the miracle God has performed.

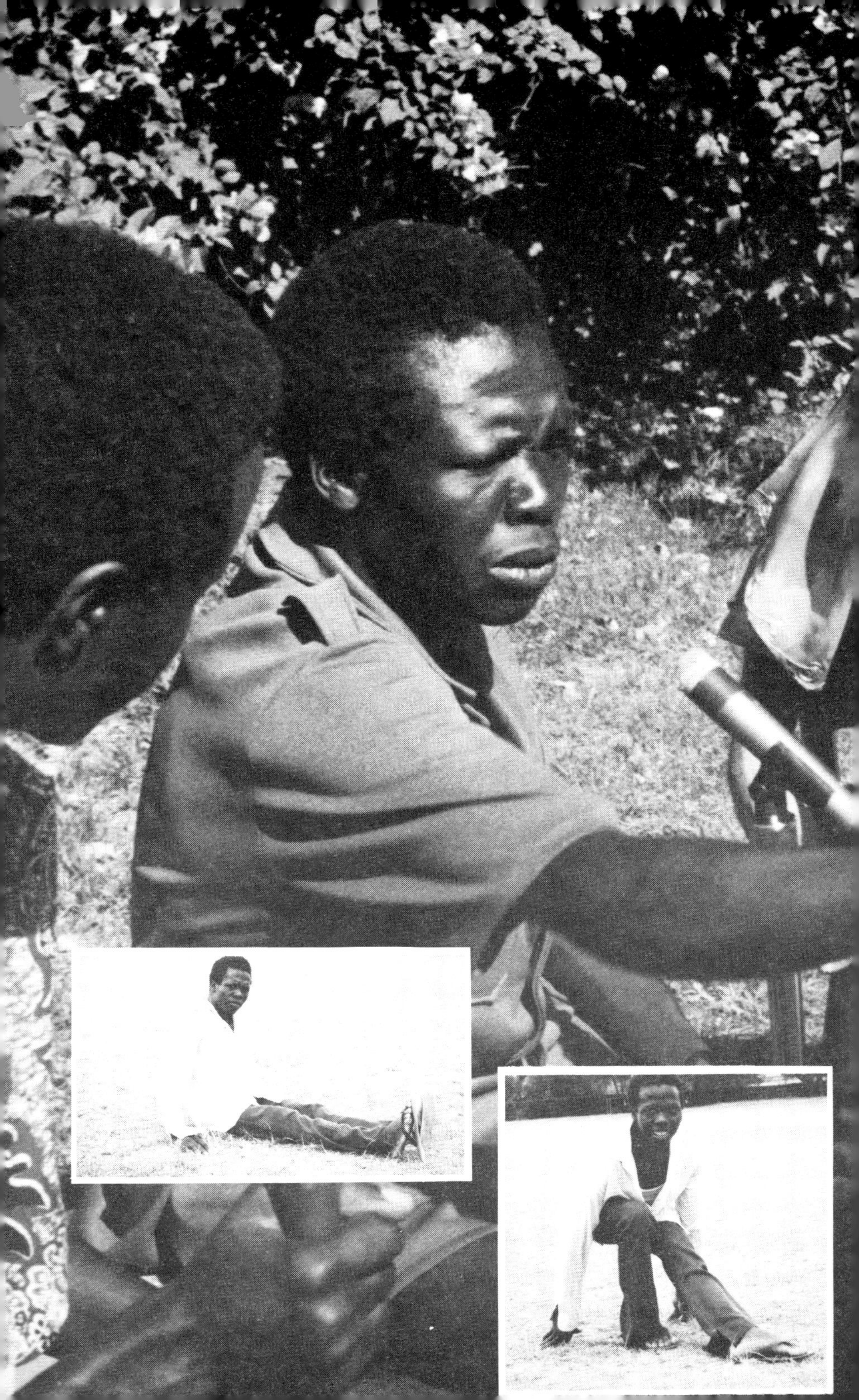

T.L. and Daisy Osborn listen as Peter Amakanji relates the pathetic story of his 23 years as a beggar, then how he came to their Nakuru Crusade and was miraculously healed.

The Osborns rejoice with Kariuki (left), the former maniac and Peter Amakanji (center), the former paralytic who had dragged on the ground for 23 years. They are two notable wonders of God in East Africa.

INSET: "Look what God did for me!" Peter tells a crippled woman to come to the Osborn Crusade where she too can be healed.

The woman came and was miraculously healed. Peter was there to rejoice with her and to confirm that he had witnessed to her.

TOP: Peter is baptized in his home village at Bendura by evangelist Chege who has trained him in evangelism. Peter uses Osborn films to attract crowds, then witnesses of his own miracle, and has given his life to preaching the gospel in Kenya (below).

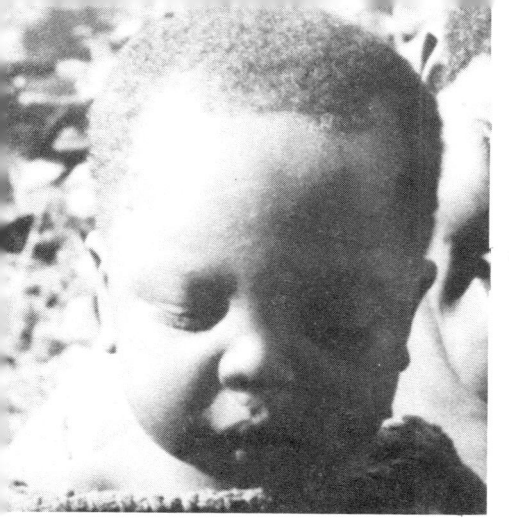

SIMEON WAS BORN WITHOUT EYES

Told by Daisy Osborn

When little Simeon was born he had no eyeballs. The family and village was saddened, until, nine months later, they heard of the Osborn Crusade in Nakuru. The child was brought by its mother. T.L. preached: *The things that are impossible with men are possible with God.* During the mass prayer, the mother believed. Within a few moments, tiny eyes formed.

The child could clearly see. By the next day, its eyes were normal — a creative miracle. One year later, our daughter, LaDonna, went with me to visit the child at its village. It is a living miracle. Hundreds of people have trekked to that village to see the boy with the miracle eyes and have been saved.

Domtilla Juma was a helpless victim of paralysis. Unable to stand or work, she crawled away from her home to die in the jungle. She was found by friends. At the hospital, several operations on her spine left her more helpless than before.

Carried to the Osborn Crusade, she heard the gospel, believed on Christ and was totally healed. She goes all over her region, showing the people what God's miracle power did for her.

T.L. OSBORN CRUSADE

When Domtilla returned to her village to show her husband how she was healed, he proudly gave her his bicycle and said: "I never want to see you carrying heavy buckets of water on your head again. I give you my bicycle. You shall ride to the river for water because God gave you back to me with a new body!"

A woman who had been a prostitute for years came weeping. She was rubbing her abdomen where a large cancerous tumor had grown. Now it was all gone, and **she was so overwhelmed that God would show mercy to a prostitute.** She did not dream that **she** could be healed. She wept aloud and finally dropped to her knees and sobbed and wept, bending her face to the floor. **Then with hands raised high and her face bathed in tears, she thanked God for His mercy.** All of the multitude was overwhelmed!

I could recount many more cases tonight. They seemed endless. It was **powerful.** God was glorified, and **the city was truly stirred to believe on Jesus Christ** and to serve Him. What an experience! What an honor to be used of God, to be part of such a visitation to a nation!

EMBU, KENYA
10th meeting

Today was a great day indeed. A great multitude crowded on the Moi Stadium grounds. I preached on **"Faith, Hope and Love."** It was perhaps the greatest crowd ever to assemble for a gospel meeting in this whole area. **After the preaching, people began being healed everywhere.** So many hundreds received Christ. I commanded cripples to raise their crutches and canes or to toss them aside and to start walking. They did what I said and, soon, we could see groups or crowds moving in four or five areas at a time as cripples were healed and crowds followed them.

It was a long time before I could get the attention of the people and get those healed to come up to the platform to testify.

I made the mistake of telling them to go out on the field and to prove what God had done for them, and that is what they did instead of coming up to testify. But finally different ones began to come and tell us what God had done for them. **They took off**

braces and threw away canes and crutches. Here and there, they handed them up to us on the platform.

Different outbursts of praise and joy would break out as others began to be healed. While crutches were being raised here and there, all of a sudden a blind man mounted the steps. His eyes were open, and he could see everything. Then an old man with crippled feet was healed. **He jumped and stomped across the platform with such joy!** He was well!

Then a mother came with her daughter who had been out of school for two years because she lost her eyesight and finally had to be led. She had been taken to the hospital at Nairobi, but nothing could help her. For eight years, she had suffered. Now her eyes were clear! She and her mother were weeping for joy.

One old woman was healed of terrible suffering in the bladder. It was touching to see how she rejoiced. There was a woman who had been bedfast for six years, unable to walk and to help herself. **Carried there in a bed and laid where she could hear us, she had been healed.** They came up the steps with her, and we all marveled at her testimony. Her name was Fosana. She was so thrilled because she could stand, and even talk. She had not been able to talk for a long time. Evidently, she had suffered a stroke of some kind. Now she walked back and forth, and everyone praised God as she told her story of deliverance.

A woman with a deaf ear was healed. She could hear a faint whisper in the ear that had been stone deaf for many years. A man who had suffered asthma for years was healed. A man who had been in an accident, and had been in pain ever since, was healed. All pain left him and he was absolutely restored! An old man came who had suffered in his back and could not bend over, as he said, **"even to eat; but now I can play like a child!"** He **stooped, squatted, doubled, bent, jumped,** and **ran** to show how completely his back was healed.

A woman with abdominal pains for seven years was healed and was well. She said: **"I have been like the woman in the Bible with the issue of blood, but now I am well. I touched Jesus today!"** She said a heat had gone through her body and all was well. Then they brought a woman who had been totally deaf. She could hear every word I whispered in either ear. She was really thrilled.

An old lady came and threw a walking stick down.

A Kikuyu father proudly witnesses to the multitude of how Jesus healed his son. The child suffered a high fever during infancy (presumably polio) and, as a result, had never been able to walk. The left leg was paralyzed. He always scooted about on the ground. BELOW: He is marching across the crusade platform, perfectly healed by God's power.

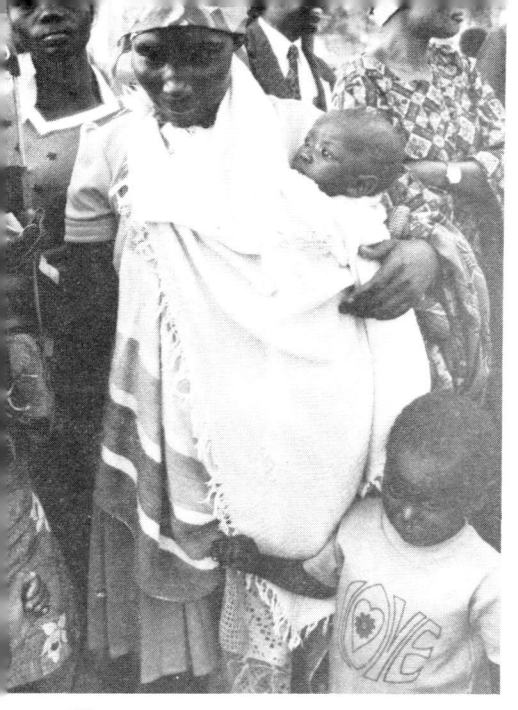

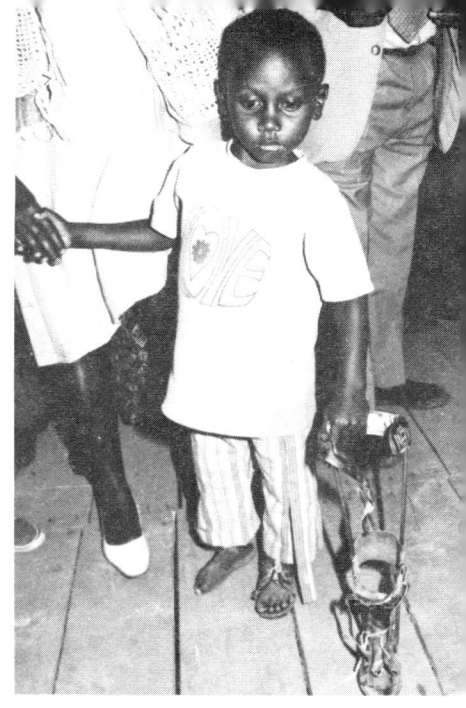

This mother's faith was rewarded by a miracle of Christ when she put her simple faith into **action.** Her little son's right leg was affected by polio, but after Jesus passed their way, they removed the steel brace and the lad was completely healed.

Her baby was raised from the dead at one of the first crusade meetings. The child had a very high fever for some days, then expired. Neighbors rushed in to tell of the crusade and the mother grabbed the child's limp body and ran to the meeting where, during prayer, it was restored to life by a miracle.

OSBORN CRUSADE

OSBORN CRUSADE

OSBORN CRUSADE

KIKUYU CAPITAL, E. AFRICA

ENUGU, NIGERIA

EMBU, KENYA

ABOVE: Two more living witnesses of Christ's miracle healing power in the Osborn Crusade at Embu. Discarded braces and crutches are evidence that Christ is unchanged.

ABOVE: Totally deaf for seven years. Now he is healed.

LEFT: Since his childhood when he had polio, he could never walk without crutches. He was instantly healed in the Embu Crusade.

She said she had suffered so much and could not walk without a cane, but now she is well and **she never wants to use that cane again.** She paraded back and forth and was so happy!

An old woman came whose hips and chest were so bad that she had barely been able to walk. Also, she was almost blind. For three weeks she had been lying at home. Now she could walk and jump and run and see clearly! Then an old mother told how that, though she lived very near, she had not been able to come because of lame legs and feet; so her friends helped her and **carried her to the grounds.** She was healed and walked like a girl and was so happy.

An epileptic lady said she knew when the epileptic spirit left her as I prayed. She knew she was healed.

A man who had noises in his head and was nearly deaf was made whole. Now all the noises are gone and his hearing is clear.

Daisy came and told about another cripple who had been healed. He was well known in the town. When he was healed, he took off his braces and threw down his crutches. But, instead of coming to the platform, he and a large group paraded out of the grounds and up the road by the market place to show the city what God had done. **A great commotion is sweeping through the town!** They sent an usher to catch him and bring him back to testify, but he said: **"No, Mr. Osborn said to go tell the people, so I am doing that."** The whole town is in an uproar and the man is well — **running, walking, jumping.** What a testimony! **How like Bible days!**

A woman who could hardly breathe and had great pain in her abdomen was healed. She had been to witchdoctors and had suffered so much. She had sold some chickens to buy a ticket to come to the hospital, but they could not help her. Then she heard of the crusade. She came and was completely made whole. She pointed to her child and said: **"Look, even my child is happy because she knows now that I am well!"**

There was no end to the wonders God has done in their lives. **It is overwhelming to hear and to see such marvels of God.** One old woman with terrible shaking palsy was perfectly healed, and her hands are as steady as a child's. What a crusade! What wonders! May God be glorified!

U.S.A.
Ministry to America

After over three decades of being absent, most of the time, from the homefront, we believe God led us to do two things: 1) Share with America, in her churches, in Christian conventions, campmeetings, conferences and seminars, some of what we have experienced already; and 2) Put into **seed** form what we have learned and what we have witnessed, so that younger generations may run with these seeds, plant with them and reap greater soul-harvests worldwide.

We saw a new miracle of love at work across America. We observed a profusion of apostolic truth being revealed and taught to millions via national Christian television networks, satellite evangelism, multiplied millions of books, audio and video cassettes, and from the pulpits of enormous faith churches flourishing across the nation.

Year after year, many of America's principle pastors and convention leaders had urged us to share more of our faith teaching and our experiences with America.

We decided to do that (between crusades and seminars abroad), because the effective evangelization of the world depends upon the partnership and faith of a strong soulwinning church at home.

As we increased our ministry across the homeland, the Holy Spirit birthed in us a great passion to encourage preachers, teachers and gospel ministers to proclaim the "G-O-O-D" news, and never to use their positions to condemn, judge, criticize or to demean human persons.

There had been a yearning in our spirits to allow Jesus Christ to manifest His love, compassion, and healing life in and through us, not only to the people but to the ministers.

Jesus did not come to **condemn** the world but to **save** the world.

God showed Daisy and me that the "faith" message in America was strong, but that the **infinite value of each human person must be discovered and emphasized,** if the people were to recognize their **self-identity** and grow in **self-value** to God, enough to put this new faith into practice.

In one convention after another, the Holy Spirit has

urged us to emphasize the fact of **God's esteem for the individual,** and of **how much He paid for each human being** in order to justify that person and to make them absolutely righteous, so that He could have them near to Him as **intimate friends and partners in His love plan for humanity.**

We have crisscrossed our homeland, with a passion to tell people that **God is not mad at them;** that He **loves** them, **needs** them, has **paid for** them, **yearns for** them, **reaches out** to them and **offers them His best.**

We have urged ministers and lay people to pledge never to **condemn** again what God has paid so much to redeem; never to **negate or reduce or impoverish** again what God treasures so dearly; never to **accuse or judge** again what God paid so much to forgive and justify; never to **harm, deteriorate or destroy** again what God paid so much to heal, restore and to save; never to **depreciate, discredit or disparage** again what God paid so much to dignify and to make royal; never to **criticize or revile** again what God esteems to be of such infinite value.

God has shown to Daisy and me that the powerful faith message in America has helped millions to become true believers, but that He wants to give a new revelation of His love and esteem for individual human persons, because His dream has never dimmed **to have YOU near Him as His partner and friend** — regardless of your sex, color or background.

We have been profoundly led of God to encourage people to understand that **each individual believer is a representative of Jesus,** and to allow His **non-judgmental love** to flow; to judge and to condemn **no one,** but to simply be gospel SEED-PLANTERS.

We have addressed some of the largest Christian conventions in America and have been able to lift thousands in a new **self-esteem** and **self-value** as Jesus-examples on this earth, and as authorized and commissioned ambassadors of the living and loving Christ.

As this passion to lift people has poured out through us by the anointing of the Holy Spirit, we have been led to write new books and to produce new cassettes emphasizing God's value of each human person — regardless of sex, race or other label.

Some of our new albums: *Faith to Change Your World, Be Alive, Super Living, Say "Yes" to God's Success, Women on Beam — Winning With*

Esteem, Two Women Who Changed the World, When Women Become Winners, and *The First Lady of Evangelism.*

Some of our new books: *Go For It, You Are God's Best, The Big Love Plan, The Power of Positive Desire, Seeds to Succeed, Opt for Opportunity, Woman — Be Free, Five Revelations for Your Own Miracle,* etc.

God has put a new song in the land and new music in the church. A new miracle of love has been transforming lives. New faith and love has healed millions. Thank God, Daisy and I have been able to be part of this new revelation.

Daisy Osborn, called of God to help women discover their position in Christ, reaches out to America in conventions, conferences and special seminars.

T.L. TEACHES AT THE COPELAND BELIEVER'S

> T.L. Osborn believes Joel's prophecy (2:28-29) is being fulfilled as women rise from traditional silence, and discover themselves in the light of total redemption.

CONVENTION — ATLANTA, GEORGIA

Photo credit: James Overrein

T.L. Osborn joins with Kenneth Copeland to pray for millions of believers worldwide. (Left: Pastor John Osteen of Houston's Lakewood Church; Pat Boone, and Charles Capps.)

BELOW: T.L. and Daisy (opposite page) minister at Lakewood Church, Houston.

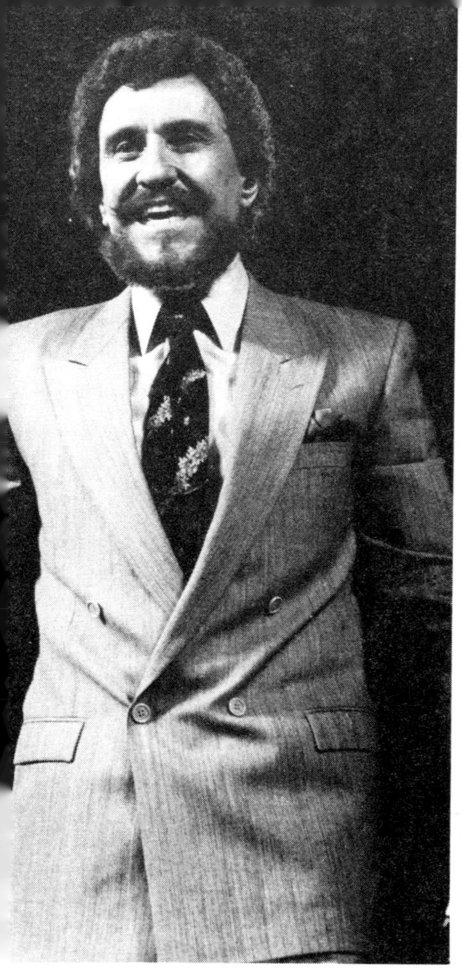
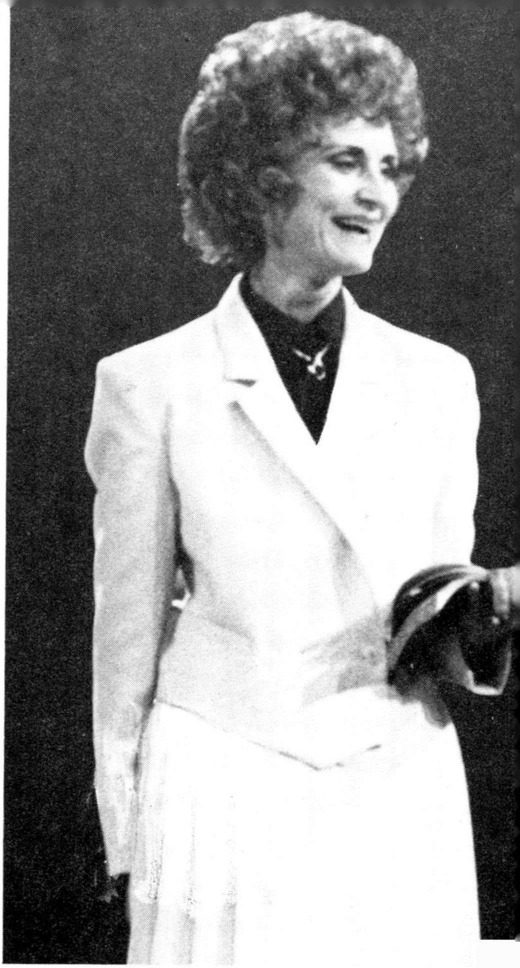
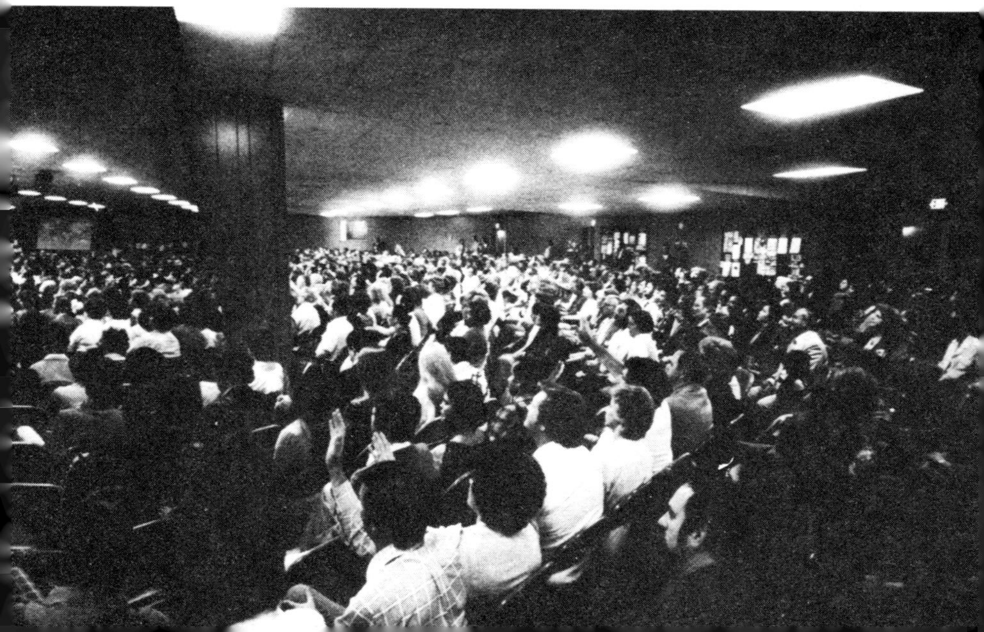

T.L. Osborn is awarded Honorary Doctorate at Oral Roberts University.

Daisy Osborn is awarded Honorary Doctorates at Zoe College in Florida ...

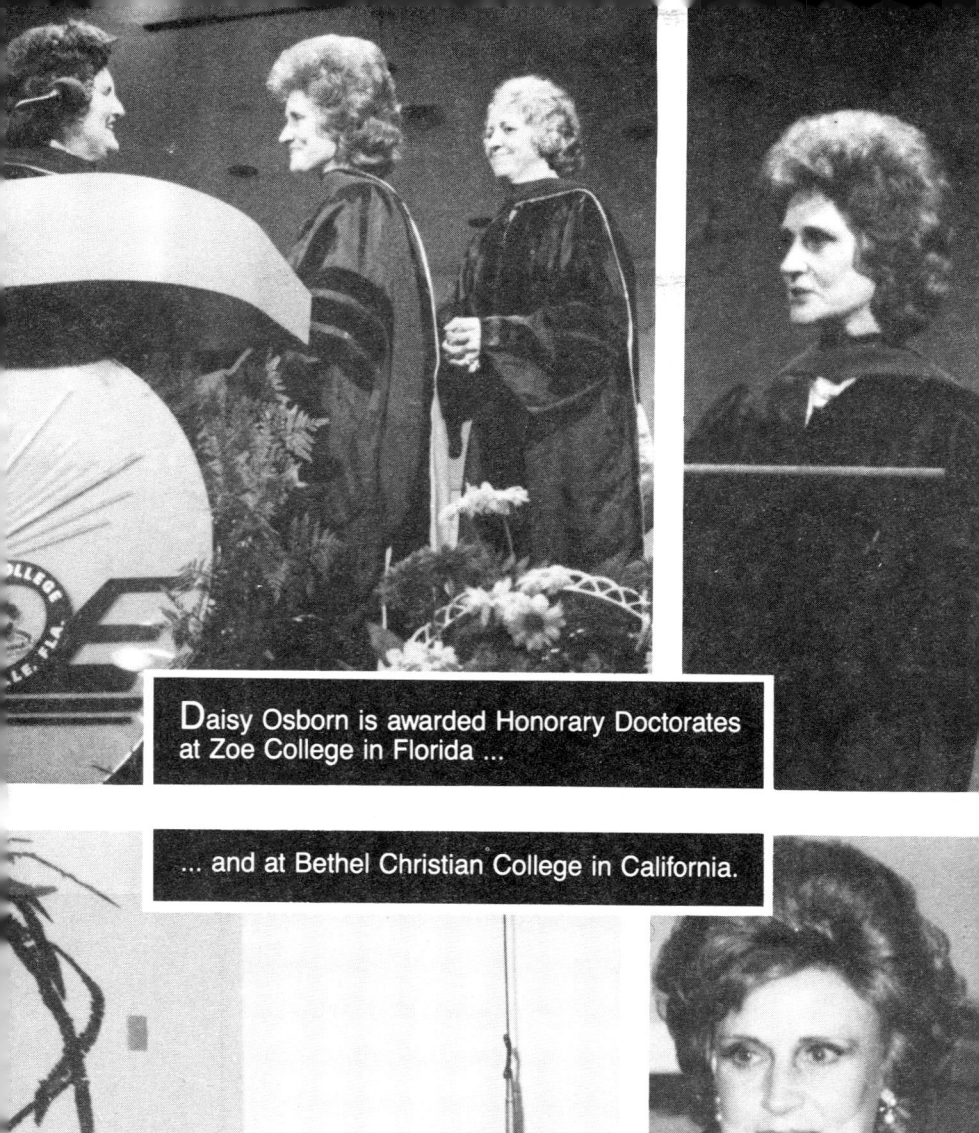

... and at Bethel Christian College in California.

At the Hagin International Campmeeting in Tulsa, Oklahoma, T.L. Osborn, Kenneth Hagin and Oral Roberts unite their faith as they pray for the thousands of men and women consecrating themselves to God's work in this generation.

Dr. T.L. Osborn addresses the graduating body at Christ For The Nations Bible Institute, Dallas, Texas.

SUPERIMPOSED PHOTOGRAPH

Dr. T.L. Osborn, one of the teachers at the Kenneth Copeland Believer's Convention, Ft. Worth, Texas, proclaims the value of each human person to God and to His plan, as proven by the price that was paid for our redemption by the death of Jesus Christ.

Doctors Daisy Osborn (left) and T.L. Osborn (right) hood Gloria Copeland and Kenneth Copeland during the ceremony at Zoe College in Jacksonville, Florida, where the Copelands were awarded Honorary Doctorates.

ACCRA, GHANA

This report on the phenomenal Ghana Crusade is a chapter in **today's Book of Acts** — like Paul wrote about his experiences.

This has been the most unusual crusade we have conducted in over three decades of mass evangelism. It began last year when Daisy was in West Africa, teaching thousands of African women from 15 nations.

The new Head of State had been on Daisy's heart for weeks. She believed God wanted her to go give him a message, so she went.

Before she left the USA, the Lord led me to say: "Honey, obey God, and when your feet touch Ghanaian soil, walk as **His** representative and **SAVE GHANA!**"

I was shocked at my words. Why did I say that?

Daisy found Ghana destitute. She never ate a bite of bread while there. There was no grain for flour.

A rigid curfew, with orders to shoot to kill violators, reigned at night. Depleted fuel stocks paralyzed transportation. Terror and animosity gripped the people.

Church leaders were shocked when the Chairman welcomed Daisy in his government headquarters.

As soldiers and the Chief of Protocol ushered Daisy in to meet the Head of State, he received her in military fatigues, armed with weapons and two radio-telephone units, flanked by guards with machine guns.

Daisy said: "Sir, I have not come to ask for anything. **I have only come to tell you that I love you,** that **God loves you,** and that **we are praying for you.**"

For over an hour she was privileged to minister to the Chairman. Then she knelt and took his hands in hers and prayed for him and for his nation. He wept as God touched his heart.

Daisy was allowed to use the government conference center daily, until curfew time. Thousands came by foot to hear her message of **love, forgiveness, hope** and **faith.**

Early one morning, God awakened Daisy and told her to go at once to the conference center. Typically, she obeyed, walked into the vast empty hall and sat down to wait for the Lord to show her why she was there.

Suddenly, a poor woman came in, clutching her baby, wandering about, as though she was stunned. Daisy discovered that **the child was dead,** and the mother was in shock.

Then, Daisy knew why God had sent her there. She managed to take the baby in her arms, and began walking back and forth, praying, praising and believing for a miracle from God for this poor distraught mother.

DR. DAISY WASHBURN OSBORN PREACHING

As she held the lifeless baby, all at once, it moved in her arms, and in a few moments, became warm and normal. Life had been restored. Then she handed it back to the mother, as they wept and thanked God together.

But the miracle was greater than Daisy realized.

The baby had been born with only one eye. As Daisy held its body, the Lord not only restored it to life, but also **created a perfect eye and new sight.** The mother was astounded.

That creative miracle was a prophecy of what was going to happen to the nation — restoration

AT GHANA'S GOVERNMENT CONFERENCE CENTER

of life and hope, and new vision for God's purpose.

The Chairman had asked Daisy to return the next evening. He sent personnel to video her teaching and to bring it to his office at once. He watched it repeatedly.

Daisy's next visit lasted nearly three hours during which the Chairman told her that she could address the nation. Her message was re-released several times, nationally.

Thousands of lives were changed and new hope was born in the hearts of destitute people, as Daisy addressed packed audiences, day after day, in that conference center. She told the Head of State, and the nation, that God had sent her, and that from the day she arrived, Ghana would have a new beginning.

Now a year has passed and here is part of the phenomenal fulfillment of her prophecy.

We were committed to go to Nigeria for mass evangelism, plus a seminar to teach over 20,000 workers from 17 African nations. We went, and the results of our mission there has exceeded our greatest dreams.

But Daisy kept saying, **"I am expecting word from Ghana, and it will be God's direction.** Last year I told the Chairman that, when the time was right, if he agreed, we would come and teach his nation."

Sure enough, a brief cable came from the Ghanaian Chief of Protocol:

> VISIT TO CHAIRMAN ARRANGED
> CONFIRM ARRIVAL
> DISPATCH PUBLICITY MATERIALS

We landed at 5 p.m., and the next six hours eclipsed any experience we have had in 35 years.

We were informed that a multitude of people were waiting for us at the official Independence Square. **This was the first indication that anything like a public gospel miracle crusade was in the program.**

We were whisked across town to the vast open public grounds by the Arch of Triumph.

Daisy and I were both overwhelmed as we neared the broad terrain and heard the voices of tens of thousands of Ghanaians singing to welcome our arrival.

There we were — barely two hours from our plane — facing a waving, singing, rejoicing multitude of Ghanaians massed on the official government celebration grounds at Independence Square. **What a spectacle of divine strategy!**

OSBORN CRUSADE

There were thousands of Ghanaians in the Accra campaign, with their arms stretched toward heaven.

The government and the news media had taken T. L. and Daisy Osborn seriously. The hour had come

ACCRA, GHANA

to see if God was really interested in Ghana. Would real miracles prove His love for the people, for the nation?

Daisy spoke masterfully and with matured wisdom, taking the meeting under control as she has done for 35 years. **Jesus was speaking through her, and she knew it,** as she told the mass of people what God had done to make this event possible.

Then I was introduced.

I knew destiny was at work. A nation's faith was at stake. I knew that if I could speak God's message simple and direct enough, a multitude would believe and a nation's faith would be reborn.

I had no time to prepare, but I never felt more certain of Christ's presence. **One after another, 5 VITAL ISSUES poured from my lips. It was God's strategy to focus what He had sent us to tell Ghana.**

1. **Why** Jesus CAME!

2. **How** do you GAIN!

3. **What** will you NAME!

4. **Who** is God's AIM!

5. **When** do you CLAIM!

That night, **it seemed like I was caught up into the third heaven.** Like Paul, I do not know if I was in the body or out of the body; only God knows. I only knew Christ was loving the people and speaking **through me.**

I seemed to lose myself. Was I in Ghana **now,** or was it three decades earlier, when we had brought West Africa's first mass evangelism crusade to Ghana?

Since that historic crusade in Ghana, there had been coup after coup, economic collapse, drought, starvation, disease, national ruin. People had lost faith in government. Confusion and near hysteria had reigned. The present Head of State had taken power for the second time, to reconstruct the nation.

That is when Daisy had come as a prophetess, with her simple but dynamic message of **God's love,** assuring him:

"From the day of my visit, sir, **Ghana will be reborn and marked by a new beginning."**

And it had happened. The rains had come. Ghana's soil had yielded abundant crops. Grain was plentiful. Rivers and waterways had overflown. The cocoa crop, vital for export, had been bountiful.

In just one year, the nation had literally been turned around. Foreign deficits had eased, imports had resumed, stores were restocked, gasoline was plentiful, transportation was restored, the curfew was lifted, hope was rekindled, a nation had experienced a new beginning.

Now, **the night of destiny had arrived.** I had addressed five major issues about God's outreach to Ghana.

Now it was time to see whether this was just holy rhetoric or if God would actually help them.

As we prayed for the multitude, the whole field of people stretched their arms heavenward, repenting of their sins of bitterness over government collapses, plundering, indiscriminate murder and rape, public looting and destruction. As they reached out for mercy, we urged them to forgive whoever had wronged them. They accepted Christ as Savior, as Healer and as their Life-Renewer.

Then, as the presence of Jesus poured into their lives, great healing miracles were experienced all over the multitude.

Deaf, blind, crippled, lame, tumors, epileptics, insane, dumb, paralyzed, cancers, fevers, crossed-eyes, crooked limbs — all kinds of miracles took place. Only God knows the details of what we witnessed.

And each night it was greater as the glory of God filled the field. **Daisy and I preached day and night. The nation's faith was reborn. Hope was lighted again.**

A distinguished gentleman wrote:

"What a wonder, your crusade at Independence Square by the Arch of Triumph! New peace and renewed faith came to the most troubled of our people. Dr. Daisy and Dr. T.L., your work is noble and invaluable, as you both point people to Jesus. You have made the Bible new in Ghana. Our nation is asking: 'Is this the same Jesus we have been worshipping?' The Jesus you proclaim is not religious, but is **Biblical,** and He has solutions for our problems. He is the talk of our city now. You two love ambassadors have re-lighted our hope and our faith in God."

That letter was typical of what was said to us by many of Ghana's leaders.

We were welcomed again by the Head of State where we ministered to him and prayed again with him. Then he directed that we be taken to his private residence, where we spent almost three more hours, ministering, testifying and praying for the first lady, the family and the nation.

When anyone follows the Holy Spirit as Paul did, an apostolic ministry is no different today than it was then.

KAMPALA, UGANDA

The Kampala, Uganda Crusade is one of the greatest and perhaps the most powerful we have experienced in almost four decades of mass evangelism in over 70 nations.

Uganda is a fabulously beautiful, landlocked country, covering an area of nearly one hundred thousand square miles, situated between Kenya and Zaire. She is bordered by Sudan on the north, and by Rwanda, Burundi and Tanzania on the south.

Over thirteen million people live in this land that straddles the equator. Until 1962 the nation was made up largely of tribal kingdoms.

Daisy's Divine Target

Then in 1966, a coup d'etat resulted in Uganda becoming a sovereign republic within the British Commonwealth. Years later, a military dictatorship took over, which proved to be a reign of terror and tragedy. Finally, invading soldiers from neighboring Tanzania overthrew General Amin's rule, but Uganda was bankrupt and in despair.

The country was fractured by different opposing forces, menaced and beleaguered by warring guerrilla troops and vigilantes, constantly subverting security and fomenting anarchy and destabilization. One of the guerrilla controlled zones extended to the edge of Kampala, the capital city.

This is the political situation into which Daisy went to attempt to organize a national crusade of Bible faith and of healing for the people and the nation.

It is difficult to imagine the psychological state of a people who have suffered lawlessness, terrorism and violence for so many years.

The Dictator's Visit

During the later years of General Amin's dictatorship, there was hope that he had changed his ways and that he might be responsive to a national gospel campaign in Uganda.

Those hopes were brightened during our historic seminar in Kisumu, Kenya, (near the Uganda border). We were conducting the largest Soulwinning Institute in Kenya's history. Over 5,000 preachers and workers were there from seven different African nations.

Suddenly a great dual-prop army helicopter swirled overhead and, to our amazement, descended upon the large field where we were teaching. It was General Amin.

While I controlled the people, Daisy, flanked by national pastors, approached the General and welcomed him to our platform where we ministered to him for half an hour, and later, for another forty-five minutes.

General Amin urged Daisy and me to come to Kampala for a campaign, promising that his government would give full backing and that he himself would encourage the people to attend.

We sought the Lord earnestly and, with no signal to proceed, left the matter in His hands.

Over 100 beautiful gospel vans, loaded and equipped with tools for evangelism have been provided FREE for mission fields worldwide, by the Osborn Ministries.

OSBORN CRUSADE — Bogota

OSBORN CRUSADE — Accra

OSBORN TEACHING — Tulsa Campmeeting

OSBORN CRUSADE — Nigeria

Hundreds of tape players — thousands of gospel tape

HUGE airlifts of **TONS** of gospel literature and evangelism tools are provided free to national pastors, leaders and to missionaries overseas, for reaching the unreached with the message of God's love.

OSBORN CRUSADE — ...yo

OSBORN CRUSADE — Kinshasa

OSBORN CRUSADE — W. Africa

OSBORN CRUSADE — Calabar

...rovided free by Osborn Ministries.

ABOVE: Largest Soulwinning Institute in Kenya's history.

ABOVE: Osborn airlift of tons of soulwinning tools — E. Africa.

5,000 preachers and workers from seven African nations.

BELOW: Osborn Seminar under Bamboo Cathedral at Kisumu.

When God Sets the Time

Because a head of state welcomes a crusade does not mean it is God's time. On the other hand, when things look the most impossible, God often shows His power in the greatest ways. When **He** is ready, nothing can stop His blessing a nation.

When we received this urgent plea from the Ugandan pastors, the Lord impressed us that, despite the hazards and even physical danger that existed, **NOW was His time for this nation.**

Rev. Bud Sickler, missionary to Mombasa, volunteers his private airplane to carry Daisy into Kampala to meet the ministers and to begin the preparations. She spends five weeks preaching in churches, halls, theaters, universities and wherever she can gather the people.

Daisy's Choice: Lugogo Stadium

Daisy faces the most awkward and impossible situations one could imagine in organizing the Kampala Crusade.

After she reviews every possible option for a location appropriate to a great crusade, she goes to **Lugogo Stadium.** It is three miles from the city center, and the entire sports field is surrounded by a huge ten foot concrete wall. As Daisy walks in on the grounds, the Lord whispers to her: **"This is the place!"**

Daisy knows the meetings would have to be conducted during daylight hours because of the risk of people being shot if they were moving about at night.

She tells the pastors: **"Wherever Jesus is, the multitude will throng Him. Even when He went into desert places, the multitude sought Him out and thronged Him.** Don't worry about the three mile distance from the city center. **If Jesus is there (and He will be), the multitudes will find Him. They will come from all over this nation, and you pastors will marvel!"**

Christian messengers volunteer to go to all the villages and towns and spread the news. Many pledge to go even into the "controlled" areas.

The Press Interview

As news spreads about the crusade preparations,

expectancy grows, and the news media assembles to interview Daisy.

QUESTION: Why have you come to Uganda?

ANSWER: We've come to conduct a national crusade of faith in God. We've come to light a fire of faith and of hope in the Ugandan people **by bringing them the good news of Christ.** If Uganda can believe that God is her best friend, and that He is powerful and loving and that He wants to help them, this will lift the people and will bring blessing to the nation.

QUESTION: What does faith in God mean?

ANSWER: Faith in God means you can have faith in one another — and in yourself. If people have faith in themselves, they can do anything. **When people lose faith in themselves, they lose faith in God too** — and vice versa. That is a sickness and it needs healing. We believe in God's miraculous healing power. **He begins by healing the individual, then He reaches out and heals the nation.** My husband and I believe that if we share the gospel of Jesus Christ, and share what we have seen Him do for people in over 70 nations, this will give new hope and courage to the people of this nation. **I can tell you, there is a new future for Uganda!**

QUESTION: What happens in these crusades?

ANSWER: Always the same. Great throngs of people attend. Great miracles take place. The lives of thousands of people are changed. **The greatest miracle is when ordinary people who think they are "nobodies",** and who have nothing, get the idea that God loves them and paid a price for them, and that He wants to bless them; when they **discover that they are important to God and are valuable to Him** — this is the greatest miracle of all. This will happen to thousands of people in this nation.

The 22 Mile Miracle Journey

The day finally comes to welcome me at the Entebbe Airport. **I receive the greatest welcome ever accorded us in any nation.** Thousands of people have managed to come to the airport to show how much they want God's blessings.

Entebbe is 22 miles from the capital city of Kampala. The Christians have spread crusade leaflets throughout the countryside and have circulated the news about our arrival.

Then we begin our 22 mile journey into the capital. The road passes through one village or small town after another.

Practically the entire distance is filled with tens of thousands of people lining both sides of the road, pushing, shoving and eagerly watching for a glimpse of the servants of God as we pass by.

They have carried their sick, led their blind and helped their needy to the roadside. Some sit on chairs, some are carried on beds, some lie or sit on the ground.

As our entourage of precious believing Ugandans creeps along, we pray for the people throughout the 22 mile journey.

In practically every service of the Kampala Crusade, **we hear reports about miracles of healing which have taken place as we passed along the roadway,** praying for the people and waving to them in the name of Jesus.

Jesus Visits Uganda

Daisy has convinced the city that Jesus Christ is alive and that nothing is impossible if they will only believe.

It seems as though the nation believes that **God has come to help them,** just because T.L. and Daisy Osborn have arrived.

God can literally love and save a nation but He has to have **human partners.**

Modern media and satellite communications can do wonderful things for millions of people. **But the poor must see Jesus among them in HUMAN FORM, in bodies which they can SEE and TOUCH and FEEL and HEAR. And that is what we are —GOD'S PARTNERS in lifting people to Him.**

The God-Uganda Connection

On the opening day of the Uganda Crusade, roads and pathways leading to the stadium are like rivers of people. They are leading the blind, carrying the sick on beds, on homemade stretchers and on their backs. Crippled and lame people are struggling to move toward the stadium using crutches, canes, limbs, sticks, braces and all sorts of concocted support.

The roads are enveloped in a heavy cloud of red dust

For 22 miles from Entebbe Airport into Kampala thousands line the road to welcome us.

from the powdery clay surface.

The amassment of people travels on foot because there is pitifully little transportation — and usually the pedestrians move faster anyway.

Daisy and I marvel at the opening day of this historic crusade. As we ascend the steps to the platform, erected on second base of the ballfield, the stadium is packed and the people are thick all the way from the grandstand to the platform — and even back of the platform.

Authorities estimate 400,000 people present at each of the services. It is an overwhelming experience to face such an encampment of needy people.

We are overwhelmed at the cry of hope and the desperate need of these forsaken people.

The Lord at Work Today

We conduct two meetings daily: Ten o'clock in the morning and two o'clock in the afternoon. The multitude is there for the morning meeting and for the afternoon. They sit under the hot equatorial sun, their attention riveted to every word preached by Daisy or me.

We wish you could be present **in just one of the great meetings** at the Lugogo Stadium in Kampala.

Neither Daisy nor I hardly ever preach a complete message **without being interrupted by remarkable miracles of healing taking place** in the lives of the people as they listen to God's word and receive faith through His promise.

The people of Uganda seem to have caught the idea that **Jesus and His power are in His word;** that when they receive His word and believe on Him, they expect Him to change their lives, to forgive their sins and to heal their bodies at once. That happens day after day in the crusade.

Each meeting is like Bible days when *it came to pass that as Jesus was teaching, the power of the Lord was present to heal.*[1] Our object in ministry is to show the people that *Jesus Christ is the same yesterday and today and forever.*[2]

The Message That Gives Life

We teach about a miracle from the Bible, expounding the many lessons contained in each story, careful to apply them to the hurting, needy people present.

We urge them **to believe** like they believed in the Bible, **to pray** like they prayed in the Bible, **to receive** Christ like they received Him in the Bible, **to call** on His name like people called on Him in the Bible, **to act** their faith like people did in the Bible and **to expect to receive** the same miracles that people received in the Bible.

That is exactly what the Ugandan people do in meeting after meeting.

If all of the miracles, signs and wonders that have been wrought during the Uganda Crusade would be recorded, it would take a very large volume to contain them.

The second day of the crusade, we almost lose control of the multitude after we preach on the healing of the cripple who was let down through the roof where Jesus was preaching.

We emphasize the fact that Jesus said to the man,

OSBORN CRUSADE, LUGOGO STADIUM,

The T.L. and Daisy Osborn crusade attracts thousands of people from

Dr. Daisy Washburn Osborn addresses over 200,000 women (besides men and children) on the historic Women's Miracle Day, in the Kampala Crusade.

JINJA ROAD, KAMPALA, UGANDA

he nations surrounding Uganda, coming to witness what God is doing.

I have forgiven your sins.[3]

The Ugandans have been so brutalized by undisciplined soldiers and lawless guerrillas, that faith in a human person has been lost. Suspicion, apprehension and fear have reigned.

What Forgiveness Means

What does it mean to proclaim to people like this the wonderful words of Jesus, *I have forgiven your sins?*

What a wonder to show them **the great fact of forgiveness, of forgetting, of burying the past, and of reaching out through God's mercy and love to a new beginning, to new faith in God and to new faith in each other.**

After we expound the powerful truth of forgiveness, then we emphasize the words of Jesus: *Rise, take up your bed and walk.*[4]

We underscore the importance of **individual faith,** and how this man took Jesus at His word, arose and was miraculously healed.

The Healing Prayer

Following the message we pray earnestly for the healing of everyone who has purposed to believe on Jesus Christ and who has accepted Him by faith.

We project ourselves, by an act of faith, out into the spirit world, where we confront every spirit of infirmity that has plagued, oppressed and besieged these dear people. **We adjure those spirits,** by the name of Jesus, to come out of the people and to leave them forever.

Then we thank God for His authority to cast out devils and to heal the sick.

We invoke the healing presence of Jesus Christ on the people and we ask that His healing virtue permeate their bodies until they are perfectly healed by the power and presence of Jesus in their lives.

We thank God for **answered** prayer. We lead the multitude in thanksgiving for God's healing presence among them.

The people are encouraged **to put their faith into action** while they continue thanking God for healing

Miracles taking place in the Osborn Uganda Crusade.

T.L. and Daisy could hardly teach or preach without being interrupted by those who were receiving miracles and who came forward to testify.

them. We tell them **to do whatever they could not do before the prayer.**

If they could not walk, **we command them to walk** in Jesus' name.

If they could not see, **we tell them to open their eyes** and to receive their sight in Jesus' name.

We tell the people to **talk into the ears of the deaf,** and to assist them in receiving miracles.

Those who had tumors, growths or cancers, **we urge to check themselves,** expecting that their growths have disappeared.

Those who had fevers or were sick, we encourage **to believe for complete recovery.**

Those who had crutches, braces or canes, we tell to **raise them in the air and to walk without them** in the name of Jesus.

Those who are invalids, sitting on chairs, boxes or lying on mats, **we command to rise up and to walk by faith** in Jesus Christ.

After the prayer and after urging the people **to put**

their faith into action, crutches, canes and braces are raised above peoples' heads.

Miracles in Evidence

There are outbursts of spontaneous praise to God. The sea of people opens as those healed press toward the platform, often preceded by some friend **parading crutches, canes or braces.**

Sometimes **a wheelchair or cot is raised above the heads of the crowd** as the healed one advances toward the platform. The packed audience opens like a river before them, amidst spontaneous handclapping, weeping and rejoicing.

This is what took place in the Bible when the crippled man who was healed was *walking, and leaping, and praising God,* and the people *were filled with wonder and amazement at that which had happened.*[5]

It is the same as it was in Bible days when *people ran through the whole region and carried about in beds those that were sick where they heard Jesus was, and besought him that they might touch if it were but the border of his garment: and as many as touched him were made whole.*[6]

We stand in amazement as we behold the wonders of God.

Celebration of Wonders

Coming toward the platform is a man **carrying a crutch.** He is yelling aloud, **"I'm healed! Look at me! I can walk!"** He is jumping and walking through the press of people, as fast as he can.

To our left is a young lady with **a large shoe and brace held high above her head.** She is coming to show what God has done for her. Both legs are now normal. Her brace and awkward shoe are no longer needed. Jesus has healed her.

In another direction a young girl is coming toward us, **carrying two crutches above her head.** She mounts the steps and parades across the platform, walking as any normal person. She is perfectly healed.

From back of the platform comes **a young lad who**

has worn a leg brace from his thigh to his foot. His leg has been affected by polio, but now it is perfectly healed and he is walking normally.

Up the steps comes a lad who had been **deaf and dumb since birth.** A pastor stops him and talks in his ear. The lad repeats every word that is spoken to him. The people are amazed.

From the other side, an older man has come up the steps, **carrying a heavy shoe and brace which he has removed from his left leg.** He has spent his life limping on that weak leg, crippled during childhood by polio.

Now the brace and the shoe are no longer needed; one leg is as strong as the other.

The Miracles Continue

A young man has come, and is weeping for joy. He has been **almost totally blind because of cataracts.** He wants to witness for Christ. He shows how he can now see everything clearly. It is a beautiful miracle of God.

One of the pastors points excitedly to the far edge of

ABOVE: Woman, healed of total blindness, reads Dr. Daisy's New Testament.
BELOW: More miracles are discovered as those healed hoist crutches and walk toward the platform to testify.

This scene from the Kampala Crusade is more proof that "the Lord works with us, confirming His word with signs following."

the crowd. **A man who has been crippled and carried here on his bed** has gotten up, is healed by the power of God, has **rolled up his mattress and raised it high in the air,** and is walking about, shouting and crying aloud for the people to see what God has done for him.

A young man in a blue and yellow shirt has been instantly healed. **From birth he has never heard or spoken.** The deaf and dumb spirit has gone out of him during the mass prayer, and he is almost hysterical with joy because of the new sounds he is hearing.

We snap our fingers by each of his ears and he jumps excitedly. We speak words and **he repeats them with amazing clarity.** Then we try short sentences, and he is able to repeat them with remarkable accuracy. It is a convincing miracle.

God's People-Priority

After each testimony we expound God's promises more and urge the people to continue in reverent expectation. We explain that with each testimony that confirms God's word, faith rises higher; that is why some of the greatest miracles take place long after the message is preached and the prayer has been prayed.

Another **blind woman is healed.** She is excited and keeps wiping away the tears so she can see. She touches my nose, then points to the people with great delight. She can see them clearly and even counts the fingers of someone in the audience. She dances and praises the Lord.

A little boy who was blind is healed. He is thrilled as he touches the nose of the ex-blind woman who just danced, and counts the fingers of her hand. Then she looks closely at the little boy's face and they rejoice together.

An older woman who has been blind for four years is healed. She is hesitant to touch my nose, but finally does it, then claps her hands with joy because she can see so well.

Then we experience the touching miracle of **an old woman who is over a hundred years old. She was led to the meeting, blind.** She has been instantly healed and gingerly pinches my nose and counts my fingers with a broad smile on her face.

She looks out and waves both of her hands at the

"It came to pass that, as we were teaching, the power of the Lord was present to heal" throughout the Uganda Crusade.

Dr. T.L. Osborn and Dr. Daisy Osborn, "teaching and preaching the gospel of the kingdom" at the Lugogo Stadium in Kampala.

people, then dances before them to give thanks to God.

Visitation — In Human Form

I think our Lord is deeply touched when He sees His blessings bestowed upon His beautiful creatures who have been so neglected, brutalized and morally prostituted. **What a wonder to be used of God to bring new hope and faith to people who have languished in such total despair.** This must be God's No. 1 Priority. They need His visitation **in human form** *(The word was made flesh and dwelt among us and we saw His glory*[7]*)* — in a form which they can **SEE** and **TOUCH** and **FEEL**. **That is what Daisy and I represent to these people.**

Suddenly here comes a wheelchair being hoisted above the people's heads. A man following it is walking and praising God.

They set the wheelchair on the platform as the healed man parades back and forth before the people, showing how he has been miraculously healed by the presence of Jesus Christ.

Then a woman testifies in tears. According to her

doctors **a tumor has been growing in her head for 15 years.** She has suffered agonizing headaches and has almost never been free of pain. Now she has been healed as she stood amidst the multitude and repeated the prayer.

A warm sensation came through her head and every pain disappeared. She is holding her head, weeping for joy as she thanks God.

More Wonders of God

A young mother arrives with her little daughter, weeping hysterically because **her child has been blind,** but now her eyes are healed and she can see everything.

An old man stands serenely as he explains to the people how **his ears became deaf ten years ago,** and how he has struggled to make a living, despite his handicap.

Now as he talks, he breaks into tears, thanking God for his miracle. He repeats each word we speak in his ears — perfectly and without hesitation. It is clearly a wonder of God.

Crippled by polio when he was a child, this man (right) has received his miracle, and the Kampala people (below) give thanks to God.

She believed the promise of God as T.L. Osborn preached the gospel. She was healed as she listened, then rushes through the crowd, to the platform, to tell the multitude.

The platform begins to be jammed with people anxious to testify. **All kinds of miracles are taking place.**

I call out to the audience, **"How many more of you have been healed?** You've received a miracle? You know you're well? It has already happened but you can't press through the crowd to get up here to the platform?"

Hundreds of hands are thrust into the air and an uproar of voices shout that they are healed.

The Blind Preacher

An old man is standing near me, barefooted. A pastor explains that **he has been blind for 15 years.** Daisy is beside him, holding his Bible which he has carried faithfully to church for years, without being able to see a word.

He never doubted that someday he would read his Bible again, and that day is **today!**

Daisy opens his Bible and hands it to him to read. He holds it lovingly and begins to read as tears pour from his eyes. **He takes a rag and wipes the tears away and**

then, as he moves his forefinger across the lines, reads aloud, to the multitude, from the small print of his Bible.

It is one of the most touching testimonies we have ever witnessed.

After a few lines, he takes that dirty rag and sops the tears from his eyes again, then continues reading. Then he stops and raises one hand to heaven and weeps as he thanks God for his restored eyesight.

We are told that he has been a preacher of the gospel and has prayed for years for God to bring the Osborns to his country. We understand why this miracle means so much to him, and we weep together.

The Gospel Works

A young lady, about 14 years old, tells the story of her years of suffering convulsions. She would fall to the ground and foam would pour from her mouth. **People have treated her as a demoniac and were afraid of her when her seizures came.**

Standing out on the field, as we commanded the

Another miracle scene unfolds in the Kampala Uganda Crusade, as the Osborns minister to thousands.

His crippled legs have been healed during the Osborn Crusade, and he is proud to show the proof of his miracle.

More miracles are witnessed as T.L. and Daisy teach faith and minister to the people.

spirits of infirmity to come out of the people, that destructive force left her and she knew she was healed. She says she **knew** when the devil left her.

A man comes **bounding through the packed crowd carrying two crutches above his head.** He presses through, anxious to testify. He tells how he has been paralyzed seven months and has not been able to walk.

He is thanking God for those who helped him to this place where Jesus has touched and completely healed him. He is shaking all over as he testifies in tears. People are amazed as he tells how the Lord has restored him.

Panorama of Miracles

A stretcher has been brought to the platform. A dear woman is presented by one of the pastors. She has been carried to the crusade in a car and placed on her stretcher on the ground. **They have brought her from the hospital where she has lain, completely paralyzed, for three weeks.**

She says, "When Rev. Osborn prayed the prayer for healing, I knew Jesus was near me. He came and touched me and **I just got up and walked.** Look at me!

Another wonder of God unfolds as someone abandons a wheelchair in the Kampala Crusade, and comes to the platform to show the multitude what the Lord has done.

Another miracle! He was crippled by polio as a child, but now he is healed at the Lugogo Stadium.

He is eager to hand his crutches and braces to the servant of God.

"**What** God has done for this man, He will do for you too. Only believe. With God, nothing is impossible."

I'm well!" She walks as well as any normal person. She put her faith in action and her faith has been rewarded.

A lady comes to testify. She has been healed of **a large goiter on her neck.** She leans her head back and pounds her throat, then couples both fists to show how big the goiter was. Now it is gone. The Lord has made her whole.

Daisy then brings a woman to the microphone who is **completely healed of cancer. She had become so emaciated that she could not walk.** Her friends carried her to the stadium and she has been lying on a straw mat during the meeting.

During the salvation prayer, she received Jesus into her life by faith and as we prayed for healing, she got up on her feet and felt strong. She has suffered for over nine months and was dying.

She has walked all the way through the crowd and up the steps of the platform, and she feels stronger every moment.

She worships the Lord and the crowd glorifies God with her for this miracle.

God's Healing Presence

A woman testifies who had broken her arm five weeks before. **The arm had seemed paralyzed and had remained helpless at her side.** During the message she suddenly realized that she had no pain.

She can now raise her arm, double it and move her fingers as perfectly as anyone. Jesus has done a real miracle for her.

A young fellow comes forward **carrying a cane on his right shoulder. For eight years he has been crippled,** following an injury. They have operated on him twice, trying to repair the broken bones in his hips.

Standing out on the field, he has been instantly healed during the prayer.

A pastor who was out in the crowd, saw him jumping and rejoicing, and told him to rush to the platform and to testify. When he was healed, he tells us that he was frightened by the presence of Jesus. But then he realized that he was perfectly well, and he had the courage to come and speak for His Lord. It is a touching testimony.

A woman brings her little child and is overcome with joy as she explains that **one of its feet was very twisted from birth.** As she joined in the mass prayer for healing, the presence of Jesus came and healed her little child. The foot is perfect now.

The Dumb and The Lame

A woman who has been dumb for five years is now speaking and repeating every word that we say in her ears. She was out in the crowd when she received her miracle.

As sound suddenly came into her ears, it frightened her. But now she is calm again and is thanking God for the miracle she has received.

A man has come to testify who has been **lame for several years.** He was involved in a serious accident which left him **crippled and obliged to walk with the aid of crutches.**

When the Lord healed him, he just dropped his crutches and has been out at the edge of the crowd, walking and running and praising the Lord. He has come

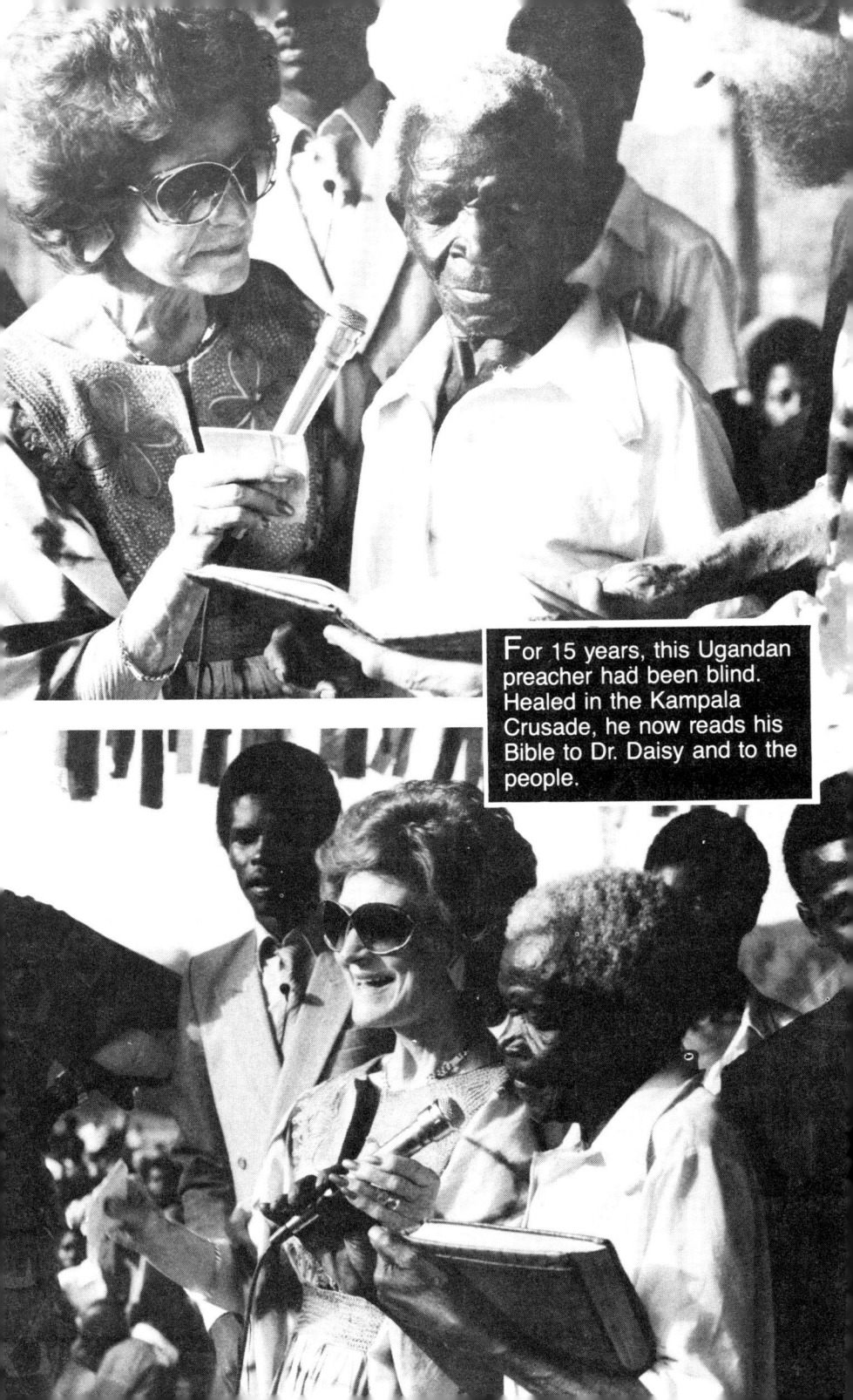

For 15 years, this Ugandan preacher had been blind. Healed in the Kampala Crusade, he now reads his Bible to Dr. Daisy and to the people.

to show what God has done for him.

When we ask him about his crutches, he says he left them out on the field; he says he threw them away because he never wants to use them again.

The Cripples Walk

An old woman testifies in great joy. **She hobbled to the crusade on two crutches,** having suffered with painful arthritis for several years.

The power of the Lord came upon her as she stood out on the field, listening to the message and the prayer.

When she was healed, she threw her crutches down and began to jump and dance for joy. Then she came to the platform to tell everyone about her miracle.

We ask her where her crutches are, and she exclaims: "Oh, I left them out there. I threw them away. I don't need them anymore." We all praise God for the miracle that has blessed this dear old woman.

A middle aged lady comes **carrying in her hand a**

shoe and a brace which she has worn on one leg since she was seven years old.

When the prayer was prayed, she simply unbuckled the brace, unlaced the shoe, removed them both and started walking in the name of Jesus. She has been completely healed and she is so thankful to be able to walk normally again.

Reliving Bible Days

Each day of this mighty crusade, we witness similar **miracles, signs and wonders.** Daisy and I cannot remember when we have seen the power of God demonstrated so mightily.

All of our crusades have been marvelous and maybe we forget the wonder of past experiences. But **it seems that nothing has compared to the dynamic manifestation of God's power here in Kampala.**

The great miracle of **Damiano** is one that has to be witnessed to comprehend its glory.

This poor beggar who staggered to the meeting on two long sticks, is now dressed in a lovely suit, wearing

A bone infection crippled this man's legs. He could not walk without crutches for three years. Now he demonstrates his perfect healing to the multitude as he weeps for joy.

He is 23 years old. Crippled by polio as an infant, he has never walked without crutches. Now he wants everyone to help him thank God for the miracle he has received in the Kampala Crusade.

Ugandan preacher, blind for 20 years, receives his sight and weeps reverently, then bursts into tearful laughter, as he looks and sees with his restored eyes.

shoes and a necktie, and is seated on the platform like a prince with God.

"Papa" Musoke who scooted on his hips, walking with his hands for years, is now a dignified looking gentleman with new hope and faith in his heart.

He was a **beggar, clad in filthy rags, who literally slept with dogs** to keep warm in the cool wet nights. Now he is a walking miracle and the whole city is amazed at what Christ has done for him.

The Voice that Spoke

A man named John struggled for six days, on two crutches, to find his way to this wonderful place which he had heard about far away in his village.

He had fallen almost 30 feet and had broken the bones in his back and hips. He was left hopelessly crippled for life.

Sitting out on the field as we preached, he heard the voice of Jesus speaking loudly from the heavens saying: **"John, stand up now and walk."** He did exactly that and was perfectly healed.

The Bolt of Power

Maria Theresa was carried to the crusade and laid on the ground. She had been abandoned as incurable, and had lain for weeks, languishing in her village on a straw mat, trying to die. She was a poor woman. There was no cure. She was waiting for death. Hearing of the crusade, she was brought by loving friends.

As Maria Theresa lay on the ground while Daisy preached, a **bolt of God's power from heaven struck her with such force that it actually blinded her for several minutes.** She literally sprang to her feet under the terror and shock of this experience.

Those nearby thought she was crazy and was having a spell. But she had been mercifully healed by our Lord.

The bolt of power so frightened her, plus the temporary loss of her sight, that she staggered about incoherently as though she was out of her mind.

I had gone down to see what was happening because the Lord had told me: **"She is not insane; I have visited her."** So I was able to help her to the platform where she tells the multitude of the wonder of God's visitation to

This woman, crippled for over ten years, is suddenly healed in the Kampala Crusade. She rushes to the platform and runs, back and forth, to show how God has restored her.

her there on the ground, during Daisy's message. It is an awesome miracle.

The Amazed Village

Throughout the area all kinds of reports come to us each day of more miracles, and of rejoicing in the villages.

One woman who was totally blind for 20 years, came to the crusade and was instantly healed. She returned to her village where her friends were astounded by what God had done.

But to add to the amazement, another woman from the same village, **attended the crusade in her wheelchair** and was instantly and miraculously healed.

Returning to her village, she pushed her own wheelchair up and down the village pathways showing the people what God had done. The blind woman heard of the miracle.

They both paraded together and the whole village marveled at what the Lord Jesus Christ had done.

Self-Esteem Regained

The greatest miracle of all is the new hope, faith and self-esteem that have been restored to multitudes of people in this sad nation.

When faith in God is gone, people sink in despair because they no longer believe in themselves.

There is no power like the power of the gospel of Jesus Christ to raise people up from the dungheap and to set them among God's royalty.

Day after day, Daisy or I stand on the platform stretching out our arms to that vast field of people, and cry:

"Uganda, God loves you! Uganda, God has not forgotten you! Uganda, you are not forsaken! Uganda, Jesus died for you! He paid the supreme price to redeem you and to bless you! He has come to tell you, 'Do not despair! Only believe! Reach out to Me! If you will call on Me, I will forgive you and heal you! And I will give you a new beginning! Uganda, I love you! I value you! I trust you! I need you!'"

Every communication we receive from pastors and

As Dr. Daisy preaches, this woman who had been crippled by polio since she was seven years old, is instantly healed, removes her brace and shoe, and comes to tell of the miracle she has received.

As in Bible days, the lame and crippled are healed, day after day, in the Osborn Crusade at Kampala.

More miracles take place as T.L. and Daisy teach the gospel in Uganda.

Christians alike, continues to confirm that Jesus Christ is truly visiting this nation and is manifesting His peace and healing power to a people who have been practically abandoned to despair.

Restoring Dignity to a Nation

New hope and faith have been relighted in the spirits of the people. Uganda has been blessed once again. God's people have realized afresh that, despite continued political turmoil and the almost insurmountable problems in government, God has not forgotten them. He loves them and He needs them.

The greatest miracle of all is that Jesus is restoring hope, faith and love to hundreds of thousands of Ugandans.

He is restoring self-dignity, self-esteem and self-worth to these multitudes of people. Faith is alive again. Love is the motivating force. Forgiveness is working its miracle in the lives of the people.

Even in the face of the persistent instability of government, **the hope of a new future for Uganda has been born. Faith in God has been restored.**

This old lady (below and opposite page) has been miraculously healed and pushes through the press of people, to reach the platform, as her daughter hoists her crutches.

Amazed by her miracle, "mama" throws her arms around Dr. T.L. then compels him to dance with her to give God praise.

That makes possible the restoring of faith in each other — **and in each one's own self.**

With this miracle being accomplished, the foundation is now established upon which the nation can be rebuilt. **She is living again!**

Your New Beginning is NOW

What God has done for Uganda (and for Ghana in West Africa), He is doing for **you** as an individual. Certainly He is interested in **nations,** but His greatest interest is in **individuals.**

Jesus is visiting **your life** by means of this apostolic report.

This has been another chapter in the continuing book of Acts **in your day.**

What He does for one, He does for **EVERYONE. And EVERYONE** means **YOU'RE THE ONE.**

He loves **you** and reaches out to **you** right now, to give YOU **His very best** as you believe on Him, call on Him and **trust Him for a new beginning.**

Scripture References
[1] Lu.5:17
[2] He. 13:8
[3] Mt.9:2 LB
[4] Mk.2:9,11
[5] Ac.3:8,10
[6] Mk.6:55-56
[7] Jn.1:14

This lad was totally blind. At first, T.L. and Daisy's white faces so frightened him that he covered his eyes in fear. Then he waves at the people with delight because he can see clearly.

This dear old woman is over 100 years old, and was led to the Kampala Crusade totally blind. Now her sight is restored by a miracle, and she rejoices.

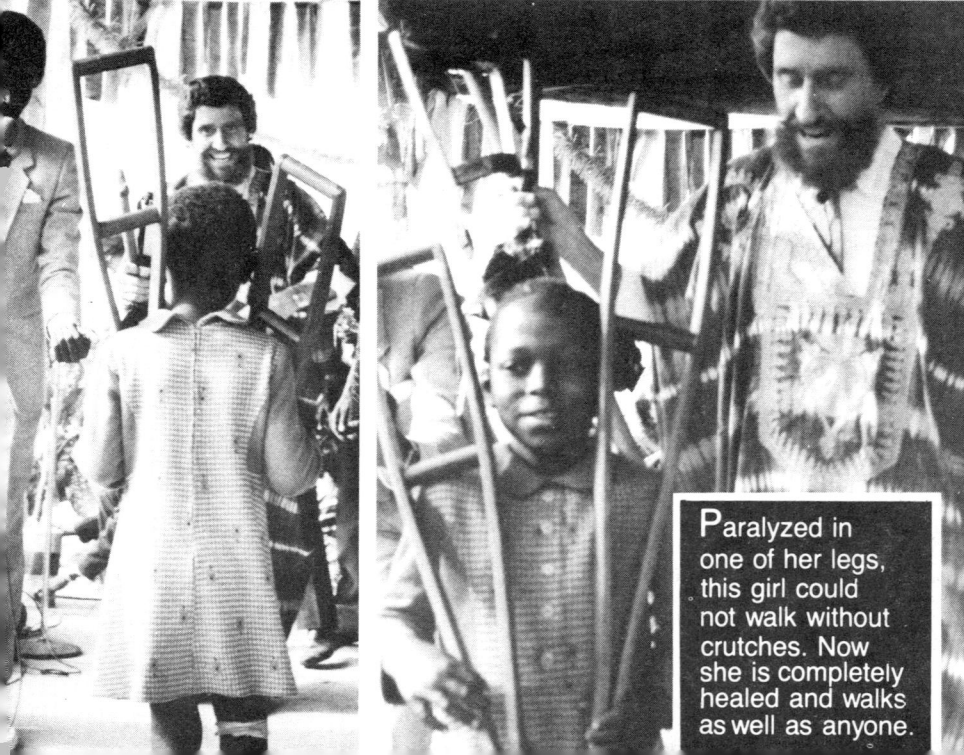

He was healed of a leg injury during the mass prayer at the stadium, and rushes to the platform to tell the people.

Paralyzed in one of her legs, this girl could not walk without crutches. Now she is completely healed and walks as well as anyone.

This young man was born deaf and dumb. Now he can hear and pronounce any word spoken by T.L. Below, he shakes hands with people to thank them for their prayers and faith in God.

Signs, miracles and wonders of God confirm the gospel at the Osborn Crusade in Kampala.

As new miracle scenes like these unfold each day during T.L. and Daisy Osborn's Kampala Crusade, thousands believe on Jesus Christ and become His followers.

Drs. T.L. and Daisy Osborn believe that the greatest miracle of all is the new hope, faith and self-esteem which the gospel restores to the people of Uganda.

Damiano Bitatinya

PART 26

DAMIANO'S MIRACLE

Damiano Bitatinya's miracle shook the city of Kampala and every one of the **multitude of people who witnessed it** take place. God impressed us to include this special miracle because the same compassion and love that touched and healed this poor, helpless man, **can touch you too** as you read about it.

This miracle account is a **modern up-to-date chapter in the continuing Book of Acts.** Read it with faith and expect to receive from God whatever you need, in Jesus' name!

I saw this poor man, clad in rags, near the Lugogo Stadium, staggering on trembling, incoherent legs, propped on two long poles, struggling alone toward our crusade grounds. Red dust was thick. The press of people was frantic. They were carrying lame and sick folks, leading the blind, etc. **But Damiano's lonely silhouette of despair would not leave my eyes.**

As I watched him from our car window, the Lord whispered to me: *"God raises the poor out of the dust, and lifts the needy out of the dunghill; that he may set him with the princes of His people."* (Ps.113:7-8)

I saw **the nation of Uganda,** in that forsaken, unloved, despairing man — alone, without hope or faith.

Daisy and I had come to this despairing, looted and brutalized nation, to tell them: **"Uganda, God loves you! God values you! God paid for you! He needs you! If you will believe on Him and reach out to Him, He will save and heal you and give you a new beginning!"**

As you read this, God is saying that to you, as much as He was saying it to those people in Uganda. His **touch of wonder** is reaching out to YOU — **now.**

We passed the poor man by as we rode in on the grounds, but when I reached the platform, **I could not erase the silhouette of that lonely, hopeless and unloved human person from my mind.**

The Lord impressed me to call for him and to make an example of him before the multitude, to underscore the fact that God paid the same price for each person, and loved each one equally, regardless of how poor or sick or sinful anyone may be.

When I went to the microphone, I described the man to the people and they found him and helped him to come to me on the platform.

There before the multitude, I used him as an object lesson. I said, **"Even if you are poor, in rags, alone and sick, God values you. He has sent Daisy and me to tell you, HE NEEDS YOU! HE PAID FOR YOU! TRUST HIM, CALL ON HIM and HE WILL SAVE and HEAL YOU; He will GIVE YOU His NEW LIFE, and A NEW BEGINNING!"**

The people clapped and wept at the same time.

I called the poor man by his name: **"Damiano, you are special to God. You've begged and crawled long enough! I bring you good news! You are not forsaken. Jesus paid for you. He needs you! In His name I love you. Only believe!"**

I told the people: "What God does for this man, He will do for every Ugandan who believes!"

I told Damiano about Jesus and **he accepted Christ.**

Dr. T.L. Osborn calls for Damiano, the beggar, to be placed on the platform so that everyone can see him.

T.L. assures the man that Jesus loves him, and will heal him, if he will accept Christ and ONLY BELIEVE.

I led him in prayer to be saved.

Then I pulled Damiano to me and I loved Him. I called out with a loud voice: **"Oh, you spirit of infirmity, leave this dear man forever, in Jesus' name!"**

Then I held him and imparted God's love and the healing presence of Jesus Christ.

I took the two poles from his hands and said, **"Damiano, you've staggered long enough. Animals crawl, but you are a man in God's image! Let's go! Walk! Jesus heals you! You are no longer a beggar! You are valuable! You are a child of God, with dignity and new life!"**

Damiano walked, taking strong steps! Then amidst tears, he broke into a glorious smile! The miracle was done!

He flung his arms around me in a grasp of love and gratitude. I'll never forget that embrace. **A beggar had become a prince in God's family!**

I said: **"Damiano, thank you for your love! Daisy and I are richer now because you are our new brother."** He was worth all that we did to bring God's love and miracle power to Uganda.

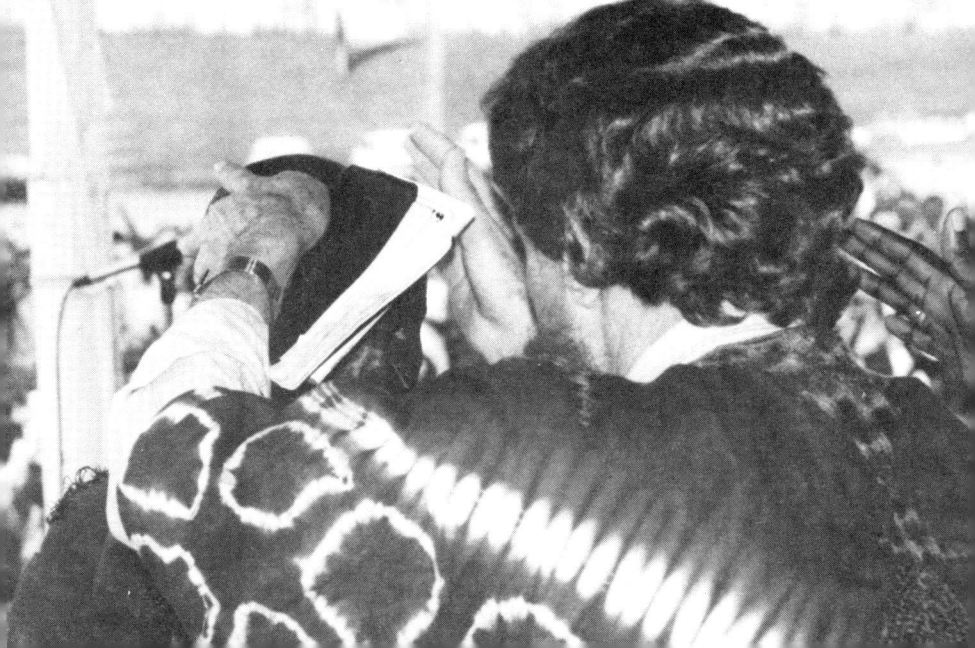

T.L. commands the spirit of infirmity to leave Damiano's body, then commands him to walk in Jesus' name.

Damiano walks with no support or help. He has been instantly healed.

To Daisy and me, **that is God's No. 1 Job!** To go to the forgotten, the lonely, the unloved, the disinherited, the sick, the fearful, those in despair ... to go in Jesus' name and **to help them discover their value to God, and to humanity; to lift and heal and save them and to give them dignity, pride and salvation.**

I told Damiano: **"Sit in my chair. You are one of God's choice people now!"** As he sat there, smiling and happy, he looked like a PRINCE.

We arranged for Damiano to have good food, a bath, a bed and new clothes. The next day, he came **looking like a re-created wonder of God's love and power.** He embraced me and laid his head on my shoulder. **We were new friends!**

Damiano is one of thousands transformed in the Kampala Crusade. For nearly four decades, in over 70 nations, we have seen **Love's miracles** like this. In preachers and workers, it is another kind of miracle. Their message is changed from **condemnation** and **judgment** to **love** and **GOOD news.**

Damiano, our new brother, has been raised from despair to become a **member of royalty** through the compassion and powerful love of Jesus Christ.

Realizing that he is healed, Damiano embraces T.L. and thanks God for his miracle.

Damiano, clad in a new suit, returns to greet T.L. and Daisy and to witness of his miracle.

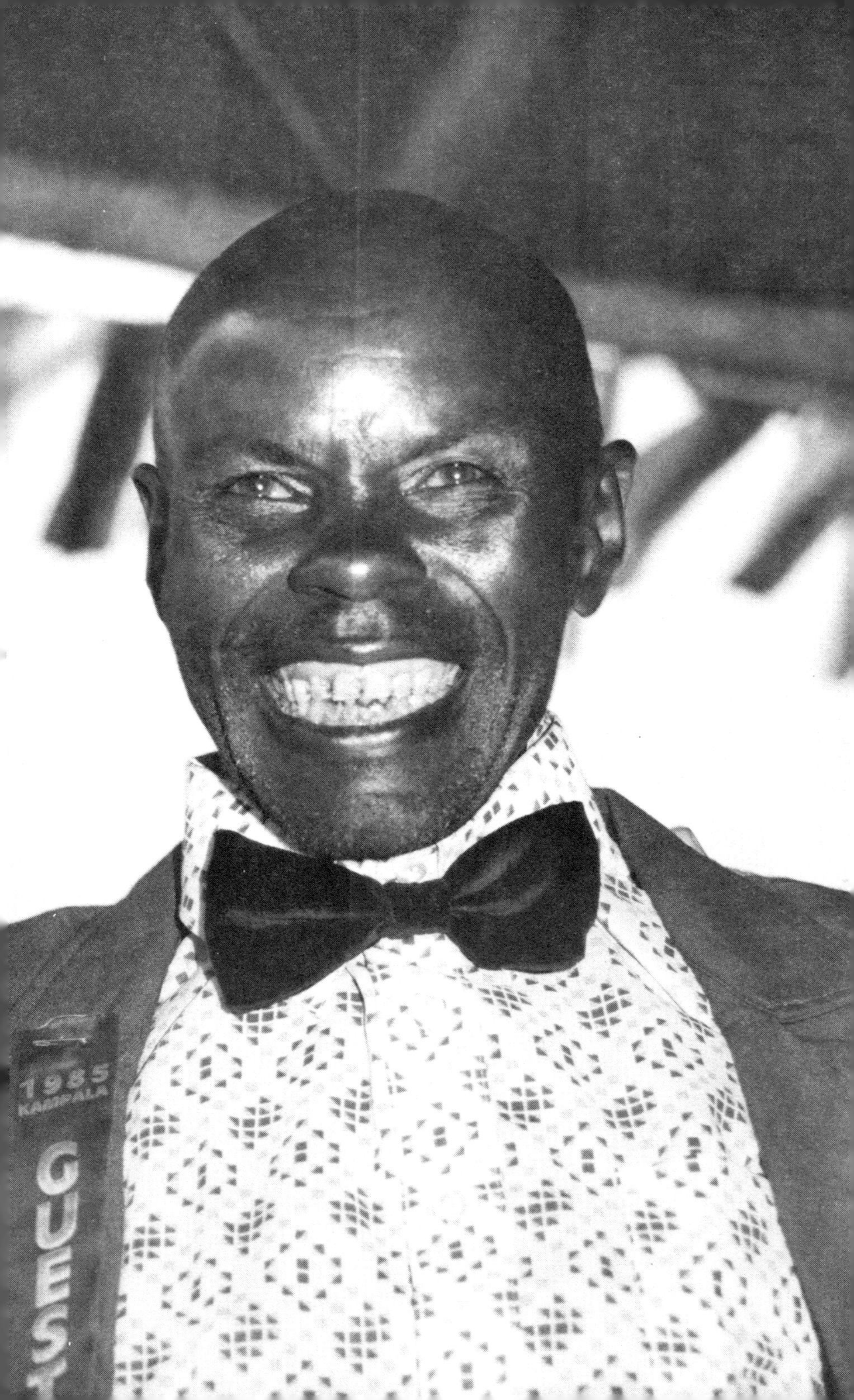
1985
KAMPALA
GUEST

Dr. T.L. Osborn rescues beggar, Peter Musoke, from being overrun in the stadium exodus.

PART 27

THE MIRACLE OF PAPA MUSOKE

Papa Musoke's miracle, during the Kampala, Uganda crusade, is **living proof of the great and beautiful wonders that God is doing through this ministry.**

Through this apostolic miracle, God is showing YOU that **Jesus is UNchanged** and that He will meet YOUR need today! Fresh, new faith for YOUR MIRACLE-NEED will be born in YOU, as you read about this wonder of God's love.

The great meeting that day had ended. Hundreds of miracles had been witnessed, and we were leaving the stadium. The vast multitude of people was bottlenecked, pushing to get out of the Lugogo Stadium grounds — and there I saw this **poor crippled beggar squeezed against the hedge, his paralyzed legs and feet about to be run over.**

Thousands of people were rushing to exit thru' the stadium gate.

BELOW: The beggar was pinned against the hedge, his crippled legs about to be overrun.

I jumped out of the car and halted the pressing river of people. As I looked at that lonely, frightened old man, the compassion of Jesus moved me to take a daring step of faith.

For years, Papa Musoke had been so lame and paralyzed in his back and legs, that he **could only move about by scooting along on his hips,** lifting and pushing himself with his hands. He had come to our crusade, but was not yet healed.

This poor beggar man was trying to scoot out of the gate in the press of people. **There he was, pinned against the bush at the wall, by a car whose wheels were about to over-run his feet.** I saw the dilemma just in time to jump out and STOP the crush of people — and the car.

I knelt in the dirt to help him and Jesus said: **"LOVE him! HEAL him and RAISE him up IN MY NAME!"** So I told him: **"Papa, Jesus loves you. God values you. He gave His Son for you. YOU are not made to crawl, but to walk like me! God paid as much for YOU as He paid for me. I will pray for you, then you can walk."**

Then I cried: "O you spirit of infirmity, come out of

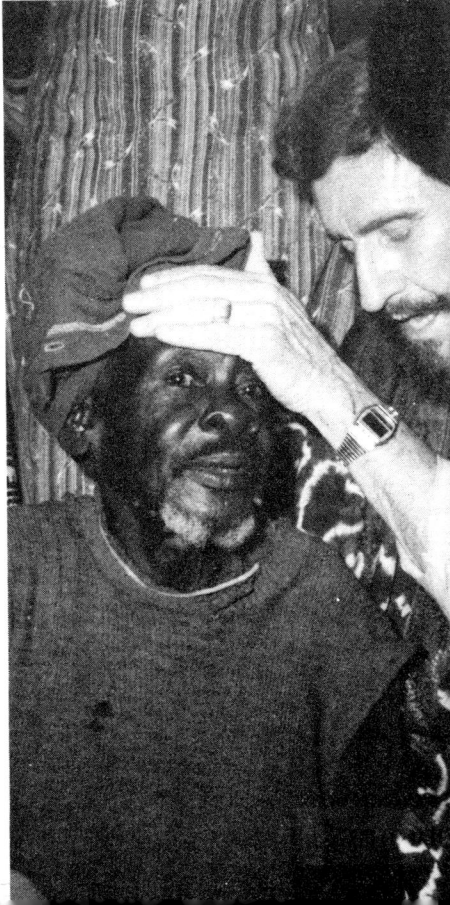

T.L. tells Papa Musoke to "ONLY BELIEVE," then he prays for his healing.

"In the name of Jesus Christ, stand up and walk!"

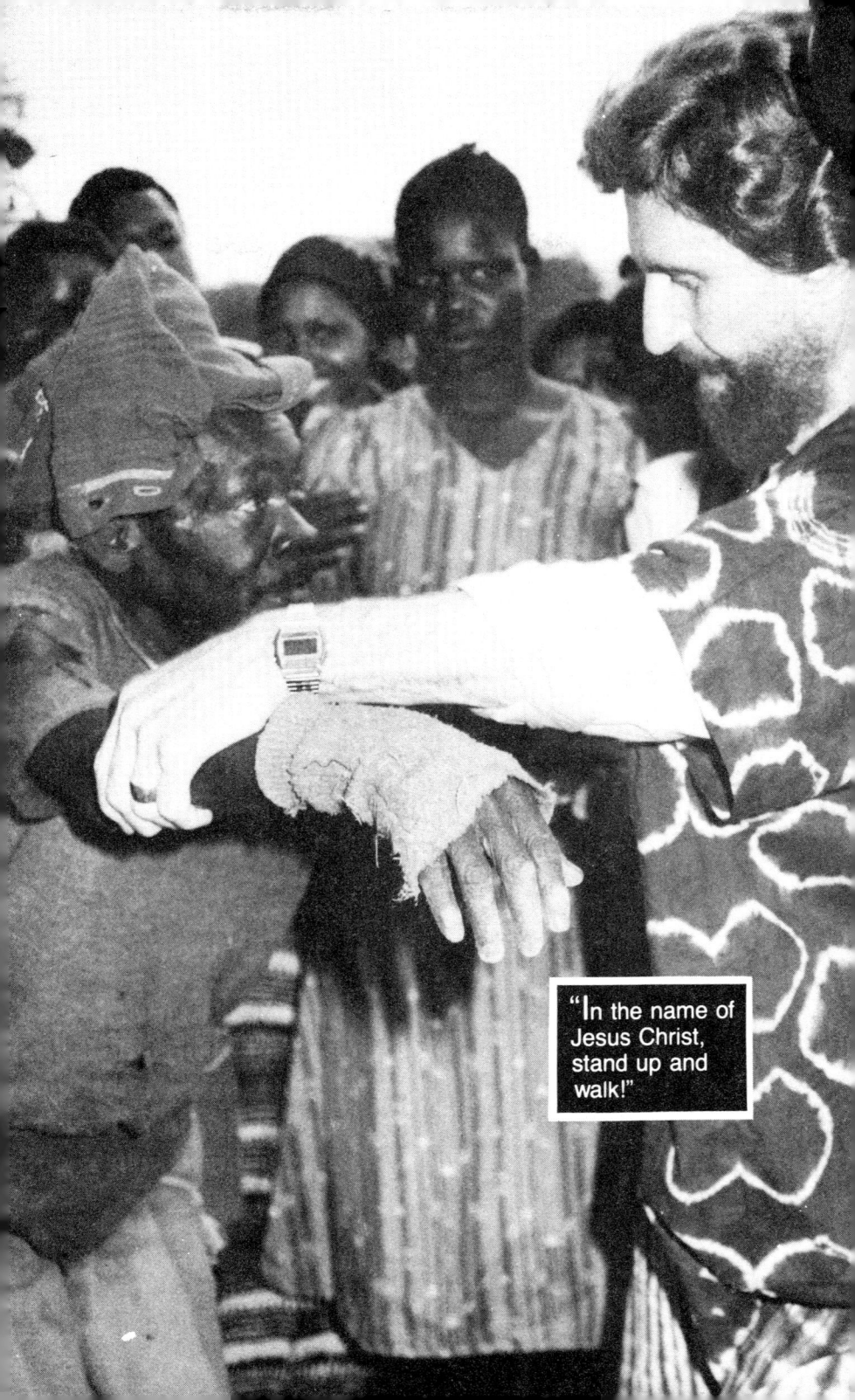

this dear man, in Jesus' name!" I KNEW it was done. I pulled him to me and I loved him, and Jesus' presence healed his bony emaciated body.

Then I took him by his arms and raised him up and HE WAS HEALED! **The press of people went wild with joy as this BIBLE-DAY MIRACLE took place right out there in the middle of the road jammed with people.** Hundreds believed on the Lord there that day.

A man volunteered to take him to his house, to feed him good food, to give him a bed to rest on, and to bring him back to the crusade so that the multitude could see him and hear him tell about his miracle.

No one had cared for him. He had no home. He had slept with some dogs that licked his hands and helped him to stay warm at night.

The next day as the mass of 200,000 to 400,000 people packed the grounds, I called for the beggar's new friend to bring Papa Musoke to the platform.

The dear old man explained how that for YEARS, he had suffered great pain and that he had to scoot on his hips to move about, and to beg for food. I asked the multitude to believe with Daisy and me for the COMPLETE MIRACLE, then we prayed again for him. As

Papa Musoke realizes that Jesus has healed him.

the healing virtue of Jesus Christ went into Musoke's body, hundreds more were healed too.

It was truly an apostolic miracle of mercy. Only God knows how many lives were changed in Uganda as that multitude **witnessed God's uncondemning, non-judgmental LOVE IN ACTION.**

I took Papa Musoke by the arm and walked with him, back and forth across the platform. As the crowd wept and applauded, the dear old man's face lit up in a smile as he realized **that this was not just a DREAM, but a REALITY.**

He was completely healed.

Then we arranged for a pastor to take charge of our new Christian brother. I told the pastor: **"Take him and give him good food, arrange for him to have a warm bath, give him a comfortable bed to sleep and to rest tonight. Then go buy him nice new clothes, shoes, a pretty necktie and whatever he needs to look nice. Bring him tomorrow for all to see!"**

The pastor did all he was told and brought to the platform, the following day, **a fine looking Christian gentleman whom no one recognized.**

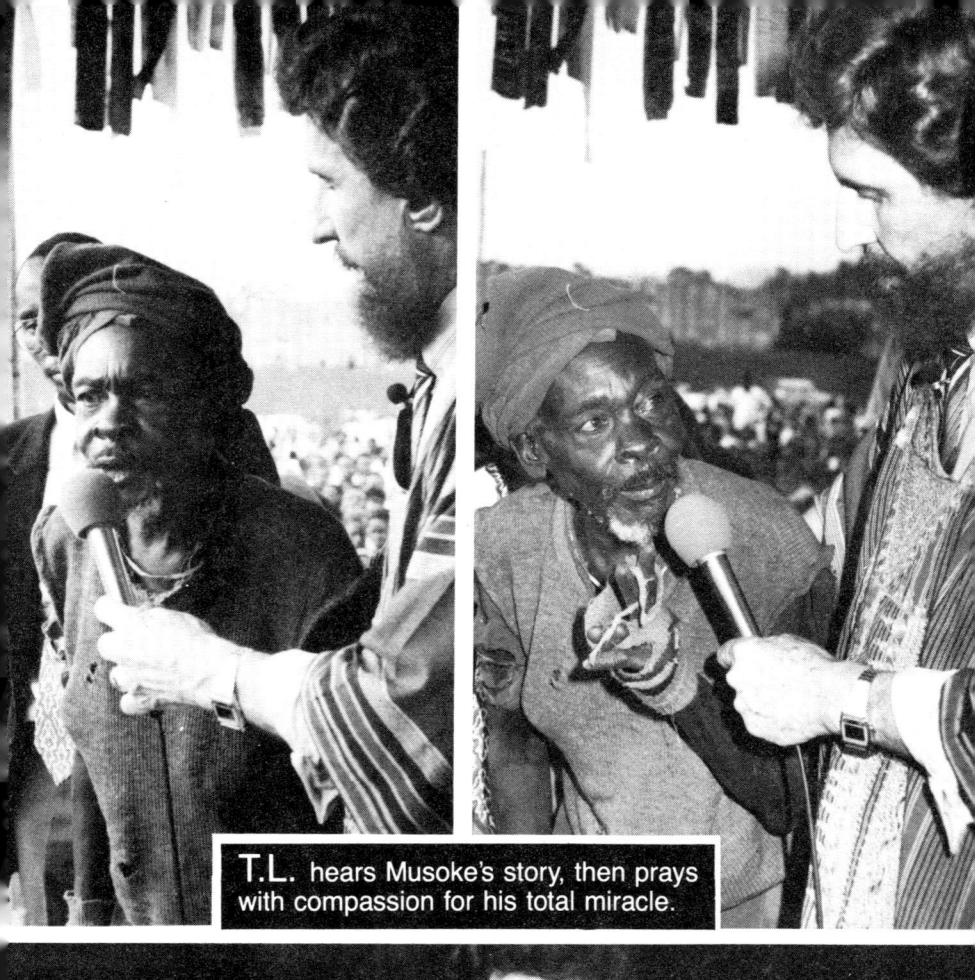

T.L. hears Musoke's story, then prays with compassion for his total miracle.

Then we called Papa Musoke to the microphone to tell the multitude what God had done for him, and when he stepped forward, everyone was shocked and broke out into spontaneous applause, rejoicing and even weeping. **They could not imagine the transformation of the ragged, despairing, crippled beggar they had seen the day before.**

Musoke was no longer scooting on his hips with his hands. He was dressed in new clothes, walking as well as anyone, and smiling with joy. **That was the GOSPEL IN ACTION — a hopeless beggar, lifted from the dust, from sleeping with the dogs, to a remarkably impressive gentleman, a redeemed, saved and healed man of God.**

The event called for photographs. We all wanted our pictures taken with Papa Musoke.

I wish the whole world could have seen **the pride and the delight which beamed in Musoke's face as he stepped by Dr. Daisy's side to be photographed with this remarkable lady of God.**

Daisy and I could hardly restrain our tears, as this wonder of God unfolded. There have been <u>so many</u> miracles for the deaf, blind, crippled, homeless, lonely and truly desperate people. It is impossible to describe the glory of the **beautiful and miraculous things we have witnessed here.**

The effect of such miracles is vital to the whole nation. Faith and hope are rekindled. Preachers are rising with new courage. The country is discovering that **the Jesus of the Bible is alive and unchanged today.**

Clad in the new clothes we got for him, Papa Musoke returns and we present him to the enormous crowd of people.

Papa Musoke gives thanks and shows the multitude how his life is now changed. Transformed by the love and power of Jesus Christ, he is now a child of God.

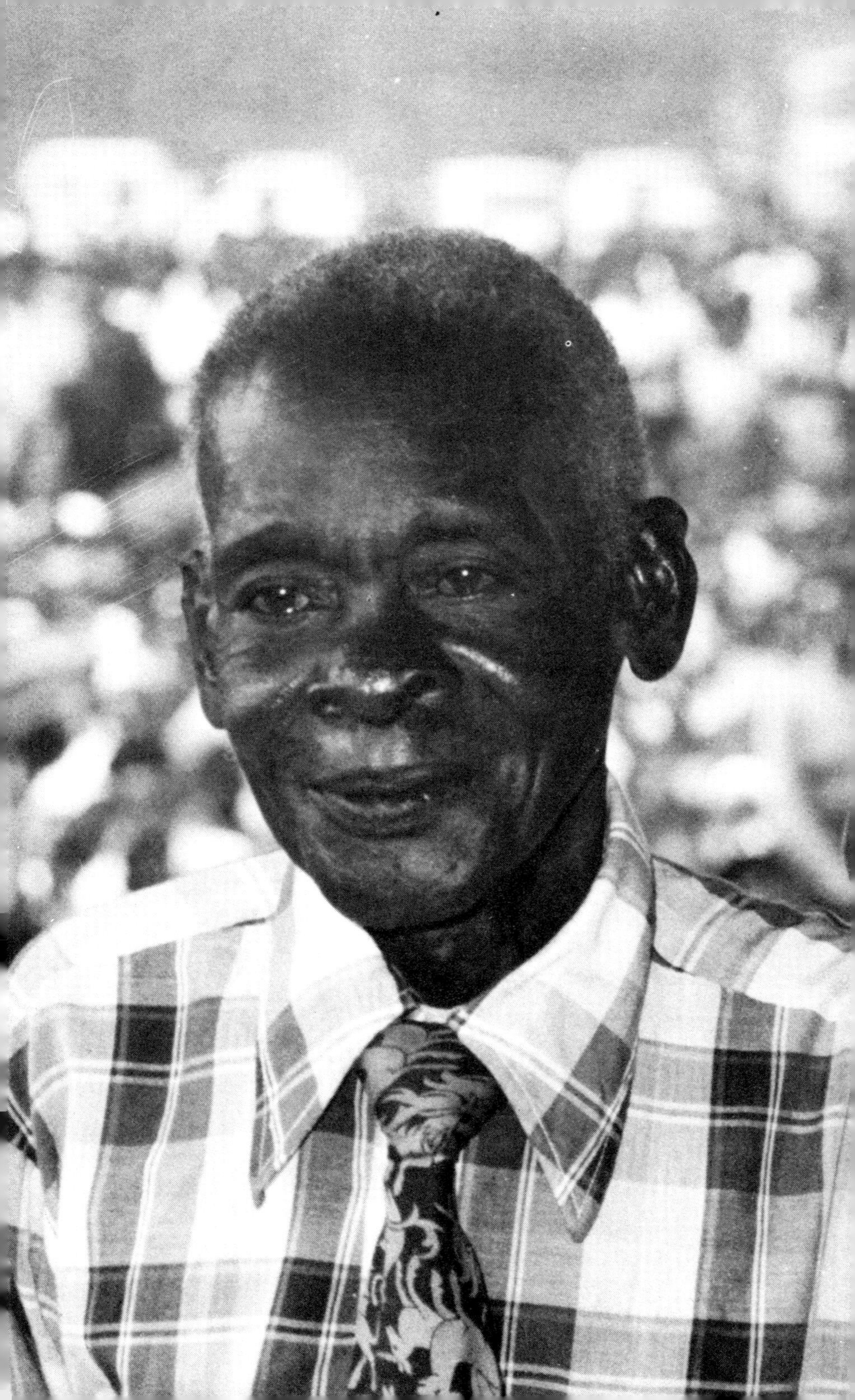

Maria Theresa, miraculously healed, and raised to her feet by a bolt of God's power from heaven, tells her remarkable story at the Osborn Crusade in Kampala.

PART 28

MARIA THERESA'S MIRACULOUS HEALING

Maria Theresa had been sent home from the hospital to die. She had **no hope of ever walking again.** Several operations left her worse than before. She prayed to die.

Then news came of our crusade. **She was carried and laid on the ground amidst the throng.** Daisy preached about the woman bent double by a "spirit of infirmity".

Maria had rolled and agonized on the ground, in anguish and suffering. A painful bone disease deteriorated her spine and hips. (One had been dislocated for months.)

When Daisy spoke Christ's words, **"WOMAN, BE FREE!,"** Maria heard no more. She thought that it **thundered** and that a **bolt of lightning had struck her.** She was shocked to her feet, and healed, but was blinded by the power. She was stunned and she screamed for fear. People thought she was insane.

I went and caught her and brought her to Daisy, and when Daisy embraced her, **her sight was restored,** and she realized that she had been healed. She shouted, jumped and danced all over the platform and the mass of people was astounded.

Maria Theresa rejoices with Daisy Osborn.

Betty Andiru's miracle deliverance from demons, after suffering 13 years of insanity.

PART 29

BETTY ANDIRU'S MIRACLE

Betty Andiru had been possessed by tormenting demon spirits. Her insanity had resulted from **hatred and bitter resentment which had raged within her** toward those who had wounded and abused her.

She had attended a convent, then guerrilla fighters and armed vigilantes had begun looting and destroying the country.

They came in the night and captured Betty, raping and debasing her. She was **brutalized** and **insulted, used** and **humiliated** until venomous hatred possessed her, and she vowed to get revenge.

As she crouched in disgrace, like a wounded animal, she **seethed with vengeance and retaliation.**

One day in her torture and anguish, **a satanic power came over Betty and she became possessed by demons.** They made her scream, bark and bite at people like a wild, wounded dog that had gone mad.

From that day, she became vicious, and no one could tame her. **She had been insane for 13 years.**

Then the news came about our crusade, and friends brought Betty to the meetings. For three days, she screamed and barked, and had to be kept beyond the crowd to prevent her from injuring anyone.

Daisy was preaching about **the Jesus life and how His love-power could give anyone a new beginning.** She urged people to **forgive** the wrongs of the past and to let Jesus change their lives.

During sane intervals, Betty cried to the Lord for mercy.

Suddenly, as Daisy preached, **the demons went out of Betty, and she was made completely whole.** The people around her knew something had happened.

The **Word of God,** spoken through Daisy, **drove those spirits out of that poor woman.**

She came to tell the multitude that she was healed. She wept and told everyone: **"Forgive your enemies!"**

Betty said, **"I was insane. Demons possessed me because of my hatred. But Jesus forgave me. Now I can forgive everyone. I am healed. I have no enemies. I love everyone now. If you will forgive your past, Jesus will give you a new beginning, as Dr. Daisy says."**

Betty is now a living witness. She goes about telling everyone the **price of HATE,** and the **reward of LOVE.**

Betty Andiru with Daisy Osborn.

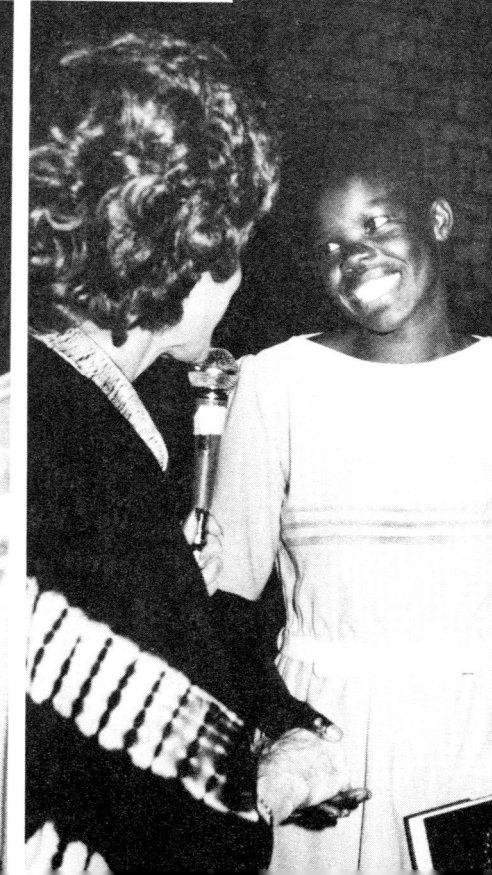

During the Osborn Crusade in Java, a Buddhist photographer captured the cloud formation in the likeness of Christ's face, above the crusade audience (below) — a wonder that has caused many to believe the gospel.

PART 30
MIRACLE OF CHRIST'S APPEARANCE

It happened during our great Crusade of Bible Faith in the South Pacific.

Tens of thousands of people were there from all over the nation. It was like Bible days when *almost the whole city came together to hear the word of God.* (Ac.13:44)

As news spread about the miracle, the report sounded like the account of Jesus' ministry in Luke 5:15: *There went a fame abroad of him: and great multitudes came together to hear, and to be healed by him of their infirmities.*

The area was 95 percent Moslem.

A great mass gospel crusade had not been conducted in the open air in over 400 years — in fact, none had ever been recorded.

The people believed that Jesus was a good man; even a gifted man of God — a prophet, a healer, a remarkable teacher — but **not the Son of God, and not risen from the dead.**

This is why so many people saw the Lord Jesus during the course of our great crusade. It was like it must have been after the resurrection of Jesus: *He showed himself ALIVE by many infallible proofs, being SEEN of THEM.* (Ac.1:3)

One beautiful afternoon as the multitude witnessed the miracles in wonder and awe, we asked everyone to be quiet and reverent, while the photographer took a great panoramic picture of the crowd.

We talked about the marvelous miracles that had been taking place, and we urged the people to think about the presence of Jesus in the crowd; to think of His crucifixion and death for our sins; to think of His RESURRECTION from the dead.

While the photographer perched himself on a tall bamboo ladder to take the audience picture, a Buddhist cameraman took a snapshot of the photographer against the somewhat strange cloud formation above the multitude. (Photos pg. 466)

The next day, he came rushing to one of the local pastors and with trembling hands showed him the photograph which he had just processed in his darkroom.

The Buddhist thought the cloud-formation resembled the face of Jesus whom we had been preaching about. The pastor, presuming the photograph enthusiast had retouched the negative, expressed surprise at his product and asked how he had done it.

The man, trembling with emotion, unrolled the freshly developed film to show the pastor. **NO retouching had been done; the picture was a print of the negative as it was exposed during the crusade.**

The Buddhist cameraman did not observe the semblance of Jesus' face when he took the picture. It was only when he developed the film and printed the photograph that he saw the image he had captured.

The photograph soon was being ridiculed as a deceitful trick to prove that Christ was risen rom the dead. Again, the reports were not unlike Bible days when, after Jesus was risen, the priests paid the soldiers money to go say, *His disciples stole him away while we slept.* (Mt.28:12-13)

However, **this phenomenal photograph remains a mystery,** unsolved by those who have scrutinized the negative. Like any unexplainable miracle done by God, unbelievers prefer to relegate it to the connivance of eccentrics rather than to believe that *Christ died for our sins, that he was buried, and that he ROSE again the third day according to the scriptures.* (1Co.15:3-4)

But *the hand of the Lord was with* (us) *and a great number believed, and turned to the Lord.* (Ac.11:21)

It was easy for Daisy and me to accept the validity of this phenomenal appearance, because **the Lord Jesus had appeared in our room one morning at 6 o'clock.** Seeing Him as clearly as any man, I lay as one dead for a long while. Water poured from my eyes though I was not conscious of weeping. The human body cannot stand the presence of the RISEN Lord. **Our lives were changed forever.**

If Jesus Christ is RISEN from the dead, it should not be strange that He would continue to show Himself ALIVE, as He did following His resurrection; as He has done throughout the centuries of church history; as He has done in our crusades;

and as He did to me personally.

In practically every crusade we have ever conducted in nearly 70 nations, the Lord Jesus has appeared to at least one, and often many, in the multitude.

Jesus said: *The one that loves me, I will love him or her and will MANIFEST* (show, reveal) *myself to him or her.* (Jn.14:21) The Lord said to Thomas, who could not believe He had risen from the dead, *Be not faithless, but believing.* (Jn.20:27) And Thomas was so overwhelmed by the nailprints and the pierced side of Jesus that he exclaimed: *My Lord and my God!* (Jn.20:28)

May YOU also believe on the Lord Jesus Christ and be converted today, *for whoever shall call on the name of the Lord shall be saved.* (Ro.10:13)

For *if you confess with your mouth the Lord Jesus, and believe in your heart that God has raised him from the dead, you shall be saved.* (Ro.10:9)

HE IS RISEN! HE IS ALIVE!

PART 31

ALIVE IN THIS CENTURY

As we go to press with this book containing **firsthand accounts of our Lord, demonstrating His power ALIVE in this century,** we can say afresh: *Jesus Christ* (is still) *the same, yesterday and today and forever* (Heb. 13:8), and by the grace of God, we are continuing to witness across the world the wonderful things *Jesus began to do and teach* (Ac. 1:1) wherever we proclaim His word.

In every country where we have gone, without exception, we have seen the same hunger and response to mass evangelism. *Great multitudes followed* (Jesus), *because they saw his miracles which he did on them that were diseased.* (Jn.6:2)

These firsthand accounts that we have shared with you are only a few of the tens of thousands of miracles we have seen with our own eyes. For almost four decades, in nearly 70 nations — night after night after night — the wonders of God have been almost as great and sometimes greater than those printed on these pages.

What a wonderful God we serve! What a gospel we proclaim! What a miracle power is manifested when anyone goes forth in His name to carry the gospel of Jesus to the world!

The ministry of proclaiming the gospel with signs following, out in the public areas — WILL **ALWAYS BE EFFECTIVE.** It is the pattern set forth by Jesus Christ and followed by the Early Church. It is the order of this generation, too, because **neither Jesus nor humankind has changed.**

Our greatest crusades are conducted in nations whose cultures differ radically. In Europe as well as in S. America, India or Africa, enormous audiences attend. Wherever we go, we find that Christ is still *moved with compassion* and people are still *eager to see* the wonders of God.

Our Lord ALWAYS confirms His word with signs and wonders wherever the gospel is preached. Those who **believe** are saved.

Among these great people of these many nations of the world, *with great power* (give we) *witness of the resurrection of the Lord Jesus: and great grace* (is) *on* (us) *all*. (Ac.4:33)

In the closing chapter of this book, we have been inspired to arrange a digest of 324 Bible verse quotations; they create an authentic, scriptural resume of what we have, and are living and experiencing.

As you read these Bible parallels for what we have taught and witnessed during almost four decades already, you will discover why we titled this unique book, **The Gospel According to T.L. and Daisy.**

PART 32

THE GOSPEL ACCORDING TO T.L. AND DAISY

(A Compendium of 324 Bible-verse Quotations)

*The **beginning** of the gospel of Jesus Christ, the Son of God, was written in the prophets.* (Mk.1:1-2) Then this *great salvation, at first spoken by the Lord,* **was confirmed to US by them that heard him,** *God also bearing* **them** *witness with signs and wonders.* (He.2:3-4)

Forasmuch as many have taken in hand to set forth a declaration of those things which **they** *saw —* those *who were eyewitnesses and ministers of the word; it seemed good* **to Daisy and** *to me also,* *to write* (Lu.1:1-3) what **we** have witnessed and experienced *concerning Jesus of Nazareth, mighty in* **deed** *and* **word** *before God and all the people.* (Lu.24:19)

We bear record *of the word of God, and of the testimony of Jesus Christ, and of the things that we have seen.* (Re.1:2)

We are disciples which testify of these things and have written these things: and we know that our testimony is true. (Jn.21:24)

We Declare Our Gospel

That which was from the beginning of our ministry, *which **WE** have **heard**, which **WE** have **seen** with **OUR** eyes, which **WE** have **looked** upon, and **OUR** hands have **handled**, of the Word of life; **declare we to you**. And these things we write to you, that your joy may be full* (1Jn.1:1,3-4) because **we declare to you glad tidings,** *how that the promise made to our fathers, God has **fulfilled the same to US** their children.* (Ac.13:32-33)

We have **re-lived Bible days in OUR generation.** Bible parallels for what **WE** have witnessed are abundant. Therefore this compendium of 324 scriptures is the best possible narrative for *THE GOSPEL ACCORDING TO T.L. AND DAISY.*

Paul talked about Jesus Christ, saying, *he was raised from the dead ACCORDING TO MY GOSPEL.* (2Ti.2:8) In Romans 2:16 and 16:25, he spoke of *MY gospel.*

This book, and this arrangement of scriptures is **OUR** witness of Jesus Christ. It is **OUR gospel.** Our account is **contemporary;** but the facts of Christ are **UNchanged.**

God said: *I am the Lord, I **change not.*** (Mal.3:6) *I AM THAT I AM. This is my name **forever,** and this is my memorial to **all** generations.* (Ex.3:14-15)

We know of a surety that *God is **not slack** concerning His promises* (2Pe.3:9) to those who believe them **today.**

Jesus Christ is the ***same** yesterday, and today, and forever,* (He.13:8) **as WE allow Him to be the same IN and THROUGH us.**

Our Witness

We have witnessed that *all that Jesus **began** both to do and teach until the day in which he was taken up,* (Ac.1:1-2) and all that the apostles **continued** to do in the book of Acts, **is still God's will today.**

Daisy and I are convinced that ***all** the promises of God in him are yes and amen,* (2Co.1:20) and that they are indeed given to ***you,** and to **your children,** and to **all** that* *are afar off, even **as many** as the Lord our God shall call.* (Ac.2:39)

As He Is, So Are We

*Christ became a **human being** and lived here on earth among us.* (Jn.1:14 LB) The angel told Mary, *he shall be called **"Emmanuel"** (meaning **"God is with us"**).* (Mt.1:23 LB) *God was **in Christ**, reconciling the world to himself.* (2Co.5:19)

*Jesus came **preaching the gospel of the kingdom** of God,* (Mk.1:14) and He told his followers to *go to all the world and **preach the gospel** to every creature* (Mk.16:15) *saying, the **kingdom** of heaven is at hand.* (Mt.10:7)

Now then, Daisy and I *are **ambassadors** for Christ* (2Co.5:20) because Jesus said, *as my Father has sent **me** to the world, **even so have I also sent you** to the world.* (Jn.20:21; 17:18)

So we say, today: *As **he is, so are we** now in this world;* (1Jn.4:17) *we are **laborers together** with God,* (1Co.3:9) *and his divine power has given to us all things* *that pertain to life and godliness, through the knowledge of him who has called us,* and He has *given to us exceeding great and precious promises: that by these we might be* **partakers of the divine nature.** (2 Pe.1:3-4)

Messengers of the Gospel

The glorious **gospel** *of the blessed God, has been* **committed to our trust,** (1Ti.1:11) *that Christ Jesus came into the world to* **save sinners.** (1Ti.1:15)

For Christ's death on the cross has made peace with God **for us all** *by his Word.* (Col.1:20 LB) *He has* **brought us back as his friends,** *and has done this through the death on the cross of his own human body, and now as a result, we are standing before God with* **nothing left against us,** *the only condition being* **that we fully believe the Truth, convinced of the Good News** *that Jesus died for us.* (Col.1:21-23 LB)

So everywhere we go, **we talk about Christ** *to all who will listen ...* **This is our work,** *and we can do it only because* **Christ's mighty energy** *is at work within us.* (Col.1:28-29 LB)

We are messengers and servants of Jesus Christ,

separated to the gospel of God. (Ro.1:1)

*We thought it good to show the **signs** and **wonders** that the high God has wrought. How great are his signs! and how mighty are his wonders!* (Da.4:2-3)

We *speak that* **we** *do **know** and testify that* **we** *have seen.* We trust that you will *receive our witness.* (Jn.3:11)

Revelation of Jesus

God ... which does great things and unsearchable; marvelous things without number, (Job 5:8-9) *has **fulfilled his word** that he has commanded,* (Lam.2:17) and *has in these last days spoken* (He.1:2) afresh to *great multitudes of people which followed him* (Mt.4:25) from many parts of the countries where we have proclaimed the good news.

*It pleased God, who separated us from our mothers' wombs, and called us by His grace, to **reveal his Son in us**, that we might **preach Him among the** non-Christian world.* (Ga.1:15-16)

*For Christ sent us to **preach the gospel:** not with*

*wisdom of words, lest the cross of Christ should be made of none effect. For the **preaching of the cross** is to them that perish foolishness; but to us which are saved it is the power of God.* (1Co.1:17-18)

*We certify you, that **the gospel** which is preached by us is not after man. For we neither received it of man, neither were we taught it, but by the **revelation of Jesus Christ**.* (Ga.1:11-12)

And we believe that *the **gospel of Christ is** the **power of God** to salvation to everyone that believes.* (Ro.1:16)

By Word and Deed

We have not ventured to include in this "gospel" *anything but what Christ has done through us to bring the* non-Christians to believe on Christ *by **word** and **deed**, by the **power of signs and wonders**, by the **power of the Holy Spirit**.* (Ro.15:18- 19 ML)

We believe that *God, who at various times and in different ways spoke in time past to the fathers by the prophets, has in these last days **spoken to us** by his Son* Jesus (He.1:1-2) *whom God anointed with the Holy Ghost and with power: who went about **doing good**, and*

healing all *that were oppressed of the devil;* (Ac.10:38) *and **we are his witnesses.*** (Ac.5:32)

*This Jesus of Nazareth was a man **approved of God** among people by **miracles** and **wonders** and **signs** which God did by him.* (Ac.2:22)

Crucified but Risen

But jealous religious opposers *reasoned in their hearts* and said, *this man speaks blasphemies.*(Mk.2:6-7) *And there was much murmuring among the people concerning him: some said, he deceives the people,* (Jn.7:12) and *they took counsel together to **put him to death.*** (Jn.11:53)

*They finally laid hold on Jesus and led him away to Caiaphas the high priest, where the scribes and the elders were assembled, and all the council sought false witnesses against him, to **put him to death**.* (Mt.26:57,59)

*They cried out, saying, Crucify him, crucify him. He ought to die, **because he makes himself the Son of God**.* (Jn.19:6-7) *And they killed the Prince of life, whom **God*** *raised from the dead; whereof **we are witnesses;*** (Ac.3:15) *God made of that same Jesus, who was crucified, both **Lord** and **Christ**.* (Ac.2:36)

*He **died** for our sins according to the scriptures, and he was **buried**, and he **rose again** the third day according to the scriptures.* (1Co.15:3-4)

In fact, *he **showed himself alive** after his passion by many **infallible proofs**, being seen of them forty days.* (Ac.1:3)

He was seen of ***Cephas**, then of **the twelve:** After that, he was seen of about **five hundred at once;** after that, he was seen of **James;** then of **all the apostles**. He was seen of **Paul also**.* (1Co.15:5-8)

And **He was seen of me** when He appeared to me in my bedroom. In like manner **He was seen of Daisy** as He came to her and told her to preach the gospel.

Then as we have gone *to all the world to preach the gospel,* (Mk.16:15) Jesus has appeared to **one** or to **several people** in almost every crusade we have ever conducted. In Thailand, over **one hundred people** saw our Lord at one time, in the same meeting, and *the people with one accord gave heed to the things which we* *spoke and there was great joy in that city.* (Ac.8:6,8)

And best of all, Jesus promised, **Lo I am with YOU alway,** *even to the end of the world.* (Mt.28:20)

So we believe that this same Jesus is **with us** wherever we go, because after *he was parted from them, and carried up into heaven* (Lu.24:51) *they went forth, and preached every where,* **the Lord working with them, confirming the word with signs following.** (Mk.16:20) We have literally experienced this in over 70 nations. *He has said, I will* **never** *leave you, or forsake you.* (He.13:5)

He Chose Us

So Daisy and I *have not chosen Christ, but* **He has chosen us,** *and* **ordained us,** *that we should go and bring forth fruit, and that our fruit shall remain: that whatever we ask of the Father in Christ's name, He may give it to us.* (Jn.15:16)

We believe that *if we abide in Christ, and if his words abide in us, we can ask what we will, and* **it shall be done** *to us.* (Jn.15:7)

Christ has clearly said: *If we believe on him, the works that he does **we shall do also** ... and whatever we shall ask in his name, he will do, that the Father may be glorified in the Son.* (Jn.14:12-13)

So, *this is the confidence that we have in him, that, if we ask **anything** according to God's will,* (or word of promise), *he hears us: and if we know that he hears us, whatever we ask, we know that **we have** the petitions that we desire of him.* (1Jn.5:14-15)

We Are His Witnesses

Daisy and I have gone to the world, during nearly four decades, *and preached **Christ** to them.* (Ac.8:5)

We believe that *this is a faithful saying and worthy of all acceptation, that **Christ came** to this world **to save sinners**.* (1Ti.1:15) So we tell the world that *God sent not his Son to the world to **condemn** the world; but that the world through him might be **saved**,* (Jn.3:17) because the great fact is that *the Son of Man is come to **seek** and to **save** that which was lost.* (Lu.19:10)

As we reach out to minister to these millions, we are

always occupied *preaching the kingdom of God, and teaching those things which concern the* **Lord Jesus Christ,** *with all confidence;* (Ac.28:31) how *he was wounded for* **our** *transgressions, he was bruised for* **our** *iniquities: the chastisement of* **our** *peace was upon him: and with his stripes* **we** *are healed.* (Is.53:5)

Great multitudes come together to hear, and to be healed by the Lord *of their infirmities,* (Lu.5:15) and we teach them how *Christ* **healed all** *that were sick: that it might be fulfilled which was spoken by Isaiah the prophet who said, himself took* **our** *infirmities, and bore* **our** *sicknesses.* (Mt.8:16-17)

And believers are the more added to the Lord, **multitudes** *both of men and women.* (Ac.5:14)

These *multitudes bring the sick to the streets* or fields or race courses or stadiums or ball parks where we preach, *and lay them on beds and couches.* (Ac.5:15) We preach to them that *as* **many** *as receive Christ receive power to become children of God,* (Jn.1:12-13) and that *as* **many as touch him** *are made perfectly whole.* (Mk.6:56)

There are also multitudes who come from *the cities round about to* our crusades, *bringing* **sick** *folks, and* *them which are vexed with **unclean spirits:** and they are healed,* (Ac.5:14-16) as they come to understand that *God forgives **all iniquities,** and he heals **all diseases.*** (Ps.103:3)

We are witnesses** of these things; and so is also the Holy Ghost;* (Ac.5:32) *God also **bearing US** witness both with **signs** and **wonders,** and **divers miracles. (He.2:4)

*We walk by **faith,** and not by **sight,*** (2Co.5:7) knowing well that *without faith, it is **impossible** to please God;* (He.11:6) that *the just shall **live by faith*** (Ro.1:17) because *Christ is the end of the law for righteousness to **everyone that believes.*** (Ro.10:4)

Our Principle Message

Our number one message is: *God so loved the world that he gave his only begotten Son, that **whoever believes** in him shall **not perish,** but shall **have everlasting life.*** (Jn.3:16) We want everyone in each multitude to know that *Jesus is the only **way,** the only **truth** and the only **life;*** that *no one can come to God except **through him;*** (Jn.14:6) that *he is able to **save to the uttermost** them* *that come to God by him, because he is alive and makes intercession for them.* (He.7:25)

As *great multitudes come together **to hear**, and **to be healed** by Christ of their infirmities,* (Lu.5:15) we know that *faith can* only *come to them **by hearing**, and hearing by the **word of God**.* (Ro.10:17) So we constantly **teach** and **preach** *the gospel of the kingdom.* (Mt.4:23)

Often, as we teach, the *power of the Lord is **present to heal**.* (Lu. 5:17) *The whole multitude seeks to touch Jesus: because virtue goes out of Him,* through His word, *and **He heals them**.* (Lu. 6:19)

*They bring **sick** folks taken with **divers diseases** and **torments**, and those **possessed with devils**, and those that are **lunatic**, and those with **palsy**, and Christ heals them.* (Mt.4:24)

In Christ's name, Daisy and I charge many *deaf and dumb spirits to **come out** and to enter no more into* the people. (Mk.9:25) Sometimes, *when the evening comes, they bring many that are possessed with devils; and we **cast out the spirits of infirmity with his word**, and Christ heals them.* (Mt.8:16) Often it seems that *the whole city comes out to meet Jesus.* (Mt.8:34)

Our message is: *For with God **all things are possible**.*

(Mk.10:27) *According to your faith, it **will** be done to you.* (Mt.9:29) *If you can believe, **all things are possible to anyone who believes**.* (Mk.9:23) ***Whatever** things you desire, when you pray, **believe** that you **receive** them and you shall **have** them.* (Mk.11:24)

We believe Jesus Christ is our principle message because He said, *and I, if I be lifted up, will draw all people to me.* (Jn.12:32) *For other foundation can no one lay than that that is laid, which is **Jesus Christ**.* (1Co.3:11) We concluded long ago: *God forbid that we should ever glory, save in the **cross of our Lord Jesus Christ** by whom the world is crucified to us, and us to the world.* (Ga.6:14)

Full of Faith and Power

We never fail to emphasize that *Jesus Christ is the same **yesterday** and **today** and **forever**,* (He.13:8) and that this was the faith of those *who had spoken to us the word of God:* and it was they whose faith we should follow, *considering the end of their conversation.* (He.13:7)

Barnabas was an example to follow. When he preached, *much people was added to the Lord,*

(Ac.11:24) *for he was a good man and **full of the Holy Ghost and of faith**.* (Ac.11:24)

Stephen was another example to emulate because *he was **full of faith and power**,* and *did **miracles** among the people.* (Ac.6:8)

That is why we believe miracles should follow our ministry; they **attract** and **convince** *much people* to be *added to the Lord.* (Ac.11:24)

When we enter a city, we *speak **boldly** in the name of the Lord, who always gives testimony to the word of his grace, and* He always *grants **signs** and **wonders** to be done.* (Ac.14:3)

The hand of the Lord is always *with us: and great numbers believe, and **turn to the Lord**.* (Ac.11:21)

As we *preach Christ to them, the people with one accord give heed to the things which we speak, **hearing** and **seeing the miracles** which are done, and there is* always *great joy in each city.* (Ac.8:6-8)

Confirming His Word

As we *speak of the things we have seen and heard,*

(Ac.4:20) we *perceive that* many *have faith to be healed* and we command the lame: **Stand up on your feet and walk.** (Ac.14:9-10)

Often they ***immediately*** *rise, take up their bed, and go their way to their house, as the multitude is amazed and glorifies God, saying, We never saw it on this fashion.* (Mk.2:11-12) Sometimes those who are healed ***leap up*** *and* ***stand*** *and* ***walk,*** and go to the churches ***walking*** *and* ***leaping*** *and* ***praising God,*** *and the people see them walking and praising God.* (Ac.3:8-9)

Unbelievers are often heard to say: *What shall we do? For that indeed a* **notable miracle** *has been done is manifest to all that dwell in the city; and* **we cannot deny it.** (Ac.4:16)

It is always evident that *the Lord is working with us,* **confirming his word** *with signs following.* (Mk.16:20) Almost always, *many of them that hear the word believe: and the number of them* is usually **thousands.** (Ac.4:4) *Believers are the more added to the Lord,* **multitudes** *both of men and women,* (Ac.5:14) and *all glorify God for what is done.* (Ac.4:21)

They See the Miracles

We implicitly obey the words of our Lord: *Go to all the world, and preach the gospel to **every** creature and these signs* always ***follow*** *them that believe. In his name we cast out devils. They* (the sick people present) *lay their hands on* their own sicknesses *and they recover.* (Mk.16:15,17-18)

The Lord has *cured many of their **infirmities** and **plagues**, and of **evil spirits**; and to many that were **blind**, he gives sight.* (Lu.7:21) People are *loosed from* their ***infirmities*** *whom Satan has bound for many years.* (Lu.13:12,16)

Some are ***immediately*** cured *and they glorify God.* (Lu.13:13) Others ***at the same hour begin*** to mend, (Jn.4:52) and some, like the lepers, are healed ***as they go.*** (Lu.17:14)

The faith of thousands is always united with us as we expect God to confirm His word *by stretching forth his hand to heal, by granting **signs and wonders** to be done in the name of his holy child Jesus.* (Ac.4:30)

All the people rejoice for all the glorious things that

are done. (Lu.13:17) *And great multitudes follow him, because **they see the miracles** which he does on them which are diseased.* (Jn.6:2)

Those who are healed are told to *go home to their friends, and to tell them how great things **the Lord has done** for them, and has had compassion on them. And they always publish in the area how great things Jesus has done for them: and all the people marvel* (Mk.5:19-20) and are *amazed and they glorify God, saying, **we never saw it on this fashion.*** (Mk.2:12)

The Gods Are Come Down

There are always some, who when they see the miracles say, of a truth these two people are gods; *the gods are come down to us in the likeness of people,* (Ac.14:11) *which when we hear of* we say, We cannot heal! We are not gods! *We are only people of like passions with you, and we preach to you that you should **turn to the living God**.* (Ac.14:15) *And with these sayings, we can scarcely restrain the people from worshiping us.* (Ac.14:18)

We always explain to them *that from* America, *round*

about to Asia and in over 70 countries *we have fully preached the **gospel of Christ**,* (Ro.15:19) *making the* non-Christians *obedient, by **word** and **deed**, through **mighty signs and wonders** by the **power of the spirit of God**.* (Ro.15:18-19)

The Gospel Is Power

Furthermore, we emphasize that we have *tried to preach **where Christ is not named** lest we build on another person's foundation.* (Ro.15:20)

We *come not to the people with excellency of speech or of wisdom, and we determine not to know anything among them, **save Jesus Christ and him crucified**.*

Our *speech and our preaching is not with enticing words of human wisdom, but in the **demonstration of the Spirit and of power**.*

We teach *that one's faith should not stand in the wisdom of people but in **the power of God**.* (1Co.2:1-5)

*We declare the gospel by which people are saved, how that Christ **died** for our sins according to the scriptures;*

*and that he was **buried**, and that he **rose** again the third day.* (1Co.15:1-4)

We believe this is vital to proclaim because *if Christ be not risen, then is **our preaching vain**, and **your faith is vain**, and we are **false witnesses** of Christ.* (1Co.15:13-15)

Two Cardinal Facts

The death and resurrection of Christ sets Christianity apart from all religions so it is vital that people believe these two facts because salvation depends on them: 1) *If you shall confess with your mouth **the Lord Jesus**, and* 2) *believe in your heart that God has **raised him from the dead**, those are the conditions on which **you will be saved**. For* 1) *with the heart you believe in* the *righteousness* of Christ *and* 2) *with your mouth, you make confession to salvation.* (Ro.10:9-10)

Believing those two facts, ***whoever** shall call on the name of the Lord shall be saved.* (Ro.10:13)

And since *faith comes by hearing the word of God,* (Ro.10:17), *how shall people hear **without a preacher?***

(Ro.10:14) That is why **we are ready to preach** the gospel, (Ro.1:15) *we are* **not ashamed** *of the gospel,* (Ro.1:16) and *we* **declare** *the gospel.* (1Co.15:1)

We can say that *we have preached the gospel of God* ***freely,*** (2 Co.11:7) because we will not ***pervert*** *the gospel.* (Ga.1:7)

Unsearchable Riches

Whenever *false brethren have tried to spy out our liberty in Christ Jesus so that they might bring us into bondage, we give no place or subjection, no, not for an hour, that the* **truth of the gospel** *might continue.* (Ga.2:4-5)

Daisy and I consistently teach and preach that *according to the* **truth of the gospel,** people *must believe in Jesus Christ, that they might be* **justified by the faith of Christ** *and not by their works.* (Ga.2:14,16)

We believe that *after people hear the* **word of truth,** *the* **gospel of salvation,** they are **sealed** *with the holy Spirit of promise,* (Ep.1:13) and that they become **heirs,** *of the same body, and* **partakers** *of the promise in Christ* *by the gospel, whereof we are made ministers, according to the gift of the grace of God given to us by the effectual working of his power. To us is this grace given, that we should preach among the* **non-Christians** *the unsearchable* **riches of Christ.** (Ep.3:6-9)

Our gospel came not (nor do we proclaim it) *in word only, but also in* **power,** *and in the* **Holy Ghost,** *and in* **much assurance.** (1Th.1:5)

Entrusted with the Gospel

We consider that *we have been allowed of God to be* **put in TRUST with the gospel,** *and so we speak it; not as pleasing people, but God.* (1Th.2:4)

Indeed we *labor night and day,* **preaching the gospel** *of God, holy and just and unblameably behaving ourselves, so that we* always *walk worthy of God, who has* **called us** *to his kingdom and glory. (*1Th.2:9-10,12)

We believe that *the word of the Lord* **endures forever.** *And this is the word by which the* **gospel** *is preached.* (1Pe.1:25)

We know that *if anyone is* **in Christ,** *he or she is a new* *creature: old things are passed away, behold all things are become new.* (2Co.5:17)

We *declare before all the people* (Lu.8:47) that ***in Christ* alone** *is life;* (Jn.1:4) *that God has given to us eternal life, and that this life is **in his Son**. Whoever has the Son **has life;** and whoever has not the Son of God **has not life**.* (1Jn.5:11-12) *As many as **receive Jesus Christ**, to them he gives power to become the children of God.* (Jn.1:12)

We say: *These things have we spoken to you that you may **know** that you **have** eternal life, and that you may **believe** on the name of the Son of God,* (1Jn.5:11-13) because *there is **no other name** under heaven given among us, by which we may be **saved**.* (Ac.4:12) *And with many other words do we testify and exhort, saying,* (Ac.2:40) ***whoever** shall call on the name of the Lord shall be **saved**.* (Ro.10:13)

We constantly recount the miracles wrought by Christ on earth, as examples for **anyone today,** and we tell them that *these **miracles are written** that the people may **believe** that Jesus is the Christ, the Son of God, and that **believing, they may have LIFE** through his name.* (Jn.20:31)

Winning with Christ

The reactions to our ministry are always varied. Some of the *priests of the temples,* and even some of the Christian religious leaders are *grieved that we teach the people, and preach through Jesus the resurrection* (Ac.4:1-2) from a dead life of sin to a **new life in Christ.**

In fact, in one of our crusades abroad, the magistrate closed the meeting in order to appease a group *which believed not. They were moved with envy and took certain lewd fellows of the baser sort, and gathered a company, and tried to set all the city in an uproar.* (Ac.17:5)

However **many** *of them which heard the word* in that city **believed,** (Ac.4:4) *and of the devout* Hindus *a great multitude, and of the women not a few.* (Ac.17:4)

Often, in our crusades abroad, *many of them which hear the word believe,* (Ac. 4:4) while others *are filled with indignation,* (Ac. 5:17) and *doubt* about the extent to which *this will grow.* (Ac. 5:24) But we always take the position that we *ought to obey* **God** *rather than people.* (Ac. 5:29)

So we continually *sound out the word of the Lord,* (1Th.1:8) preaching that *in the name of Jesus Christ of Nazareth* people can *rise up and walk;* (Ac.3:6) that *his name through faith in his name,* can make people *strong.* (Ac.3:16)

Of course, *the multitude of those who believe are of one heart and of one soul,* (Ac.4:32) and *the hand of the Lord* is **always** *with us.* (Ac.11:21)

We believe *the Holy Ghost has fallen* on us **the same as it fell** on those *at the beginning* in Jerusalem, (Ac.11:15) so being united in our faith, we are aware that *great grace is upon* us both. (Ac.4:33)

Let God Be True

But people sometimes *stagger at the promises of God through* **unbelief.** (Ro.4:20)

Some seem to have fear and unbelief, and *think that it is a thing* **incredible** *that God should* perform miracles in this age. (Ac.26:8)

Some think that mass evangelism was alright in the

book of Acts, but that it is not God's program for this day. There are people who even believe that miracles were only for the Apostles. Of course through their unbelief *no mighty works* are done among them, (Mk.6:5) and the Lord, no doubt, *marvels because of their* **unbelief.** (Mk.6:6)

We feel, however, that even *if some do not believe, their unbelief should* **not** *make the faith of God without effect.* We feel that we should *let* **God be true**, *but every person a liar.* (Ro.3:3-4)

In spite of these reactions here and there, *we continue to this day, witnessing both to small and great, saying none other things than those which the prophets said should come: That Christ should* **suffer** *and that he should* **rise** *from the dead and should* **show light** *to the* non- Christians. (Ac.26:22-23)

We proclaim that Jesus Christ *himself took* **our** *infirmities, and bore* **our** *sicknesses,* (Mt.8:17) and that *with his stripes* **we** *are healed* (Is.53:5); and that He, *himself bore* **our** *sins in his own body on the cross so that* **we**, *being dead to sins, should* **live to righteousness**. (1Pe.2:24)

In non-Christian nations, we have even faced leaders

who consider our ministry a *sect that is spoken against.* (Ac.28:22)

But wherever people **accept the gospel,** they *fear, lest a promise being left, any of them should seem to come short of it.* (He.4:1) They rejoice that *the* **gospel** *is preached to them* but they regret that *the word preached does not profit* those who believe not, *not being **mixed with faith** in them that heard it.* (He.4:2)

Notable Miracles

So as it was in the days of the Bible, we observe that it is the same in our day: Some would not believe, but those who ***believe, see** the glory of God,* (Jn.11:40) and we continue to *heal the sick, to cleanse the lepers, to raise the dead and to cast out devils* (Mt.10:8) wherever we announce the gospel, since Jesus commanded it and has given us *power over all the power of the enemy.* (Lu.10:19; Mk.3:15)

The healing ministry of Christ is of great importance because miracles cause *the people to **run together,** greatly wondering.* (Ac.3:11) Miracles cause the people to ***give heed** to the things that we teach.* (Ac.8:6)

Notable miracles are done which are *manifest to all them that are in* the cities wherever we go, *and no one can deny them.* (Ac.4:16)

As great miracles take place, *many see them, and **turn to the Lord.*** (Ac.9:35) *And as* these things become *known throughout the area, many **believe** in the Lord.* (Ac.9:42)

When those healed testify, *others also, which have diseases come, and are healed.* (Ac.28:9)

Only seldom do we encounter those who are *filled with envy and speak against these things.* (Ac.13:45) Most people *are **glad,** and **glorify** the word of the Lord.* (Ac.13:48)

Tens of thousands *are **amazed** and **glorify** God, saying: We never saw it on this fashion.* (Mk.2:12)

It is wonderful *when great multitudes come, having with them those who are lame, blind, maimed, and many others, and cast them down at Jesus' feet;* ***and He heals them:*** *Insomuch that the multitudes wonder, when they see the dumb to speak, the maimed to be whole, the lame to walk, and the blind to see: and they glorify the God of Israel.* (Mt.15:30-31)

Thank God, *believers are the more **added to the Lord**, multitudes both of men and women.* (Ac.5:14)

*The word of God **increases**; and the number of the disciples **multiply** in each area greatly; and a **great company** of* those of non-Christian religions *are obedient to the faith,* (Ac.6:7) *so mightily **grows** the word of God and **prevails**.* (Ac.19:20) Also *the name of the Lord Jesus is **magnified**.* (Ac.19:17)

If God Said It, He Will Do It

These things *now have **WE seen** with our eyes,* (Zec.9:8) as we constantly teach that *there has not failed **one word** of all God's good promise which He has promised.* (1K.8:56)

We emphasize that *God is not a man, that he should **lie**; neither the Son of man, that he should **repent**: If he has said it, **he will do it**. If he has spoken, **he will make it good**,* (Nu.23:19) because He has said, *I am the Lord: I will speak, and the word that I shall speak **shall come to pass**; I will say the word, and **will perform it**.* (Eze.12:25) He says, *the word which I have spoken **shall be done**.* (Eze.12:28)

We constantly teach the multitudes in our meetings

the faithfulness of God to fulfill His word. *The Lord will do the thing that he has promised.* (Is.38:7) He says, *Yes, I have spoken it, and **I will also bring it to pass;** I have purposed it, and **I will also do it.*** (Is.46:11) We love to assure the people that *heaven and earth shall pass away, but Christ's words **shall not** pass away.* (Mt.24:35)

Receive Our Witness

To teach and convince these masses about Jesus Christ, God always keeps us *full of **faith** and **power**,* then He can do *great **wonders** and **miracles** among the people.* (Ac.6:8)

We report what **we** have seen Jesus do, like John's disciples reported what they had seen Him do: *The **blind** receive their sight, and the **lame** walk, the **lepers** are cleansed, and the **deaf** hear, the **dead** are raised up, and the **poor** have the gospel preached to them.* (Mt.11:5)

Truly, the vital message of our Lord is, *The time is fulfilled, and the kingdom of God is at hand: repent and **believe the gospel,*** (Mk.1:15) because *if the mighty works which were done* in your days *had been done* in many previous generations, *they would have repented long ago.* (Mt.11:21)

Now Is the Time

We urge *you* to **believe** *on the Lord Jesus Christ* right now *and you shall be* **saved,** *and your house.* (Ac.16:31)

Since **now** *is the accepted time, and* **now** *is the day of salvation,* (2Co.6:2) you can *repent and be converted, that your sins may be blotted out* (Ac.3:19) by **looking to Jesus** *the author and finisher of your faith* (He.12:2) who *has redeemed* **you** *to God,* (Re.5:9) because *he loved* **you** *and washed* **you** *from* **your** *sins in his own blood* (Re.1:5) *of the new testament, which is shed for many for the* **remission of sins.** (Mt.26:28)

It is wonderful to know that after *Christ died for the ungodly,* (Ro.5:6) *God, having raised up his Son,* **sent him to bless you,** *in turning you away from your iniquities.* (Ac.3:26)

God commends his love toward you, in that, while you were still a sinner, **Christ died for you.** *Now being justified by his blood,* **you will be saved** *from all wrath.* (Ro.5:8-9)

So reckon yourself **dead indeed to sin,** *but* **alive to God** *through Jesus Christ your Lord, for the wages of sin is* **death;** *but the gift of God is* **eternal life** *through Jesus*

Christ our Lord. (Ro.6:11,23)

You *are in Christ Jesus, who of God is made* **to you** *wisdom, and righteousness, and sanctification, and redemption.* (1Co.1:30)

The life of Jesus is also made manifest in **your mortal flesh,** (2Co.4:10) because **your body** *is the temple of the Holy Ghost* (1Co.6:19) and *you are a member of Christ's* **body,** *of his* **flesh,** *and of his* **bones.** (Ep.5:30)

His Desire for You

His desire is not only to *forgive all of* **your** *iniquities,* but also to *heal all of* **your** *diseases* (Ps.103:3) because, *himself took* **your** *infirmities and bore* **your** *sicknesses* (Mt.8:17) the same as *he bore* **your** *sins in his own body on the cross.* (1Pe.2:24)

Since Christ bore **your** sins, **you** can have *remission of sins* (Mt.26:28) — NOW. Since He bore your sicknesses, *by his stripes* **you** *are healed* (1Pe.2:24) — NOW. Therefore His words to you are: ***I have forgiven your sins,*** (Mt.9:2 LB) and also, *arise* if you are sick, **take up your bed, and walk.** (Mk.2:9)

He says to you, *Beloved, I wish above all things that you may **prosper** and be in **health**, even as your **soul prospers**.* (3Jn.2)

This Is Our Gospel

THIS IS OUR GOSPEL which we proclaim to the world.

THIS IS THE GOOD NEWS which we are *anointed by the Spirit of the Lord to proclaim.*

*He has sent us to **heal** the brokenhearted, to preach **deliverance** to the captives, and **recovering of sight** to the blind, to **set at liberty** them that are bruised, and to preach the **acceptable** year of the Lord.* (Lu.4:18-19)

THIS IS THE MESSAGE *which is **the power of God to salvation** to EVERYONE who believes.* (Ro.1:16) And **EVERYONE** means **YOU'RE THE ONE!**

THIS IS THE GOSPEL which we are to *preach in all the world, to every creature.* (Mk.16:15)

THIS IS THE GOSPEL which *Jesus Christ **confirms** with signs following. Amen!* (Mk.16:20)

"The preaching of the cross is to them who perish foolishness; but to those who believe and are saved, it is the power of God." 1 Corinthians 1:18

SUPERIMPOSED PHOTOGRAPH

ON THE GO LIFTING PEOPLE.

From their soulwinning youth, to their phenomenal success in world evangelism, Doctors T.L. and Daisy Osborn live their remarkable lives, ON THE GO, lifting people who need God's help, showing them how to get GOD'S BEST.

BOOKS BY THE OSBORNS

BELIEVERS IN ACTION—*Apostolic-Rejuvenating*
FIVE CHOICES FOR WOMEN WHO WIN—
21st Century Options
GOD'S LOVE PLAN—*The Awesome Discovery*
HEALING THE SICK—*A Living Classic*
HOW TO BE BORN AGAIN—*The Miracle Book*
JESUS and WOMEN—*Big Questions Answered*
LIFE— TRIUMPH OVER TRAGEDY—
A True Story of Life After Death
NEW LIFE FOR WOMEN—*Reality Re-focused*
BIBLICAL HEALING—*Seven Miracle Keys*
4 Visions–50+ yrs. of Proof–324 Merged Bible Vs.
SOULWINNING–OUTSIDE THE SANCTUARY—
A Classic on Biblical Christianity & Human Dignity
THE BEST OF LIFE—*Seven Energizing Dynamics*
GOD'S BIG PICTURE—*An Impelling Gospel Classic*
THE GOOD LIFE—*A Mini-Bible School–1,467 Ref.*
THE GOSPEL ACCORDING TO T.L. & DAISY—
Their Life & World Ministry–510 pg. Pictorial
THE MESSAGE THAT WORKS—
T.L.'s Revealing Manifesto on Biblical Faith
THE POWER OF POSITIVE DESIRE—
An Invigorating Faith Perspective
THE WOMAN BELIEVER—
Awareness of God's Design
WOMAN WITHOUT LIMITS—
Unmuzzled—Unfettered—Unimpeded
WOMEN & SELF-ESTEEM—
Divine Royalty Unrestrained
YOU ARE GOD'S BEST—
Transforming Life Discoveries

GLOBAL PUBLISHER

OSBORN PUBLICATIONS
P.O. Box 10
Tulsa, OK 74102 USA

✧✧✧

FRENCH DISTRIBUTOR

ÉDITIONS
MINISTÈRES MULTILINGUES
909, Boul. Roland-Therrien
Longueuil, Québec J4J 4L3
CANADA

✧✧✧

GERMAN PUBLISHER

SHALOM — VERLAG
Pachlinger Strrasse 10
D-93486 Runding, CHAM, Germany

✧✧✧

PORTUGUESE PUBLISHER

GRACA EDITORIAL
Caixa Postal 1815
Rio de Janiero–RJ–20001, Brazil

✧✧✧

SPANISH PUBLISHER

LIBROS DESAFIO, Apdo. 29724
Bogota, Colombia

✧✧✧

(For Quantity Orders, Request Discount Prices.)